TOP 101

INDUSTRY EXPERTS

A GLIMPSE INTO THE MINDS OF
ACCOMPLISHED PROFESSIONALS

Cambridge Who's Who®
© 2010 Cambridge Who's Who® Publishing, Inc.
ISBN: 978-1-60758-112-3
LCCN: 2010940739

For information, contact:
  Cambridge Who's Who® Publishing, Inc.
  498 RXR Plaza
  West Tower
  Uniondale, NY 11556

Manufactured in the United States of America.
Cambridge Who's Who® is not Associated or Affiliated with any other Who's Who Publication or Organization.

CAMBRIDGE WHO'S WHO®
MANAGEMENT AND STAFF

MANAGEMENT TEAM

PRESIDENT
Randy Narod

CHIEF OPERATING OFFICER
Erica Lee

CHIEF TECHNOLOGY OFFICER
Jerry Mott

EXECUTIVE VICE PRESIDENT, HUMAN RESOURCES AND DEVELOPMENT
Deb Morrissey

SENIOR HUMAN RESOURCES GENERALIST
Michelle Trabucchi

DIRECTOR, EDITORIAL CONTENT AND DEVELOPMENT
Meredith Foster

DIRECTOR, PRODUCT AND PROCESS MANAGEMENT
Elaine Joseph

MANAGER, COPY EDITING AND PROOFREADING
Kristen Giani

DIRECTOR, PRODUCT AND CONTENT DEVELOPMENT
Kara Lee

DIRECTOR, ONLINE CONTENT DEVELOPMENT
Nikki Masih

DIRECTOR, COMPLIANCE AND QUALITY ASSURANCE
Denice Mussillo

PRODUCTION STAFF

SENIOR EDITOR, "TOP 101 INDUSTRY EXPERTS"
Danielle Blanchard

ASSOCIATE EDITOR
Amy Fisher

GRAPHIC DESIGNER
Matthew Gianturco

PREMIER MEMBER SERVICES

SENIOR DIRECTOR, PREMIER MEMBER SERVICES
Sandra Anderson
Tara Siciliano

ACCOUNT DIRECTOR, PREMIER MEMBER SERVICES

Mindy Black	Michele LeFurgy
Awilda Cruz	Angie Loeffler
Stacey Drew	Pamela Marshall
Jill Gerdes	Daniel Metzger
Rose Marie Grossman	Julie Mosher
Bette Anne Healy	Glynn Nolan
Paula Kaiser	Stephanie Standish
Robert Kalaf	Jon Storey
Linda Kinsman-Saegert	Carina Tom
Joan Kroener	Susan Tyson
	Roger Waldeck

TABLE OF CONTENTS

FOREWORD

by Donald Trump Jr.

I am pleased to present the latest edition of "Top 101 Industry Experts," a collection of biographies and exclusive interviews with leading Cambridge Who's Who® members. Over the past 30 years, my family has invested its time and resources into establishing a global, iconic and luxury brand. We've focused primarily on real estate, but there are plenty of lessons I have learned as Executive Vice President of Development and Acquisitions for The Trump Organization that apply to all industries and areas of business.

My career has taken me around the world and enabled me to speak publicly about business, entrepreneurship, branding, networking and marketing, because these are the core elements of success in any field. I welcomed the unique opportunity to team up with Cambridge Who's Who as a way to communicate my ideas to a much wider audience of professionals. Through our new relationship, I'm applying my business acumen to help members gain greater opportunities for career growth. When Cambridge asked me to pen the foreword to "Top 101 Industry Experts," I was galvanized to share my perspectives on personal branding and global networking — two aspects that I've found are essential to becoming successful in any career.

It takes a considerable amount of manpower and resources to construct a building, but to be known as the best at what you do is another feat entirely — it happens only when you take a proactive and creative approach to branding and networking. Since every individual has a unique set of skills, characteristics and abilities that separates him or her from everyone else, a public representation of you — known as your personal brand — is an important facet of your career requiring constant attention and cultivation. Building a professional reputation takes time. Once you begin to establish your individual brand, your professional network will be invaluable — it will enable you to market your expertise to as many people as possible.

Success begets success, and gaining recognition is important to triggering this self-fulfilling cycle. My father has built his reputation, in part, by acknowledging his own accomplishments. He insists that if he does not do it, no one else will do it for him. People don't tout your triumphs because either they don't know enough about them or they're your competitors. But when you position yourself as a force in your industry, you will get noticed, become sought after and gain greater opportunities for exposure.

I always say, "If you're going to learn from someone, learn from the best." I was fortunate enough to be taught by the best — my father — by watching him, working by his side and listening to his advice throughout my life. That said, I wholeheartedly recommend that you read "Top 101 Industry Experts" from cover-to-cover. The individuals featured in this book have a tremendous amount of wisdom and experience to impart to you, as my father did to me.

Sincerely,

Donald Trump Jr.
Executive Director of Global Branding and Networking
Cambridge Who's Who®

Top 101 Industry Experts

Introduction by

Danielle Blanchard

Liz Wolgemuth's December 2009 article in U.S. News & World Report attempted to highlight the 50 best careers of 2010 by isolating the most promising vocational opportunities given the unstable financial and economic climate of the time. Biomedical engineering, the output of which is equipment that preserves health, was the occupation with the most rapid growth rate across multiple industries. Overall, the health care industry in particular saw an increase in jobs and pay scales, while some creative souls broke free from their corporate constraints and became full-time artists, curators, technical writers, and entrepreneurs. Still others answered the call for more general and special education teachers to improve test scores and train well-rounded students to enter the real world. Whether they were able to remain in positions they had held for years or found themselves traversing uncharted waters, many professionals saw this difficult 18-month period as an opportunity for reinvention.

For those who kept their occupations, this was a time of affirmation, a chance to reconnect with that which ignited their fervor in the first place. Learning to adapt to higher prices, less resources, and flux across the board proved in some to strengthen a resolve to succeed, and spurred the evolution of traditional roles. Real estate agents for example, at one point faced with dismal projections for purchasing rates, developed new marketing techniques aimed at regaining consumer trust. One expert featured in this book declared that her employer aggressively recruited fresh new talent with a specific skill set to accommodate the shifting needs of their market, reasoning that acquiring a well-constructed workforce is the first step to fulfilling consumer needs.

As various companies begin to emerge from the crunch and re-establish themselves in a global economy that still requires enough timidness to scale back in some areas, the individuals highlighted herein have actually taken the initiative to solidify their places at the forefront of their respective fields. The medical workers who brighten hospital corridors with compassionate bedside manners do not do so only to gain sparkling performance reviews, and as many educators would attest, sometimes a classroom is more daunting than the boardroom. What makes these people experts, however, is not their staying power in times of hardship. Rather, it is their ingenuity, their unique proficiencies, and their comparable work ethic that shine through as remarkable.

Expertise, for these selected members, is neither a testament to how many accolades they have attached to their names nor an indication that they have completely mastered a particular subject. Their humility initially caused many to comment that they were not, in fact, experts, and instead were merely following their hearts — doing what came naturally. It is a widely accepted notion that we do best what we love most, and the sincerest effort yields the greatest results. Though an ample paycheck is not likely to be absent from the list of factors that affect job satisfaction for most individuals, personal and career success as the result of self-motivation is certainly a comparable reward.

The mission of Cambridge Who's Who is to provide our members with some of the resources necessary to connect with a network of knowledgeable, dedicated and upward-moving professionals. The discussions you will read convey emotion and passion that are not only refreshing, but stirring to anyone who has had a dream and envisioned it coming true. I learned much from these interviews, and have been moved by some of the trajectories that led each person to their current situations. The performers, scientists, medical technologists, engineers, financial executives, government officials, and military personnel compiled in this book share scores of similarities: leadership, innovation, zeal, sustainability. Their qualifications read as not only impressive, but expected. Each has something to offer to help you reach your own pinnacle of achievement.

Best regards,

Danielle Blanchard
Senior Editor, "Top 101 Industry Experts"
Cambridge Who's Who®

INDUSTRY KEY

Your Guide to Our Experts

While Cambridge Who's Who® members share similar industries, they each excel in a particular field. The visual key below depicts the 24 major industries into which our members are categorized.

	ADVERTISING/ MARKETING/ PUBLIC RELATIONS	INSURANCE	
	AGRICULTURE	LAW	
	ARCHITECTURE/ CONSTRUCTION	LEISURE	
	ARTS	MANUFACTURING	
	BUSINESS SERVICES	MEDIA & ENTERTAINMENT	
	EDUCATION	NONPROFIT	
	ENERGY	REAL ESTATE	
	FINANCE	RETAIL / WHOLESALE / DISTRIBUTION / SALES	
	GOVERNMENT	SCIENCES	
	HEALTH CARE	SOCIAL SERVICES	
	HOLISTIC HEALTH	TECHNOLOGY	
	HUMAN RESOURCES	TRANSPORTATION	

TOP 101

INDUSTRY EXPERTS

BIOGRAPHIES

Sports and Trauma Psychology

Dr. Cynthia A. Spanier

Owner, Creator, Health, Trauma and Sports Psychologist
Psychological Health & Behavioral Medicine
Penn Avenue
Pittsburgh, PA 15221 USA
cyndiespanier@aol.com

Dr. Cynthia A. Spanier is a health, trauma and sports psychologist. She founded and operates Psychological Health & Behavioral Medicine, a private practice that offers therapy for mind-body illnesses and includes help for traumatic stress due to stressful life events. Working from a humanistic perspective, Dr. Spanier specializes in helping people who suffer from traumatic stress disorders, where she focuses on different cognitive, emotional and behavioral strategies that clients can learn and apply to their lives.

Before she became a psychologist, Dr. Spanier was a speech therapist with a collection of experiences that yielded her a strong communication and brain-behavior background. Building on this foundation as a psychologist by allowing clients to grieve and acknowledge cosmic losses, Dr. Spanier finds that resiliency and optimism come into play in many of her clients' cases. But sometimes, the continuous care becomes difficult for clients, regardless of their progress. At this point, she urges a client to persist; she also applies her extensive knowledge of the nervous system and the human response to stressful situations to help a client self-soothe to a tranquil state, continue healing, and recover.

Her method of caring for individuals who suffer from grief, loss and (often) betrayal is multi-tiered: she deals first with the grief and loss, and then other, often interpersonal, issues that arise. "It is a matter of asking a client, 'How do you move on to the next phases of your life?'" she describes. One of the critical points she helps her patients realize is that being a victim doesn't imply one has to inherit a demeaning role in life; it means that a critical incident or series of critical incidents occurred or continues to occur that is not the client's fault. She uses person-to-person medicine: that is, her goal is to help ease human suffering and help a person live life to its fullest potential.

Dr. Spanier has written a number of journal and chapter publications and has an extensive background in clinical research and training. She lectures on topics ranging from depression and psychotherapy to smoking cessation. She has just started using Spring Forest Qigong, which is a form of active exercise meditation that she recommends.

Dr. Spanier completed an internship in clinical psychology in 1997 at the Clinical Psychology Training Consortium of the Brown University Department of Psychiatry and Human Behavior. She received a Ph.D. in Psychology in 1997 from the University of Pittsburgh, a Master of Science in Communication Disorders in 1982 from Marquette University, and a Bachelor of Science in Communication in 1981 from Marquette University. Dr. Spanier completed further psychology training as a postdoctoral fellow in cancer clinical research at the University of Pittsburgh Cancer Institute in 1999. She is a member of the International Society for Traumatic Stress Studies, the Posttraumatic Stress Disorder National Professional Network, the Pittsburgh Chapter of the American Association of University Women, and the Psychology Division of the National Institute of Sports Professionals. She is also a National Association of Sports Psychologists Diplomat in Sports Psychology.

CONVERSATION WITH DR. CYNTHIA A. SPANIER

CAMBRIDGE WHO'S WHO: What would you like to promote most about yourself or your business?
CYNTHIA A. SPANIER: My professional responsibilities involve trauma work with war and terrorism survivors. I'm also working a great deal with people who are survivors of crime and others with post-traumatic stress. I work with both men and women, although often my clients are women.

I work with all kinds of cases and I belong to the International Society for the Study of Traumatic Stress [ISTSS]. I am still involved with sports psychology and continue to work with coaches and players, especially in the sport of tennis. Mainly because this, too, is all about change and adaptation. However, most of my referrals are in the area of trauma.

On what topic(s) do you consider yourself to be an expert?
As a clinical and trauma psychologist, with further training and study, I've become an expert in trauma. I am also an expert in mood disorders, relationships, anxiety, health psychology, and sports psychology. I deal with traumatic stress, which could be from any number of reasons. It could be severe, prolonged and repetitive physical instances dating back to the client's childhood or a one-time severe stressor like a car accident, shooting or gang fight. It could be a war crime in which the client or someone they knew was involved. It could be an instance where a family member was killed in front of the client. It could be anything; it could be a recurring kind of event, which is called multiple incident complex post-traumatic stress disorder, versus simple post-traumatic stress disorder, which focuses on a single incident. There are different kinds of post-traumatic stress disorders.

How do you remain current in your profession?
I read extensively and stay very active. I am very much an athlete and come from a family of athletes. I personally live out my sports and health psychology every day with myself and my family. I read journals such as the Journal of Traumatic Stress, which is published by the ISTSS. Recently, I read a journal article about reparative healing, which focused in on when soldiers return from war. I was profoundly moved and changed by my understanding of this

construct. Reparative justice is really a necessary part of the healing process after massive trauma. That kind of acknowledgement is essential for the healing process.

Since the early days of my childhood, I have always been a vast reader. As a result, I have a colossal imagination.

What makes you a valuable resource in your industry?
I'm genuinely committed and I care deeply. Also, I care a great deal about people and I want to make the world a better place. I believe in justice for my clients, my family and myself. I am a victim of a car accident; my daughter and I were hit head-on in a car accident. I believe in altruism and making the world a better place, so compassion is a key element. I want to make a positive difference in the world, not only for today's generation, but for the generations to come.

What is the most significant issue facing your profession today?
Managed care and insurmountable paperwork in place of patient care and clinical research.

What advice can you offer fellow members who work in your industry?
You really need to keep abreast of what's going on because so many changes are happening so rapidly with technology. Things are happening behind the scenes that we don't know about technically and, as these applications become available in the public domain (they are currently available behind the scenes), it is important to keep up. Keep your eyes and ears open. It is a classic case of technology getting ahead of the laws and regulations needed to control its proper safe use for humanity. What I am saying is that we have great technology, more than most even know about; however, the problem is that the laws, the wisdom, the judgment, the morals and ethics need to be in place first so that these tools are used properly and not as weapons to destroy one another. Stay sharp and keep your continued education going. Be ready for change because it is definitely happening.

What advice can you offer people aspiring to work in this profession?
Be prepared for a long journey and hard work. It takes many years of training and practice, but it's well worth it if you love it. You have to be a good listener. Listening is a skill and you have to learn how to be a good listener just like everything else.

What are you passionate about?
Reparative justice, curing traumatic stress, doubles tennis, parenting, education, planting, purchasing and the consumption of organic food.

Who have been your mentors or people who have greatly influenced you?
The clinical internship in which I participated at Brown University undisputedly influenced me. My philosophical and moral background education at Marquette University and the many friends I made there. My dear family and friends, including my soul mates, Jeff and Rose: "Mes amour merveilleux."

Do you have a motto?
"Say yes to life." I try to have a positive attitude and speak highly of people all the time if it is legitimate for me to do so.

Advertising and Brand Development

John G. Most

President, Chief Executive Officer
MOST Brand Development + Advertising
25 Enterprise
Suite 250
Aliso Viejo, CA 92656 USA
john@mostagency.com
http://www.mostagency.com

John G. Most is the president and CEO of MOST Brand Development + Advertising, a highly awarded advertising and brand development agency that in 2010 was ranked #107 in Inc. magazine's annual 500 list of the nation's fastest-growing companies. His company also had the distinction of having the biggest leap on the Inc. magazine 500 list that year. MOST, in 2009, was the top-ranked small company in The Orange County Business Journal's inaugural Best Places to Work and returned to the top rankings again in 2010. Also, in 2010, MOST was named their third fastest-growing privately held company — a distinction it has earned for the third straight year. Mr. Most, one of only 25 certified brand strategists nationwide, is responsible for overseeing the brand discovery and development of current and prospective clients' brands. He combines honesty, common sense, hard work, and a relentless commitment to meet the needs of his clients. The clients expect and MOST delivers superior results with strong brand plans and result-oriented creative solutions. In the six years that MOST has been in existence, they have garnered more than 36 industry achievement Awards for Creative Excellence — most notably, a Summit International Marketing Effectiveness Award, received in 2009, which is the best of category award.

Building brands, and strong business and personal relationships takes top priority for Mr. Most, whose commitment to his clients and employees — a practice of "doing business the way people should be doing business" — can best be summed up by his mantra: "Good enough...isn't." He takes cues from his successful relationship with The National Association of Realtors, one of his top, longstanding clients of nearly 15 years. "NAR has nearly 1.2 million members and while I haven't met them all," he jokes, "I go to their key meetings and conventions, where I meet with the best the profession have to offer." Despite a severe downturn in the real estate market, particularly for the past three years, Realtors seem to agree that the work MOST delivers is making a difference with consumers and relevant to the changing markets they face, especially in the way the company promotes their professionalism and image.

Mr. Most received a bachelor's degree, with a dual-minor in business administration and advertising in 1979, from the University of Bridgeport. He believes deeply in giving back and is a recognized community leader. He is the former chairman of the Board of Trustees for the Orange County Chapter of the National Multiple Sclerosis Society; the planning committee chairman of the MS Bike event, which annually raises more than $2 million per year; and a perennial top fundraiser for the 100-mile bike event, in addition to the MS Walk and 50-mile Challenge Walk events. In 2005, he was named the NMSS Orange County Chapter's Volunteer of the Year. He is active in many other national and local charities and gives generously to a number of causes. He was also awarded an Emmy for his role in the United Way of America's national pro bono account and was runner-up for Volunteer of the Year for the G.D. Crain Award presented by The Advertising Council.

CONVERSATION WITH JOHN G. MOST

CAMBRIDGE WHO'S WHO: What characteristics help to separate your company from other competitors?
JOHN G. MOST: We are an agency, but not an agency in the way clients have, unfortunately, come to think of them. While typical advertising agencies "do advertisements," we discover and develop brands and are able to successfully complete the job by creating the communications that reach the client's target prospect most meaningfully and memorably — in their head and in their heart — with positive business results on a more cost-efficient basis.

What is your greatest professional accomplishment to date?
While most people look back at my time as developing the Grey Poupon Dijon Mustard brand and their famous Rolls Royce advertisement campaigns, my greatest professional accomplishment is our work with the National Association of Realtors. I have been leading, from my company, their brand development from ground zero to where it is today — it's been a more than 14-year relationship. The program has been extraordinarily successful and has been well received by their members. I'm honored that Realtors think of me as a part of the NAR family.

What are your short-term and long-term career goals?
[My goals are to] stay within a manageable size and scope on growth where I can continue to have hands-on influence on our client businesses and their success. We're looking for "a few great clients" interested in mutually beneficial relationships, where the client values our contributions and where we, in turn, can do our best work to make sure that they exceed their goals. Simply stated, we're not successful unless they are.

What is the most rewarding aspect of your career?
I never intended to have my own business, so owning a successful company is right up there, but I take a lot of pride in how we developed our award-winning environment and culture from the employee perspective. After all, until six years ago, I was an employee. I really care about our people and their families — their children. We do the right thing for our people, who are the primary assets of our business.

ARCHITECTURAL MANAGEMENT AND DESIGN

ROBERT BRUCE FARIS
Owner, President
Design Futures
10837 Ballah Road
Orient, OH 43146 USA
designfutures@sbcglobal.net

When it comes to thinking outside the box, maintaining positive people relations and delivering inspired designs to clients, Robert Bruce Faris has proven to be one of the architecture industry's reliable agents. He is the president and owner of Design Futures, a private firm that has provided corporate and commercial architectural management and designs for the past three years. Mr. Faris brings more than a quarter of a century of experience to his employers and is responsible for the full gamut of architectural services, including managing business operations, marketing, negotiating contracts, and business development planning. He has several key strengths that have enabled him to establish a great name in the architecture industry, which include loyalty, trustworthiness, passion, emotional intelligence and efficiency.

After receiving a Bachelor of Science in Architecture in 1985 from The Ohio State University, Mr. Faris worked in a variety of roles that are crucial for the development and growth of a company. This includes a stint as vice president of retail and renovations for Goliver and Associates, Inc., as principal and, director of marketing for East Europe, and process design leader for leading architecture firm NBBJ, leading up to his current consultancy. Working in a private firm, he aspires to continue diversifying his contributions to the field, while growing the company to great heights.

From Ohio to Moscow, Mr. Faris feels most satisfied that his career has taken him around the globe. His experience extends from residential design in the community to small commercial projects within the Columbus metropolitan area, to large-scale projects in the Middle East, China and Russia, et al. Select architectural projects include a 12-story tower addition to Crowne Plaza in Columbus, Ohio, project management of a mixed-use development in Moscow, and construction administration of Huntington National Bank's Business Service Center in Columbus, Ohio. Mr. Faris, who resides in Columbus, drives past the structures on which he worked every day. "Building something in your town is great," he beams.

In his spare time, Mr. Faris enjoys traveling and spending time with his children on his farm.

CONVERSATION WITH ROBERT BRUCE FARIS

CAMBRIDGE WHO'S WHO: What are your short-term and long-term career goals?
ROBERT BRUCE FARIS: My short-term goal is to get my consulting business moving forward through diversification and relationship building. My long-term goal has always been to explore architecture through all aspects of the practice. While my career is important, my short- and long-term goals must be achieved through the balance of family, faith, personal and professional goals.

And what specific steps have you taken toward achieving these goals?
I've begun my journey to create a global consulting practice that encompasses various aspects of the architectural field – from land acquisitions and development opportunities to leading projects from a technical and process point of view and overseeing construction administration duties – all while continuing to build and nurture relationships.

On what topic(s) do you consider yourself to be an expert?
Architects are by definition jacks-of-all-trades and masters of none. I enjoy learning about new ideas, possibilities and opportunities. I internalize those learnings and once I understand them, I try to reassemble them into something new. It's a new way of looking at something. I possess a unique perspective on the architectural practice in that I've experienced and have been accountable with most aspects within it.

How do you remain current in your profession?
I attend seminars regarding building codes, new products and a variety of other topics that relate to architecture. Trade publications and books are a great way to remain current on particular trends within the industry – whether they are design- or even business-related. One of the best ways to remain current is to use your network of friends and colleagues in architecture and talk about products, projects, your success stories and failures.

What makes you a valuable resource in your industry?
The breadth of my experience, which is beyond my knowledge foundation about the design process (this includes facilitating the conceptual design of

complex structures to following through with their construction). My understanding and experience in international marketing, combined with my leading the operational and financial aspects of the design studio, are pretty unique in our industry. I've also attended and coached a number of leadership programs, some of them lasting as long as nine months.

What is the most significant issue facing your profession today?
The economy is the most significant issue at this point in time. Some firms that have maintained a healthy practice in government, civic works or hospitals have managed to survive. It's a struggle for larger firms all the way down to the one-man shops. The generalist architect seems to be a thing of the past.

What advice can you offer fellow members who work in your industry?
The lean times, such as what we are experiencing now, can help purify and refine our industry since we tend to see the worst architecture done in the best of times. We have the opportunity to recreate our industry to meet the goals of the emerging global market and economy; also, to integrate sustainable design into the soul of our practice, rather than merely filling out a checklist.

What advice can you offer people aspiring to work in this profession?
Maintain a positive attitude and work hard. Understand where you want to go within the profession and manage your own course. Take an active role in your long-term strategic career planning and utilize even the littlest opportunities that may arise as you accomplish your goals. There are four agreements that I have adopted from Don Miguel Ruiz: 1. Be impeccable with your word; 2. Don't take anything personally; 3. Don't make assumptions; and 4. Always do your best.

What are you passionate about?
Family, faith and the balance of life. I am also passionate about experiencing nature through outdoor activities, living on my farm and tending the soil of the earth.

Who have been your mentors or people who have greatly influenced you?
My parents laid the foundation for the journey, the Boy Scouts of America provided key growth opportunities in the areas of self-esteem, confidence and leadership, and my family, including my ex-wife and children, inspired me to continue to walk the path. Another mentor I had was my friend Friedel Bome, who constantly asked "Where do you really want to go?" And finally, for inspiration and guidance, Jesus Christ, who has been walking with me every step of the way.

What prompted you into this industry?
I started in aerospace engineering, but didn't feel I had a creative connection with the field. Architecture created the connection, but with practical applications.

Do you have a favorite quote?
"You work that you may keep pace with the earth and the soul of the earth. For to be idle is to become a stranger unto the seasons, and a step out of life's procession, that marches in majesty and proud submission toward the infinite." – an excerpt from "The Prophet" by Kahlil Gibran

What is your greatest professional accomplishment to date?
Achieving the majority of my goal of becoming a generalist architect, with experience in small and large companies, domestically and internationally. Individually, it would be a couple of local projects that I have done in Columbus, Ohio.

What is the most difficult obstacle or challenge you have faced in pursuit of your goals?
Architecture is a stressful profession, especially in a larger firm. The balance in life is something that you have to work on daily. If you don't set that as a goal, you will burn out, lose your family and friends, or give yourself health issues.

Authorship, Artistry and Music Composition

Patti Forté
Writer, Author, Artist, Entrepreneur
pcforte@earthlink.net
http://www.pattiforte.com

Patti Forté is an author, artist and entrepreneur who, after more than 21 years in the profession, is taking her artistic vision to bold new heights. She presently is working on three concurrent professional operations: she designs CD covers and jackets, is using her new painting techniques to express her feelings, and is writing and doing research on her second book, "The Missing Medulla." As her creative outlook matures, Ms. Forté is looking forward to unleashing greater volumes of art to the world in robust, powerful waves.

As many artists would attest, their creations are very personal. In 2002, Ms. Forté published a book and a music CD entitled "Parting the Mist," and wanted to keep the art originals for herself and her family. But another side of Ms. Forté believes she has got to let go in order to continue. She remarks that for the first time, she's stepping out of her comfort zone. "At first, I was doing it to heal myself, but right now other people are wanting these," she says, speaking of the handiwork that has given her the confidence to break out of her self-imposed barriers and quickly discover an inspired place.

Ms. Forté, who attributes her success to her intense passion for the arts, has also completed a collaborative screenplay titled "Caryatid Porch," which examines women in power. She hopes to explore publishing opportunities with it in the near future. With regards to the work she does on an easel or blank canvas, she is presently painting more with her hands, rather than a paintbrush. This is something novel and very exciting for the creative expert, wherein she has learned to explore the tremendous healing powers of her hands and translate that energy into her paintings.

Ms. Forté received a bachelor's degree in elementary education from San José State University. Throughout her career, she has worked for the Junior Center of Art and Science, the Family Service Guild, and eWomenNetwork, Inc. She is a member of the American Business Women's Association and the International Poetry Society. She is a founding laureate member of the International Society of Poets.

Conversation with Patti Forté

Cambridge Who's Who: What is the most rewarding aspect of your career?
Patti Forté: I love being able to express myself through writing, poetry, music, painting and other mediums — it's cathartic. This creation comes from a place deep within my soul. I like the way the world is shifting and changing, because it gives me insight into a new perspective that I can express and put on canvas. My most recent paintings are based on my love of nature, and I use my memory and imagination to create landscapes not necessarily seen but felt. I feel blessed that I have this creativity inside to be able to express myself.

What is the most difficult obstacle or challenge you have faced in pursuit of your goals?
The most difficult challenge is that, from one moment to the next, I never know what I am going to be able to express. There's always this feeling of, "Oh my gosh, can I do this again?" I was just talking about this to a friend the other day. I know that I will be able to express something, but I keep thinking, "What if I lose this ability?" It's a little daunting not knowing what to expect, or what's going to come out next.

On what topics do you consider yourself to be an expert?
My art is always exploratory, and explorers don't consider themselves to be experts. They are always looking for the next adventure. If you consider yourself an expert, you may slow your growth. An artist's goal is not to be an expert, but to achieve greater personal growth

What are your short-term and long-term career goals?
Actually, my short-term and long-term goals are the same. My goals are to continue exploring my spirituality and expressing it through my writings and artwork.

What advice would you give to other people who aspire to be a writer, artist or creator?
Stay open and let your artistic energy flow. Keep letting go; go deep within, and believe in yourself. Don't do it for other people; do it for yourself, just to have fun. I truly believe we all are artists with something inside to discover.

As I look back, I now realize some of my favorite paintings were done before I ever took my first art class. Everyone has something to express and should take the time to develop that part of themselves.

What is your motivation for creating artwork?
I do it for my own personal gratification. I do it for the joy it gives to me and others. Creating art is like falling in love — it comes from your soul and you can't help it when it happens. It's exhilarating and fulfilling.

Who have been your mentors or people who have greatly influenced you?
My friend, Joan Cochran, was and is my mentor. She believed in me way before I ever believed in myself. I remember taking an outdoor painting and sketching class with her and she said my trees looked like Rembrandt etchings. Another time, she showed me how a few brush strokes could turn one of my paintings into my favorite painting. Joan has encouraged me from the moment I started painting, and she is also one of the best painters I know.

What makes you a valuable resource in your industry?
I'm willing to listen, and I'm always positive and encouraging. I truly believe that the more we believe in ourselves, the more everything comes together.

PASTEL PAINTING

ANN OSBORN GENDREAU
United States Customs Inspector (Retired)
United States Customs Service
Fort Kent, ME 04743 USA
ann.gendreau@cwwemail.com

Ann Osborn Gendreau is a retired customs inspector for the United States Customs Service, a government organization that provides inspections to vehicles traveling to and from the country. She served the organization loyally for almost 15 years, stationed in Madawaska and Fort Kent leading up to her retirement in 1997. While giving up her profession has afforded her the blessing of free time, she remains as busy as ever, creating eye-pleasing works of art as well as providing much-needed service to the elderly and needy in the community.

Through the years, her artwork has been displayed and sold at local craft fairs and has gained a decent amount of exposure. While Ms. Gendreau has partaken in artistic endeavors the past 14 years, her appreciation for the craft stems back beyond that. "I have done art all of my life," she states, remembering when she co-owned a gallery with 10 other artists and taught art classes for four years through an adult education program. Ms. Gendreau, who attributes her success to her incredible zest for life, truly enjoys painting with pastels, although she started with oil and acrylic. She feels most inspired by items in nature, including bodies of water such as lakes, streams, rivers and ponds. Oftentimes, she can be found frequenting scenic locales, taking photographs that will serve as inspiration for her future paintings. Additionally, she is adept at painting human portraits.

Ms. Gendreau received a Bachelor of Science in Education, magna cum laude, in 1979 from The University of Maine at Fort Kent. She is the former president of the American Legion Auxiliary. In her spare time, Ms. Gendreau enjoys four-wheeling, the arts and spending time with her family. She also donates her time and resources to St. Jude Children's Research Hospital, local animal rights groups, The American Society for the Prevention of Cruelty to Animals, The Humane Society of the United States, the World Life Foundation and The Smile Train.

Conversation with Ann Osborn Gendreau

Cambridge Who's Who: What would you like to promote most about yourself or your business?
Ann Osborn Gendreau: My artwork.

What is the most rewarding aspect of your career?
I had my own real estate business, of which I was proud. I had about seven or eight people working for me with two offices in Connecticut. I had that business for about 12 years.

On what topic(s) do you consider yourself to be an expert?
Volunteering and painting.

How do you remain current in your profession?
I get all the artist magazines, The Pastel Journal, and American Artist. I also read TIME, Newsweek, National Geographic and Smithsonian.

What are your short-term and long-term career goals?
I volunteer to cook for about 37 senior citizens who live in their own homes. We will be having a big 30-mile tag sale, all the way from Fort Kent to Madawaska this summer, and we are trying to get that organized. I'm simplifying my life and getting rid of all of these nice things that are in good shape. I want to give them away because I have no more use for them.

Do you have a favorite quote?
"A good laugh with friends is the best healing in the world."

What are you passionate about?
My animals — my charities are all for animals or for the children — and rescue missions. I am also passionate about nature and conservation.

What advice can you offer people aspiring to work in this profession?
I like people and what I loved about customs was meeting new people. I enjoy listening to others. Every person has a wonderful story that's completely different from your whole life.

Program Coordination

Beth Stormont, DMA, MA, BA
Manager, Program Director
Bowers House Writers Retreat
P.O. Box 74
100 Depot Street
Canon, GA 30520 USA

Dr. Beth Stormont, a manager and program director of Bowers House Writers Retreat, has 56 years of professional experience. Throughout her career, she has worked in a variety of vocations, including teacher for Los Angeles County Schools, professor for Glendale Community College, and professional organist and choir director for various liturgical churches in California. Her academic background and desire to experience vastly different things in life prompted her to accept the position at Bowers House Writers Retreat in Canon, Ga.

The Bowers House Writers Retreat, located in the farm country of northeast Georgia, is a picturesque home where writers come to quench their thirst for creating their art form. As program director and manager, Dr. Stormont helps to continue founder Laura Bowers Foreman's wish to maintain the house so residing writers may find the peace and seclusion necessary to complete their work. Ms. Foreman invited Stephen Corey, the editor of The Georgia Review, to be associated with what was originally a literary center in order to help it gain credibility and the interest of the journal's authors along with its readership. After lying dormant for five years, the beautifully restored historic home has been transformed into a full-fledged resilient residence and meeting place for writers.

Dr. Stormont's previous position was as coordinator of the RISE Lifelong Learning program for Rio Salado College in Arizona. It currently has more than 1,000 active members and offers 100-plus classes each term for the enrichment of retired mature adults. Much of its success can be attributed to Dr. Stormont's work with the program for the past five years.

Dr. Stormont received a Doctor of Musical Arts in Performing Arts from the University of Southern California, a Master of Arts in Music from Occidental College and a Bachelor of Arts in Education from California State University at Long Beach. Her recent organizational memberships have included The Theosophical Society in America, Toastmasters International, Friendship Force International, West Valley Women (Business Women of Arizona), and the American Association of University Women.

Dr. Stormont's many activities also include leading spiritual discussion groups; traveling domestically and internationally; writing philosophical and spiritual prose and poetry; listening to, creating and performing classical music (piano, organ, harp, orchestral string bass); and directing choral groups.

CONVERSATION WITH BETH STORMONT, DMA, MA, BA

CAMBRIDGE WHO'S WHO: What would you like to promote most about yourself or your business?
BETH STORMONT: I moved from Arizona to Georgia in June 2010. I am now the manager and program director of Bowers House Writers Retreat, where I will be creating and implementing a varied program in both the fields of writing and education. I am especially promoting the many potentialities of Bowers House Writers Retreat.

What is the most rewarding aspect of your career?
Creating something wonderful to benefit people. I didn't realize how successful I had been with the RISE program until after I had left – that is the most rewarding thing to me. The RISE program is part of the Lifelong Learning program that is nationwide and usually connected with colleagues and universities. The specific RISE Lifelong Learning program, of which I was coordinator for the past five years, is geared toward retired adults to whom classes are offered free of charge all year long for an annual $45 membership fee.

What is your greatest professional accomplishment to date?
I feel I have been more successful coordinating the RISE Lifelong Learning program — in terms of really impacting the lives of many people — than anything I have ever done before.

What are your short-term and long-term career goals?
I follow the new law of manifestation, which means that I let my visions evolve and manifest in the way that is natural to them. Like my evolution, the RISE program has also evolved; I was the vehicle through which it could create itself. For my new position, my short-term goal is to successfully manage the Bowers House Writers Retreat, carrying out the ideals of the owner and having writers come to finish their works here. Additionally, there will be workshops and seminars to oversee. I also envision coordinating and directing an outlet for lifelong learning. The expansion of the program would be my long-term goal. I have no career goals for myself as such.

What is the most difficult obstacle or challenge you have faced in pursuit of your goals?
Combating limitations placed on the carrying out of my work by short-sighted organizational leaders, which, in turn, has made me stronger and more resilient.

On what topics do you consider yourself to be an expert?
Education, spirituality and classical music.

What makes you a valuable resource in your industry?
Not only my background of education and experience, but also much of what I do comes from my inner knowledge.

What advice can you offer fellow members who work in your industry?
Be focused, detail-oriented and dedicated, but always keep in mind the big picture. My dedication, I know, has been a major factor in making me successful. People know that I "live, eat and breathe" what I do.

What advice can you offer people aspiring to work in this profession?
If you are looking at it for money, forget it. It is a calling – one to which I have always felt I was called.

What are you passionate about?
I am passionate about the people with whom I work – they are my family and closest friends. I am also passionate about the work that I am given to do. Just about everything I choose to do in life, I do with passion!

Who have been your mentors or people who have greatly influenced you?
The people who have been brought into my life for a meaningful purpose and those with whom I have lived and worked with closely and sincerely.

Do you have a motto or principle that guides your work?
Share your passion.

Glassmaking and Education

Amanda Taylor
Co-Owner
OATKA School of Glass and Glass Studio c/o Egami Inc.
56 Harvester Avenue
Batavia, NY 14020 USA
amanda@oatkaglass.com
http://www.oatkaglass.com

Of the many different art forms one can choose from to express oneself, Amanda Taylor has opted to make a living by creating beautiful works out of glass and teaching others to do the same. Located in one of the farthest regions of western New York state, the OATKA School of Glass and Glass Studio specializes in bringing students of all nationalities and talent levels together to produce their finest pieces. The school has evolved from humble beginnings in Mrs. Taylor's home to a first-class studio housed in a historic 19th century warehouse near the Corning Museum of Glass, which features 35 centuries of outstanding glass art.

As co-owner in partnership with her husband Lance, Mrs. Taylor provides students with an opportunity to learn about the history of glassmaking and various techniques while enriching their creative spirits. The name Oatka, which is a North American Indian word loosely translated as "through an opening" or "approaching an opening," holds a dual meaning for the studio. The first and most obvious refers to the translucence of glass and one's ability to see through it, while the second describes Mrs. Taylor's mission to guide her students through a breach – one that exposes them to new ways of thinking, creating and relating to the world. Near the studio, she and her husband host a bed and breakfast where they house students and international artists who come to visit or teach specialized classes at the school.

The recipient of a Bachelor of Fine Arts, Mrs. Taylor has always maintained an intense interest in arts and crafts since she was a child. When opening the school, she wanted to provide a learning facility where students and instructors had the freedom to explore their respective visions without hindrances or interruptions from outside forces. Additionally, their array of classes in kiln casting, lamp working, glass mosaics, fritography (the use of crushed glass pieces to create fused artwork), and glass vessel sinks proffers a vast selection from which students can glean inspiration.

Mrs. Taylor is a board member of the Glass Art Association of Canada and a member of the Glass Art Society and the International Society of Glass Beadmakers. In the near future, she hopes to organize more events and expand the gallery to include more artists and features.

CONVERSATION WITH AMANDA TAYLOR

CAMBRIDGE WHO'S WHO: What would you like to promote most about yourself or your business?
AMANDA TAYLOR: We will be trying to bring in artists who use different mediums such as ceramics and metals. In the upcoming year, our main focus is to promote the school portion of our business.

What is the most rewarding aspect of your career?
I love working with glass and having my own business. I love being challenged and the teaching aspect is very rewarding. It is a great thing when you can see excitement and pride in students' eyes when they see and feel their finished work.

What has been your greatest professional accomplishment to date?
Starting the glass school and managing 12,000 square feet of studio space with my husband and co-founder. Operating the school, making artwork to sell, marketing and having a presence is a great accomplishment when you consider that there are only two or three of us managing it all. My studio used to be in my basement before I moved to New York and expanded it.

What are your short-term and long-term career goals?
My short-term goal is to build a network of students who keep coming back to take more classes and buy supplies from us. My long-term goal is to continue progressing with my own work. I also want to push our marketing strategies so that my artwork will get more exposure in galleries and stores.

Have you taken any specific steps toward achieving these goals?
I have become more diversified with classes we offer, substantially increased our marketing on the Internet, and opened a store where we carry specialty manufacturers' products.

What is the most difficult obstacle or challenge you have faced in pursuit of your goals?
We are only two people running a large studio in addition to running and renovating the bed and breakfast we purchased in 2008. We house visiting instructors and out-of-town students there. The renovation of the 1825 home will be an ongoing project.

On what topics do you consider yourself to be an expert?
I was a geophysical technologist for 30 years, where I specialized in seismic data management and geophysical systems management. During that time, I wrote a data management program and sold it to my clients for use in their companies. I have been working with kiln-formed glass since 1994 and my work includes many of the techniques I have been taught over the years.

How do you remain current in your profession?
Since we host workshops at our school, I am constantly learning new things that I can apply to my own work. We also belong to various art-related societies and partake in their conferences on a yearly basis.

What makes you a valuable resource in your industry?
We have amazing instructors teaching at our school on a monthly basis. The classes that we teach are structured in a way that greatly enhances the students' learning abilities. Having the bed and breakfast offers another dimension to our business.

What is the most significant issue facing your profession today?
In this economy, people consider learning an art form as a bit of a luxury expense. We have seen a gradual improvement in the class enrollment over the past year. Also, there are many other glass studios teaching, but we feel we are unique. Getting the word out is always a challenge at the start. Cost of materials is always something to be factored in.

What advice can you offer people aspiring to work in this profession?
Spend time, experiment and don't undersell yourself. Your value is in yourself and your time.

Who have been your mentors or people who have greatly influenced you?
Robert Leather Barrow was my first kiln-formed glass instructor in Calgary, Alberta. He is well-known glass artist. Patty Gray and Rebecca Bergsina are friends and glass artists who inspired me to go to the max with my work. And last but not least, my psychic friend, Chad Smith, who told me I had a calling and if I didn't use it, I would lose it.

Do you have any exciting news or upcoming ventures?
Some of my work is being published in an upcoming book by Danijela Kracun called "Creative Glass," which features work from several glass artists.

What is your motto or favorite saying?
Go big or go home!

Trade Show and Event Production

Sandra K. Campbell-Flippin
Trade Show, Event Sales and Production Manager
A-Classic Expo Design
1625 Southeastern Avenue
Indianapolis, IN 46201 USA
scamp45450@aol.com
http://www.635-expo.com

As a trade show and event sales and production manager for A-Classic Expo Design, Sandra K. Campbell-Flippin is well aware that as people return to annual events, they need to experience something new and different each time. For that reason, she works hand-in-hand with producers and clients to ensure that they never design the same event for attendees. "I encourage people to think outside the box because people have experienced what I've already done," she states.

In 1990, Ms. Campbell-Flippin started working in corporate motorsports public relations and marketing. As she started managing events for racing teams and professional racecar drivers, she began working with a company that was a sponsor for one of the racecars. She was approached by Jack Bayt and Jack Hawkins, owners of A-Classic Expo Design, to start an expo section of their business, BRI Inc., an opportunity that would offer their employees work during the off-season. Along with Exhibit City News, these people served as her mentors and helped her to keep up with the changes in industry trends.

An industry veteran, she does not view obstacles as barriers but rather ways to work through challenges. She advises other women who want to enter her industry to give themselves the time to learn and determine how they can fit into the system, rather than try to change the world. One of Ms. Campbell-Flippin's techniques is to always give members her cell phone number so that she is accessible and reliable to customers.

Ms. Campbell-Flippin, who reads Special Events, Tradeshow Week, and Meetings & Conventions, is a certified meeting professional and exhibition manager. She has started her own home-based Internet company, ProductsWithoutDelays.com, which is an eBay business composed of the contents of foreclosed stores and estates made available for resale. Through auction, Products Without Delays will provide more than 50,000 products including audio, video, marine audio, home electronics, iPod, gaming, music, DJ and lighting tools, and jeweler's supplies.

Conversation with Sandra K. Campbell-Flippin

Cambridge Who's Who: What would you like to promote most about yourself or your business?
Sandra K. Campbell-Flippin: A lot of what I want to do is provide everyone with the best service possible. With the economy, everyone is trying to save money, so we try to work within things, and not just on a yearly basis. You are always changing events and mixing things up, doing something different and adding something new.

What is the most rewarding aspect of your career?
Watching people walk in and go, "Wow!" The wow factor is the most successful aspect of my career.

On what topic(s) do you consider yourself to be an expert?
I love corporate events and trade shows. These people just want it to be the best it could be and their jobs are on the line – they have high expectations. I have designed and set up a whole crew of people who work with me. My team knows what I expect and I know what they expect; we work very closely as a group so that we bring that vision to the client.

What is your greatest professional accomplishment to date?
My greatest professional accomplishments are having the respect of fellow meeting, event and convention professionals. They all look up to me or call me when they are stumped or need assistance in getting their events together.

How do you remain current in your profession?
I attend a lot of trade shows focused around the style of events that I handle. The key is really finding out what works. I will attend shows to which people invite me and I am able to see the things that they do. I will also bring my team to see what we might need to try.

Do you have a motto?
"Do unto others as you would have them do unto you." That is how my father raised me.

What advice can you offer fellow members who work in your industry?
Stop and listen to your customer. Don't take control of their event; let them have the feel of control, even if they really don't have it. Spend time building their vision and not your vision. You can always learn from your clients. Always follow through and listen to what they say.

What are you passionate about?
Doing things right – there's a wide variety of things that I do.

What is the most significant issue facing your profession today?
The economy drives everything and a lot of the trade industrial shows have really felt [the recession] this year. I'm starting to take notice of where people are selling more floor space. Also, I'm beginning to see a process where more of the exhibitors are coming back because they can't afford to be away.

Who have been your mentors or people who have greatly influenced you?
I really drew inspiration from my father. He was a very caring person – not by giving money, but by giving love.

What is the most difficult obstacle or challenge you have faced in pursuit of your goals?
Competition is tough; so many companies are hungry due to the economy and they are bidding events so low that they are only covering costs with no profits. I am not in business to break even. We work way too hard to not make money.

What makes you a valuable resource in your industry?
I feel that what makes me a valuable resource in my industry is knowing what is new and how to work it into clients' budgets. You can dream up a $100,000 event, but the client only has a $10,000 budget. You have to keep everything within perspective to your client.

Trade magazines and the Internet are very helpful with the trends that are new and upcoming. You must change what you do as the trends change. If you do not, someone else will.

ORGANIZATIONAL DEVELOPMENT

René Montoya Lado, MS, NCC
President, Founder
Strategic Designs for Learning
165 S. Union Boulevard
Suite 270
Lakewood, CO 80228
rlado@strategicdesigns.net
http://www.strategicdesigns.net

René Montoya Lado of Strategic Designs for Learning has 30 years of experience as an organizational development professional. She had over 25 years of corporate experience before she evolved to consulting with businesses to build their capacity for organizational renewal. She also enjoys a small private therapy practice in which she primarily works with children. Since starting SDL in 1999, she has become quite adept at her trade and gained substantial experience working exclusively with family-owned businesses.

After working as a senior executive in an international professional services firm, Ms. Lado found her niche in the field of family-owned business and decided to start her own firm. Her husband and his family had a big influence on her in that they owned a family business. Ms. Lado's proximity to their daily lives enabled her to witness firsthand how a business can eclipse a family and threaten their stability. She vowed from that point to help other families address the issues that may be overlooked due to the constant pressure to maintain the business.

Working closely with her clients, who are in the manufacturing, energy, retail, finance, and information technology sectors, Ms. Lado utilizes her expertise in organizational behavior to coach executives, counsel employees and family members, and help companies with such issues as change management and succession planning. After recently relocating to Denver, Colo. Ms. Lado is not one to retire just yet. She intends to continue coaching with families, their C-level executives, and their governance boards. She will also continue to enjoy her private clinical practice with children. Additionally, she would like to do some pro bono work in adult literacy.

Ms. Lado received a Master of Arts in Political Science from the University of Colorado, summa cum laude, and a Master of Science in Pastoral Counseling from Loyola College, cum laude. She is certified in the use of the Myers-Briggs Type Indicator and the HR Chally instrument, and has completed the Designed Learning "Empowered Manager" series and the Center for Creative Leadership's

"Benchmarks" program. She is also a member of the Association for the Management of Organizational Design, the American Counseling Association, the Family Firm Institute, Inc., the American Psychological Association and the Organizational Development Network.

Conversation with René Montoya Lado, MS, NCC

Cambridge Who's Who: What would you like to promote most about yourself or your business?
René Montoya Lado: It is difficult enough to have an effective business and maintain a family, but when you have a family business, it's useful to get outside help from advisers — whether they are financial planners or estate attorneys. We help family-owned businesses navigate some of the stickier [situations], such as succession or executive coaching. I am also clinically trained as a pastoral-psychotherapist, so I bring a useful "family systems" approach to my work as well.

What do you find to be the most rewarding about your profession?
Being able to contribute to healing that needs to occur within families when the business has eclipsed them. Another rewarding aspect is being able to make a contribution so the clients feel that they have their family back, without having to give up the obvious financial advantages of a successful business.

What is your greatest professional accomplishment to date?
There is a family that I work with who owns and operates a fourth-generation manufacturing company. When I started working with them five years ago, there were four siblings and no identified successor. There was not much hope that this group of siblings could cooperate or collaborate together to decide on one of them. Through my work with this family, the sibling group has come together, now supports each other, and has allowed their father to identify one of them as his successor; the rest of them will work in the business. They are working well together and I feel very grateful to have advised them; I believe I have made a huge contribution.

What are your short-term and long-term career goals?
I am reaching the last phase of my professional career and it is important to me to continue to be able to help family-owned businesses, especially those that cannot afford a firm such as mine. Therefore my short-term goals are to provide coaching and training to other practitioners who are business consultants and advisers who are working or want to work with family businesses. Family businesses have some important differences, and if a consultant is not aware of those differences, they could inadvertently do harm.

And what specific steps have you taken toward achieving these goals?
We are putting together a certification course for other advisers to avail

themselves of. I'm very excited about putting what I have learned to more use so that an increased number of businesses can succeed and have a healthy family as well as a successful business.

What is the most difficult obstacle or challenge you have faced in pursuit of your goals?
Given that it's me and a few other consultants — and, according to the U.S. Bureau of the Census, approximately 90 percent of American businesses are family-owned or controlled and 60 percent of all publicly traded companies in the U.S. retain some level of family control — there is an enormous demand for this kind of work. Bandwidth limits me to working with five or six clients at a time. It is very important for others to expand their business consultancies to include family work.

On what topics do you consider yourself to be an expert?
Family-owned business and family system dynamics, executive coaching, framework, organizational change, communication, and assessment of leadership.

How do you remain current in your profession?
I read, and train independent contractors to work with my firm as consultants, and constantly provide them with insights and information. I also have a blog that I author: familyworkblog.com. I review literature on the industry or vertical market that my clients are in, so that I can learn about the context of their work. I do a biannual literature review on certain topics such as succession and executive development. I send copies of relevant articles to my clients; they will frequently respond by saying that they were insightful.

What makes you a valuable resource in your industry?
I am extremely fluid, open to change and willing to customize my offerings to fit every client's needs. I don't have a cookie-cutter approach. I pretty much go in and do an individualized assessment. We are constantly assessing and ensuring that we have appropriately customized our responses to our clients. Not everybody has that facility, but that's the way that I like to work with clients — we are constantly evolving as they are changing.

What is the most significant issue facing your profession today?
There is pressure on family-owned businesses, in particular, as a result of our unstable economy. A lot of times, they don't have the same investment diversity; they feel more pressured to pull in. They go into survival mode instead of realizing that they need to reflect and invest in their firm, just as they would invest in their portfolio. The unstable economy is a major threat to family-owned businesses and to overhead costs, such as family advisors.

What advice can you offer fellow members who work in your industry?
The family comes first. You really need to look inside, find out what the points of undernourishment are and get some sustenance to those points as soon as you can. When the family is feeling well-nourished and well-connected, you can get to work. Many times, colleagues of mine go right to the business-related problem; it becomes a point of failure because nobody in the family has received the nourishment to actually work on the problem. If you don't tend to the family's needs, you won't be successful.

What motivates you?
Contribution motivates me. I have the ability to give people the thing that they long for the most, which is a connection back to their family.

Who have been your mentors or people who have greatly influenced you?
I had managers and "rabbis" who believed in me. There are also people whom I looked up to in graduate school and in my company. The people I worked with at IBM were particularly influential to me because they were really hard on me; they pushed me to go beyond my own expectations.

I was also greatly influenced by my mother and father, who worked hard to bring us out of poverty and into the working class. Work became an honorable thing, no matter what it was. They really taught me to accept people for who they are and not what they have. My son has influenced me a lot because his mind is so rich and inquiring and he doesn't make a lot of assumptions. He asks a lot of questions and I admire the way he thinks.

Do you have a motto or favorite quote?
This is a variation of something from the Bible: "Who do you say that you are?" I ask myself a lot: Is everything in my life lined up in congruence with this, and am I in integrity with who I say that I am?"

What are some questions that an individual interested in your services can ask to ensure a more productive relationship?
You have to ask yourself if you are strong and resilient enough to do this work. You have to be quite grounded and stable because you will experience a maelstrom of emotions, thoughts, damage, history and baggage. You have to be able to sort through all of that objectively and not get sucked into some of the amazing drama that occurs in these families. You must also withstand that kind of undertow. If you aren't able to do this all the while maintaining critical distance, then you probably shouldn't do it.

What is your favorite or least favorite work-related task to do and why?
The documentation and administrative stuff are my least favorite tasks. I love to do family work sessions and team building. I am very good at designing a mode of treatment, but I hate the mechanical part of it, such as the presentations themselves.

Did you ever consider pursuing a different career path or profession? If yes, how did you end up working in your current field?
No, I've always loved making a contribution. My professional career has always lined up around that theme.

How has being a leader of your own business benefited you personally as well as professionally?
Personally, we have done very well financially. It has allowed me and my husband to be important resources for our extended family who have not done well financially. We are also able to give away a lot of money. Professionally I don't think there is anything like running or owning your own business in terms of how it contributes to one's confidence. I'm not afraid of anything and I don't imagine encountering something that would stop me. Running your own business gives you 100 degrees of freedom to be as entrepreneurial and risk-taking as you want, thereby giving you the freedom to be as successful as you choose.

Human Resources Consulting

Kimberly K. Logan, MA
President
Signature Management Group, Inc.
40 Greenhouse Place
Huntingtown, MD 20639 USA
kim@signaturemanagement1.com
http://www.signaturemanagementinc.com

When it comes to running a successful business, it pays to invest from within. Kimberly K. Logan exemplifies this philosophy as president of her company, Signature Management Group, Inc., and treats her employees with respect and kindness. In turn, her company teaches others the benefits of such practices by providing consulting nationally to private industry and government clients, thus showing them how to commit to their employees. They provide training, which is vital to any business, and their mission is to transform businesses into extraordinary enterprises by optimizing organizational performance and client service delivery. Leadership development and trust are major factors when getting a business off the ground and keeping it steady. "You have to communicate and not be afraid to share and put yourself out there," says Ms. Logan, who feels that communication is the backbone of the relationship between leaders and their employees, who then transfer that dedication onto the clients.

Ms. Logan was always involved in human resources, finance and accounting and wanted to focus on internal customer needs. The task her company takes on is helping other organizations and establishments to analyze their strengths and weaknesses within their own workforce while developing opportunities and strategies that will allow business leaders to proactively manage human capital. With 18 years of experience in business management, Ms. Logan uses her knowledge in strategic planning to run a corporation where the employees are fully engaged and express their loyalty to the company. She believes that promoting employee engagement is one of the most critical aspects in the success or failure in the achievement of an organization's goals. "People still have to run the business and if they feel undervalued or that they are not connected, you are only going to get what you're going to get, and it's not going to be 100 percent," she says.

Ms. Logan received a Bachelor of Business Administration in 1989, then a master's degree in administration and management in 1993 from Bowie State University. She was given the 50 Most Powerful CEOs and Corporate

Executives Award from the Minority Enterprise Council and was recently featured in the September/October issue of Minority Enterprise, which is distributed in the Washington, D.C. area. In the future, she would like to train, mentor and conduct business coaching to extend programs to people with learning disabilities or other challenges.

CONVERSATION WITH KIMBERLY K. LOGAN, MA

CAMBRIDGE WHO'S WHO: What would you like to promote most about yourself or your business?
KIMBERLY K. LOGAN: I have been an Inc. 500 winner for four consecutive years, from 2006 to 2009. During my career, I have helped to take a waste management company and an information technology company from small-business status into multimillion dollar businesses. I started my business on the basic truth that there is no leadership without a partnership. My company has a team of experts with over 50 years of combined experience, a network of more than 500 professionals in the United States and about 15 internationally.

What is the most rewarding aspect of your career?
My ability to be successful without having to compromise my integrity. Equally, it is having a reputation of trust and empowerment to other people.

What is your greatest professional accomplishment to date?
Establishing my own company and helping two other businesses that were already established to grow even further. I also created my own mission and values and hired my own staff.

What are your short-term and long-term career goals?
My short-term goal is to expand my business and sell it to my employees by the time I'm 50 years old. My long-term goal is to teach entrepreneurial skills to students at a college or university.

And what specific steps have you taken toward achieving these goals?
Setting up the company originally, I created an infrastructure and strategy from the beginning so that the end goal would be easier to attain. You have to look at things in terms of where you want to end. If I want to end up selling my company to my employees, there are some things I need to do on the front end when the company has little to no value, so that when it does have the value that we're looking for, we already have the plan in place.

What is the most difficult obstacle or challenge you have faced in pursuit of your goals?
In terms of the mission of my business, the hardest thing is getting people to understand the need to have the employees fully engaged in an organization

to make sure that they are feeling as though the company is just as loyal to them as they are to the company. It is obtaining and maintaining control of your executive management buy-in to stress the importance of employee engagement on the bottom line. Even though you can show them performance measurements and data, because it's not something that is completely tangible, they have a very difficult time believing that the way we treat our employees really has a major impact on the performance and production.

On what topic(s) do you consider yourself to be an expert?
I consider myself an expert on corporate infrastructure, how to set up a company from the very beginning to plan for the end game, and how to obtain trust, employee engagement and leadership development. I also have a very strong background in government contracting and information technology management.

How do you remain current in your profession?
Part of what my company does is training; you can't offer training unless you have a lot of training yourself. I am an avid reader — that's what takes up most of my time, but it's what I enjoy the most. I am a member of many associations and not just ones from my industry, such as the National Association of Female Executives, so I understand women and business. I am also a member of many government contract organizations because you have to understand how the government works and be able to work with it. I have a mentorship program within my organization. I also read the Washington Business Journal and receive journals so I can keep abreast of not just what's going on here, but across the country.

What makes you a valuable resource in your industry?
My years of experience and the fact that I have a background in turning small businesses into multimillion dollar companies. I started working for my dad, who owned a waste management company, when I was 12 years old and he sent me to school, but when I came back, I had to start from the ground up. I didn't start at an executive position. When I mentor my students, whether they are in high school or college, I always tell them I believe that while they are in college, they need to have some work experience. I also have expertise from the female's perspective in a male-dominated industry and know how to handle myself in a [difficult] situation.

What is the most significant issue facing your profession today?
It is the way that the majority of businesses have been run over the last 20 years. They have always been about profit margins, executive management compensation packages, and no sharing of the wealth for reinvesting people on the ground. This is the reason why we are in the economic situation that

we are. I believe greed and not sharing or reinvesting has caused our infrastructure to fail. We really need to get to the point of understanding and knowing that you can't throw away money or see people as if they are just machines.

What advice can you offer fellow members who work in your industry?
If you are going to start a company, you have to understand that not everybody is supposed to run a company. Be OK with and understand that may not be your gift or calling; really try to spend some time to figure out what that is. I'm 44 years old and would not want to be this age not knowing what I'm supposed to do.

What advice can you offer people aspiring to work in this profession?
In terms of the work, just really know who you are, figure out what your comfort zones are, and don't try to run a company because someone else makes it look easy for them. You really have to spend the time to get to know yourself and know what it is that comes naturally for you. You need to use that natural gift because we are all put here to do something very specific.

What are you passionate about?
I'm passionate about education, but I'm more passionate about providing our young people with the tools they really need to be successful in the world — everything is not about books. I don't believe the school system can teach them everything, such as management and communication skills that they need to have in terms of being successful. .Public service and volunteerism are important for students to see how they can impact the world. They need to be able to engage that feeling and use all their senses. They have to get connected to the environment and the world around them.

Who have been your mentors or people who have greatly influenced you?
My father and my husband Michael. My husband gets me and gives me all the space I need to be me.

Do you have any weblogs, websites or links to articles you would like listed?
I am starting a blog, and I want it to be passages for a book. The website will be on my business website.

Do you have a motto?
My business motto is "We put PEOPLE back in business." My personal motto is "Be true to yourself and true to others." Always be trustworthy and treat yourself and others with integrity. That's what people will remember.

Human Resources Management

Jennifer B. Mosholder, M.Ed.
Managing Director
Leading Org Solutions, LLC
Highlands Ranch, CO 80129 USA
jennifer@leadingorgsolutions.com
http://www.leadingorgsolutions.com

If human resources management is the glue that holds a company together, Jennifer B. Mosholder is the Elmer's of the industry. The career coach and human resources consultant has dedicated the past 15 years of her life to bringing positive change to individuals and companies alike. As the president and career coach for Leading Org Solutions, LLC, Ms. Mosholder helps employees and employers through transition management, human resource process improvement and career coaching. Ms. Mosholder looks to the saying "We must become the change we want to see," by Mohandas Gandhi for inspiration. In a nutshell, the phrase sums up her strong desire to attain a satisfying workplace for her clients.

Ms. Mosholder has developed a military-to-corporate transition management training program in partnership with Paramount Transitions, LLC that provides former military personnel with effective tools and strategies to transition into the corporate work environment. Additionally, her company, Leading Org Solutions, LLC, is dedicated to contributing time and resources to philanthropic efforts focused on skill-building, resume improvement and job search mechanics — all a part of her quest for self-improvement and lifelong learning.

According to Ms. Mosholder, a company must start with its employees if they want to have any sort of valuable change or growth. "On average, the typical person changes careers three to five times and spends more than 100,000 hours working during his or her lifetime," she points out. "The worst part is that more than 60 percent of people do not enjoy their work or their jobs." Her advice is to discover what you love to do and make it a point to find a job that fits that description because when you love what you're doing, it doesn't feel like work anymore. Ms. Mosholder continues to traverse the challenging terrain of human resources due to her desire to make sure every employee she encounters is satisfied with their workplace. "As companies move forward, the only way to attract employees is to start from the heart because companies are not going to be able to thrive unless they have motivated employees," she says.

In 1997, Ms. Mosholder received a master's degree in education and training from Pepperdine University; in 1992, she obtained a bachelor's degree in business administration with an emphasis in international business from Loyola Marymount University.

Conversation with Jennifer B. Mosholder, M.Ed.

Cambridge Who's Who: What is your greatest professional accomplishment to date?

Jennifer B. Mosholder: I'm so blessed to have such a great career, with wonderful experiences and mentors along the way. I believe that there are so many things that I have accomplished working with such great teams. My biggest accomplishment has been establishing human resources functions and driving change throughout an organization. I'm especially proud of setting up my own company — delivering great programs that support company and individual success — especially with military-to-corporate transitions.

What is the most difficult obstacle or challenge you have faced in pursuit of your goals?

Nobody's perfect, but I take challenges as they come and try to work through the solutions. I face challenges every day that are different in nature but in the midst of it, I leverage my strengths and the working relationships that I have.

What are your short-term and long-term career goals?

My short-term goal is to support the company with which I'm currently working in setting up a successful talent organization. I strive to be a part of a company, make a difference, and have an impact within that group. But I also work directly with leadership and know that my impact is not only on the employee base, but also on the leadership aspect and future of the company. I want to help them set their culture and vision, mission and values as they move forward. My long-term goal is to continue to impact positive change in companies and individuals. I would love to be able to leverage my talents to give back to the community by setting up a philanthropic foundation to support individuals in their quest for change and transition.

On what topic(s) do you consider yourself to be an expert?

I consider myself an expert on setting up an integrative talent strategy, which includes recruitment, training, planning, and talent management. I can also speak on the importance of having strategic human resource professionals within an organization and how that impacts the future growth and strategy of that company. I can certainly speak on company culture and helping to set that, and working directly with leaders.

What would you like to promote most about yourself or your business?

I would like to promote Leading Org Solutions as a true human resource consulting firm that brings effective solutions and positive change to companies. I would also like to promote myself as an expert in my field in terms of talent strategy in human resources. Change isn't just an event; it is a journey that we all go through both personally and professionally. It is critical to make the transition internally in order to be success both as an individual and within a company.

What is the most significant issue facing your profession today?

What hinders individuals from getting into a company is not having the mindset of business; individuals need to be a businessperson first and really understand the business and industry they are representing, essentially be able to "talk the talk." In order to be successful in human resources within a company, the individual has to really understand what the business people are going through so they can help guide them. They need to create something that will add value and drive their performance.

How do you remain current in your profession?

I collaborate a lot with different people. I read all the time and right now I'm reading "Leadership Pipeline" by Ram Charan, Stephen Drotter and James Noel, which is about how companies need to constantly groom their best people at every level of the organization to become future leaders. It is about providing the right kind of development opportunities and training to support their readiness to keep moving up into more complex management roles.

What advice can you offer people aspiring to work in this profession?

Gain a solid business background. If you want to focus on human resources, you have to have a strong business degree and make sure that you are collaborating and networking with others within the industry. Look for internships with human resource leaders in your area so that you can gain a deeper understanding of what they really do. You need to see the strategic side of human resources, which is really all about driving performance through talent or "the people" within an organization.

What advice can you offer fellow members who work in your industry?

Over 70 to 80 percent of the reason why people leave their company is because of their manager and the company culture. If you're not happy with your company, I advocate for you to find a company that aligns with your values and the culture that you want. After all, you spend most of your waking hours at work. If you want a fast-paced, energized company with a great leader, then you need to start looking for that.

Who have been your mentors or people who have greatly influenced you?
Two of my old bosses were the best mentors to me and still are. What was so great about them is that they gave me REAL feedback, the feedback that I may not have received from others. It was helpful for me even though some of it was painful to listen to. I have become a better person because of it.

What is the most rewarding aspect of your career?
Being able to influence and make positive change within a company and to make a difference in the lives of individuals I coached, both formally and informally. The highlight of my career was being able to work and travel internationally.

What are you passionate about?
I spend a lot of time with my son, Dylan. Family is very important to me and I am very close to them.

Global Project Management

Vas Nair, MBA
Vice President, Chief Learning Officer
Schering-Plough
Union, NJ USA
vna11r@yahoo.com

Vas Nair is a global project management professional with more than 15 years of experience. As the former vice president and chief learning officer for Schering-Plough (which merged with Merck & Co., Inc. on November 4, 2009), she established the company's global learning and development function and infrastructure from scratch — a drastic inception, which set off a series of changes that profoundly improved the culture at this pharmaceutical corporation. During her years working at Schering-Plough (2003 to 2009), she instilled several important initiatives that include a leader behaviors program, the company's first global performance management protocol, a behavioral competency framework, and a process for management optimization during corporate merger-and-acquisition activities.

Ms. Nair also helped to create Schering-Plough's first Women's Network and later became the network's first chairperson. The role required that she attend many speaking engagements at events and business schools (including Rutgers, The State University of New Jersey) on their behalf. She became well recommended, as consulting firms saw her as an ideal speaker on the challenges of being a woman in corporate America. To this day, Ms. Nair speaks publicly, anywhere from six to 12 times a year. The experience has helped her to remain abreast of new developments in her field, due to the extensive preparation required. "I try and make my presentations very practical and 'real' for the audience," she says.

A profound passion for learning and development, combined with a desire to positively impact people's lives while bringing competitive advantage to companies prompted Ms. Nair to become involved in her profession. She worked as a bank manager at Australia and New Zealand Banking Group Limited, and in 1997 came to work in the United States at Pharmacia, which merged with Pfizer, Inc. in 2003 as a global management and development professional. She gradually took on increased responsibilities, including the design, piloting and implementation of a front-line management program at 25 global locations.

Ms. Nair received a Master of Business Administration from the University of New England, Australia and a Bachelor of Commerce from the University of Wollongong, Australia. She is a steering committee member of the Council on Learning, Development and Organizational Performance and a peer review board member of the Human Resource and Organizational Development Roundtable. She is also a member of The Conference Board Inc. and the Healthcare Businesswomen's Association. In 2005, she was awarded the Tribute to Women and Industry Award by the YWCA of New Jersey.

CONVERSATION WITH VAS NAIR, MBA

CAMBRIDGE WHO'S WHO: What would you like to promote most about yourself or your business?
VAS NAIR: The fact that I have global experience when it comes to my area of work, and more significantly, that I have successfully implemented global programs. It is about scope and reach worldwide and secondly, where the more challenging side of our work comes into play, understanding the cultural nuances that make it a successful global implementation. This is in terms of establishing the learning and talent platform.

My most recent experiences have been within the pharmaceutical industry and, as chief learning officer, you have a global role. I have to ask myself, "How do you implement and establish a learning and talent foundation that is truly effective globally, when you are thinking of 100 or more countries?"

What are your short-term and long-term career goals?
My short-term career goal is to help an organization to create a corporate university and a solid learning culture. Looking at my long-term goals, the plan is to successfully integrate a people strategy that can capture the talent management and learning challenges addressing the multigenerational workforce within a corporation. I think the exciting part about that is being able to solidify relationships with the business schools. I really want to get to a place where corporate America partners with business schools and effectively manages talent. In many ways, this will have a positive impact on the community.

And what specific steps have you taken toward achieving these goals?
I have moved from one management development role to the next, while increasing my responsibility. The last seven to 12 years, I've had extensive experience from the learning and talent management perspective. In terms of the long-term goal, I'm now starting to reach out to business schools to try to figure out what it is that graduates are afraid of when they think about starting their own business or working in corporate America.

For me, it's about trying to get these graduates to be a lot more effective before they join a company or start a business. I'm starting to hear a lot more in education about a lack of focus on people and "soft skills." It's everything, from how to be effective on a team, to leading a team without being a team leader, and influencing skills. These abilities are not mastered in high school or at the university level to the extent that they should. The reality is, today you are getting individuals prepared for the corporate world from a technical standpoint. A balance is struck when they obtain skills to effectively undertake a leadership role. If you have corporate America focused on giving back to those business schools and colleges, I believe it's a solid way of moving along that track.

On what topic(s) do you consider yourself to be an expert?
I consider myself an expert on global project management, learning and development, and talent management.

What is your greatest professional accomplishment to date?
I created a global learning and talent development platform within a major pharmaceutical company. I truly started with very little; it wasn't about walking in and cleaning up something that someone else had done. It was about creating that platform for 50,000 people.

What is the most rewarding aspect of your career?
One of the most rewarding things having worked for Schering-Plough was connecting with the American Red Cross. I am now on the board for the American Red Cross and take a very hands-on role, advising the organization on their staff and learning issues. Whatever I've been able to put to practice at Schering-Plough, I am now putting to a good cause.

How do you remain current in your profession?
I find that the best way to stay current is to attend and speak at seminars and conferences. For one thing, you have to get yourself very polished and prepared; second, when the audience throws questions at you, you find where the real challenges are and you get into "solution mode."

I tend to take a more practical approach to a lot of things in my career. It's not just about being a participant, but actually putting my hand up and saying I will speak about certain things. Recently, at a CLO Summit, I spoke about the challenges of being agile in a merger and acquisition situation. It's a very hot topic right now, so I tried to blend how to create an agile learning environment with going through a merger.

What makes you a valuable resource in your industry?
I've lived, studied and worked in three different continents, including Asia and Australia. This experience has given me a global perspective when designing programs and solving problems.

What is the most difficult obstacle or challenge you have faced in pursuit of your goals?
When I relocated to the United States from Australia in 2002, I moved here on my own and didn't have family here to support me. It was challenging on many levels. After a month having moved here, the company that I worked for had been acquired by another company. Overcoming these obstacles makes one more informed and agile. The thing about planning is you always have to have a plan B. You've always got to think, "What if plan A doesn't happen?" Be very clear about your deadlines and priorities.

Another challenge was when I joined a company that was literally tanking. I worked for a CEO who had a passion for people and people development. It was a risk, but the amazing experience was to come in and significantly change the organization and know that you made a difference.

What is the most significant issue facing your profession today?
During tough economic times, it's getting harder to quickly show a return on investments, from a people and learning strategy. In today's world, since we are so tight in terms of wanting to be successful with minimal dollars, what may have taken three years to do may be allotted half the time. The biggest challenge we have as learning professionals is getting out there and getting a strategy to work very quickly; also, being able to very quickly prove your business case and return on the investment dollar to the stakeholders.

What advice can you offer fellow members who work in your industry?
Be creative. Have a very short-term strategy followed by a long-term strategy and focus on excellence in execution. My previous CEO used to say that your execution is your strategy. You have to know your company, industry and competitors. Keep raising the bar.

What are you passionate about?
Spending quality time with loved ones affords me the passion for my work. They bring out the best in me. I'm also passionate about traveling. Every time I travel, I always discover something new about myself.

Do you have a motto or mantra that guides your work?
Never having to say "I regret."

MARKETING AND BUSINESS ADMINISTRATION

DOREEN SAMS
Assistant Professor
Georgia College & State University
210 Hancock Street
Milledgeville, GA 31061 USA
doreen.sams@gcsu.edu
http://hercules.gcsu.edu/~dsams

Dr. Doreen Sams, an assistant professor in Georgia College & State University's department of information and technology, possesses a wealth of experience and knowledge in many aspects of business management, including recruitment, marketing, program development and budget control. The former vice president of sales for Innovative Benefit Consultants and head of the office of enrollment management at East Tennessee State University worked in numerous settings before entering academia, which strengthened her leadership abilities and skill for functioning among diverse groups. At East Tennessee University, she managed part-time personnel in admission activities and recruitment, and participated in software development initiatives that ushered the institution into a new age of technological advancement.

Dr. Sams' copious record of published articles is the result of several collaborations with other authorities on business practices and extensive research into methods of process improvement for managers and high-level executives. These include "The Importance of an Internal Marketing Orientation in Social Services," with Cynthia Rodriguez Cano in the International Journal of Nonprofit and Voluntary Sector Marketing; "Is Socially Responsible Behavior Good Business? An Investigation of Tomorrow's Business Leaders," with Cynthia Rodriguez Cano and Joe Schwartz in the Journal of Social Responsibility; and "The Effect of Law Enforcement Stress on Organizational Commitment," with Fernando Jaramillo and Robert Nixon in Policing: An International Journal of Police Strategies and Management. In addition to her writings, she has presented her papers and views at scholarly conferences geared toward improving higher education standards and the use of technology and marketing in an ever-evolving world.

In 1998, Dr. Sams received a Bachelor of Arts in Marketing from the University of South Florida, which she followed with a master's degree and doctorate in business administration from the same institution. Her course load consists of classes in high-level marketing theory and applications, business ethics, global responsibility, international business and marketing, and principles of marketing that prepare students for upcoming internships and careers. She is a representative of the education committee in the J. Whitney Bunting School of Business, and a member of the Academy of Marketing Science, the American Marketing Association, the Association for Consumer Research, and the Society for Marketing Advances.

Conversation with Doreen Sams

Cambridge Who's Who: What is the most rewarding aspect of your career?
Doreen Sams: The most rewarding aspect is when students get great jobs and recognize the contributions from their professors.

What is your greatest professional accomplishment to date?
My greatest professional accomplishment is [contributing to] five publications in four years.

What are your short-term and long-term career goals?
Promotion is my short-term goal and my long-term goal is to get published in a highly recognized international journal.

And what specific steps have you taken toward achieving these goals?
I am going through professional requirements to get to the necessary point for promotion. As for the long term, I'm working with professors from other countries on publications.

What is the most difficult obstacle or challenge you have faced in pursuit of your goals?
The most difficult obstacle I have faced was overcoming a near-fatal auto accident in 1996.

On what topics do you consider yourself to be an expert?
Marketing research, international marketing, business ethics, and service marketing.

How do you remain current in your profession?
I am constantly reading journals and attending conferences.

What makes you a valuable resource in your industry?
My experience and degrees make me a valuable resource.

What is the most significant issue facing your profession today?
Budget cuts – we are working with less money to do more, and that is very difficult.

What advice can you offer fellow members who work in your industry?
The most important thing is to team up and work with others who fill the gap where you are not as strong.

What advice can you offer people aspiring to work in this profession?
You need to be persistent. Keep moving forward because it is very trying.

What are you passionate about?
International relations and sustainability.

Who have been your mentors or people who have greatly influenced you?
Dr. David Ortinau and Dr. Miriam Stamps from the University of South Florida.

ADMINISTRATIVE SERVICES

SUSANNE J. STEPP
Secretary
County of San Bernardino
825 E. Third Street
San Bernardino, CA 92415 USA
roundypoet1@aol.com
http://www.co.san-bernardino.ca.us

Susanne J. Stepp is the division secretary of the County of San Bernardino's Federal Projects/Flood Control Engineering Division, providing administrative and clerical support to a division chief and four section chiefs. She has more than 15 years of professional experience in secretarial work and has gained a high level of proficiency and expertise in communications management, customer service and clerical support. Throughout her career, she has offered administrative support for several important undertakings. She began her career with the County of San Bernardino as a public information clerk II in the treasurer-tax collector's office. In this position, she provided information to the public over the phone and at the public counter regarding property tax issues — specifically current and prior year taxes, property tax sale guidance, and payment plans to pay back taxes and void their property from going to tax sale. In 1996 she went to the District Attorney's Office criminal division, where she provided receptionist and frontline clerical support to more than 20 deputy district attorneys; she also provided information to the public and law enforcement agencies including local police departments, the Department of Justice and the FBI, and notified the court of the status of pending warrants for defendants.

In 2000 she was promoted to secretary to the county surveyor. She provided administrative and clerical support to the surveyor and land development divisions. She honed her customer service skills by acting as a liaison between property owners and county departments, notarizing documents for the public and verifying that grant of easement requirements had been met. This enabled the property owners to complete their final inspections and take possession of their new homes.

As a poet and scribe who has published more than 50 poems, Ms. Stepp searched for a vocation where she could apply her knack for writing and communication. Becoming a secretary seemed like a natural extension of her craft, whereby she could communicate with others effectively, whether verbally or by the written word. She is inspired by a famous quote from Norman

Vincent Peale, who said, "When you throw your heart over the bar, the body will follow." Taking these words personally, Ms. Stepp remains dedicated to helping others within the community achieve their goals.

The County of San Bernardino's Federal Projects/Flood Control Engineering Division is charged with preparing and specifying flood containment initiatives, which includes collaboration with the U.S. Army Corps of Engineers, serving the San Bernardino County Flood Control District. The organization is also responsible for reviewing plans and proposals put forth by third-party consultants and other government agencies (via the District's Flood Control Permits Office) to ensure compliance with the District's protocol.

Ms. Stepp is currently pursuing an associate degree in arts and humanities. She is the recipient of the Lifetime Achievement Award and the International Peace Prize in 2008 from the United Cultural Convention. In 2007, she received a Gold Medal from the American Biographical Institute and the Best Poems and Poets title from Who's Who in Poetry. She is a three-time recipient (2006-2008) of the Woman of the Year award by the American Biographical Institute. In her spare time, she enjoys writing poetry, reading biographies and creating crafts.

CONVERSATION WITH SUSANNE J. STEPP

CAMBRIDGE WHO'S WHO: What would you like to promote most about yourself or your business?
SUSANNE J. STEPP: I have a talent for writing poetry. The ability to put thoughts and emotions into words can be a challenge when searching for the right words to express what is in your heart; it is always exhilarating when the final product mirrors exactly what you are feeling at the time.

What is the most rewarding aspect of your career?
One of the most fulfilling experiences is when I can assist others in accomplishing their objectives, whether it is notarizing a document for the public or helping one of my co-workers to complete their projects.

What is your greatest professional accomplishment to date?
I have been honored with several awards for my poetry. Among my most cherished are the Lifetime Achievement and International Peace Prize awards from the United Cultural Convention. I am also proud to have been named Woman of the Year three years in a row by the American Biographical Institute.

On what topics do you consider yourself to be an expert?
I excel in customer service and in the area of communication, both verbal and written. I have the ability to communicate clearly and concisely with the public, my co-workers, and outside agencies – this is vital to completing my many tasks.

What are your short-term and long-term career goals?
In my career with the county, I want to return to law enforcement. It is a positive way to serve others. I would like to be promoted to executive secretary when the opportunity arises. I also have plans to compile and publish a collection of my poetry.

And what specific steps have you taken toward achieving these goals?
I network within the county and with outside contacts. When the workload and division budget permits, I take employer-sponsored training. I just completed the state-mandated training and testing requirement to renew my notary commission.

What makes you a valuable resource in your industry?
I have a positive "can do" attitude and am always willing to learn new things and assist others in the department.

What is the most difficult obstacle or challenge you have faced in pursuit of your goals?
The most difficult obstacle was overcoming the negative environment in which I was raised. One of the benefits of making an effort to get to the other side is that I have become a more loving and supportive mother to my two beautiful daughters; I have succeeded in showing them an alternative way to do things.

How do you remain current in your profession?
I have read many books pertaining to my current position; another valuable resource consists of the other secretaries in our department – we all pool our collective knowledge together.

What is the most significant issue facing your profession today?
As with most industries during this time, budget cuts are an issue.

What advice can you offer fellow members who work in your industry?
Take responsibility for your mistakes. Apologize and do everything you can do to rectify the situation; learn from it and let it go. When you succeed, be sure to share the glory. In truth, you may be the one that finished the task, but it would not have gotten done without the help of others.

What are you passionate about?
My passion is writing poetry.

Who have been your mentors or people who have greatly influenced you?
I have been blessed to have several people in my lifetime who have mentored me. There is one man who changed my life, my father Gibb Stepp.

What advice can you offer people aspiring to work in this profession?
Keep reading for your brass ring and never give up!

Do you have a motto?
My motto is "Do no harm," to others and myself.

INTERIOR DESIGN

SHIRLEY STIVERS LUCCI
Author
798 Big Ridge Road
Bakersville, NC 28705 USA
moutainmamma1@verizon.net

After more than 50 years as an interior designer, Shirley Stivers Lucci has worked with many clients, but none were as memorable as the mayor of Sunrise, Fla. "I was playing around with his carpet on my hands and knees looking absolutely lovely, and Frank Sinatra [walked] in the front door," she says. "I thought I was going to faint and fall on my face." While perfecting the final details, she overheard Mr. Sinatra compliment her work on the kitchen, and that experience created one of the greatest memories of her career.

Mrs. Stivers Lucci has dabbled in a number of areas, including public advocacy when she made several radio appearances and successfully lobbied for a mandatory education law in Kentucky. Though visually impaired, she has published two novels entitled "Amberstone" and "Return to Amberstone," both of which she hopes will inspire others to read and enjoy life's fruitfulness. Her self-confidence, persistence and courage when facing challenges have propelled her to a level of success commensurate with her dedication, which remains potent as ever in her 80th year on this earth. Within the next five years, she would like to publish her third novel, "The Awkward Age, 80 Years Old," at a time when many people would be content to live out their days in rest and tranquility. One of the most rewarding aspects of her career has been sustaining various personal and professional relationships, all of which contributed to her sense of fulfillment.

A member of Kappa Alpha Theta, Mrs. Stivers Lucci received a Bachelor of Science in Interior Design from the University of Kentucky in 1947. She received a Reader's Digest National Award and an award from a local community mental health center. She is the founder of the Apple Festival with The Garden Club of North Carolina, Inc. and volunteers with the Big Sandy Horse Show.

Conversation with Shirley Stivers Lucci

Cambridge Who's Who: What is the most rewarding aspect of your career?
Shirley Stivers Lucci: I love to look at a job when I'm finished with it. Getting to that point is really something. It's just fun to sit there and write the words that pop into my head.

What is your greatest professional accomplishment to date?
Writing my two books and having them published. Another accomplishment [took place] was when I was going to work with the governor of Kentucky, who was the husband of one of my friends. I went to him and told him that we were one of 11 states that did not have a mandatory education law. He said he would help me write the bill if I would get in there and push for it. I spent that year running around and lobbying for that it. I got the bill passed after two years and I will never forget the day when they passed it. I am most proud of that because I knew nothing about politics. It took another year, but we got funding for it.

What would you like to promote most about yourself or your business?
I would like to promote my two books, "Amberstone" and "Return to Amberstone." I have also been an interior designer for 54 years.

What are your short-term and long-term career goals?
I would like to write more in the future. I have thought about writing a children's book about cats. My husband had 26 cats and we had to have a special cage behind our house for them. The most gratifying thing would be to make a movie out of my books.

What is the most difficult obstacle or challenge you have faced in pursuit of your goals?
One thing you face as an interior designer (if you are a bit attractive), is that you have to have the wives get over the fact that you're attractive. They are not sure if they want their husbands to talk to you, but they've heard that you are good and they want to work with you.

My eyes started to go bad in 1994; I am now legally blind and my eyes are getting worse. Another challenge was coming from a little town in eastern

Kentucky. I didn't get much practice being an interior designer there, but I did have a lovely department in the furniture store with all of my samples and books. I would have to take the few people that I had and drive them to Chicago to help them pick out good furniture. I lived there for 23 years and received my customers mostly by word of mouth.

On what topics do you consider yourself to be an expert?
I consider myself an expert on color selection.

How do you remain current in your profession?
I used to read magazines on interior design, such as Better Homes and Gardens.

What is the most significant issue facing your profession today?
Getting people to read my books is a significant issue. What I'm finding out is that very few younger people read anymore. They are on their cell phones and playing with their computer. I'm surprised at the ignorance of people nowadays.

What advice can you offer people aspiring to work in this profession?
It's hard to get rich in something like this. I've been sued many times and you really have to be a good judge of character so you can decide what kind of people you are talking to before you do business with them.

What are you passionate about?
I'm passionate about my house and where I live. I'm not a city dweller; I'm living on a mountain right now.

Who have been your mentors or people who have greatly influenced you?
My teacher during my first year of college told me that I had talent and was trying to get me into journalism to be a writer, but I told her I liked art and wanted to be an interior designer. That was in 1945 to 1946. When I was writing this [third] book, the things she said to me came back to me and I tried to do what she told me to do. The thing she said that made the biggest impression on me was, "Leave them [the readers] hanging and anxious to go to the next chapter." That's where most writers fail.

Do you have a motto or favorite quote?
"Every day is a new adventure," and "There is something to love about every day."

STATISTICAL RESEARCH

SHIFRA R. WICE
President (Retired)
SRW Interviewing Service
2160 Greentree Road
Condo 411-W
Pittsburgh, PA 15220 USA

In order to succeed in any business, it is necessary to identify with its target market and consumers, and formulate the best methods for reaching them to sell a product. As Shifra R. Wice discovered after 20 years of running SRW Interviewing Service, heading such an operation takes effort, dedication and a keen sense of current and emergent trends. Mrs. Wice offered statistical research as her main service, helping companies to acquire vital information that increased their profits and offered more channels toward success. This complicated process involved more than just examining existing developments and using them to make educated decisions; detailed, time-consuming work went into making sure that all evaluations were accurate and derived from the most trustworthy sources.

Today, Mrs. Wice reasons that the prevalent attitude of seeking quick fixes to solutions has affected the quality of services offered by some companies whose main interest is the bottom line. She believes in working hard toward a goal and earning hands-on experience before jumping into something blindly to gain immediate gratification and results. After all, one's livelihood should be based on interest and a desire to help others, not solely on monetary gain. Although she was able to achieve a considerable amount of success that allowed her to put all five of her daughters (Andrea, Betsy, Candace, Debby and Ellen) through school, she was more concerned with growing more solid in her profession as the result of interactions with each client she encountered. The support she received from her late husband Gene, family, friends and colleagues was more than enough motivation to continue seeking knowledge even after her business had gained a reputation of excellence.

In her retirement, Mrs. Wice is free to enjoy many of her favorite pastimes, which include collecting coins, bowling, listening to music, playing bridge and bingo, knitting, traveling, and teaching piano lessons. She also volunteers at a local mental hospital and belongs to the National Council of Jewish Women, a faith-based volunteer organization.

CONVERSATION WITH SHIFRA R. WICE

CAMBRIDGE WHO'S WHO: What has been the most rewarding aspect of your career?
SHIFRA R. WICE: I have prepared for all of them myself. My education and volunteer work since I was a teen have given me substantial experience dealing with people.

What is your greatest professional accomplishment to date?
The most wonderful accomplishments I have are my five beautiful daughters Andrea, Betsy, Candace, Debby and Ellen, who knew all through school how to earn money, save money and spend money. They have never asked me to borrow money after they graduated from college.

How would you like to be remembered by your peers?
As being a lot of fun, dependable, independent, and helpful. My husband was a big mentor for me and never held me back from doing what I wanted to do.

What was the most difficult obstacle or challenge you have faced in pursuit of your goals?
I mastered anything that was a challenge to me. I was able to take care of difficult things as well as easy things, and so was my family.

On what topics do you consider yourself to be an expert?
I wouldn't say I'm an expert on anything, but getting along well with people is one of my priorities.

What is the most significant issue facing your profession today?
The economy is a big problem now because businesses don't have any extra money and it's a shame. Even the federal government looks into statistics before they spend any money on anything.

What advice can you offer to people aspiring to become involved in this profession?
I want young people to be willing to work at a project in order to see if they are good for that particular business.

What advice can you offer to people working in your industry?

If they're too young to retire and want to work, there's room for more questions and thoughts from people in this business. Even though the economy is down, people are still doing business and they still need your opinion. You can't believe how many letters I still get from companies in the catalog business, for instance, that want my opinion. They offer me all kinds of presents to participate because that's how important it is for their success.

Do you have any interesting hobbies?

I'm an expert knitter and I've knitted beautiful cocktail clothes since I was about 12 years old. When I got married, I knitted a ribbon dress and my whole salary was spent on that. My husband asked, "What did you do?" I told him and he said, "Don't you ever give that dress away." That was 60 years ago and I still have it.

What makes you a valuable resource in your industry?

I enjoy learning new things. The statistical research I have done is most important, combined with my ability to go through questions and give honest answers.

What would you like to highlight most about yourself or SRW Interviewing Service?

SRW [reflects me as a person] because I developed it at the time I was 9 years old. I feel that [my work] is something that is not hard to learn, but if you're honest and patient, you can be a good producer of the statistics that people want to have for their business.

SPECIAL NEEDS ENRICHMENT

ANN ALEXANDER
Special Education Teacher
Lafayette Parish School System
113 Chaplin Drive
Lafayette, LA 70508 USA
Annaal8@aol.com

Ann Alexander is a special education teacher for the Lafayette Parish School System. For more than 35 years, she has proven to be a determined individual who will stop at nothing to endure the burden of instructing special needs children. But to the veteran educator, her job is not a burden but a gift. Ms. Alexander, who attributes her success to her love for challenges, has a unique talent for building student and parent relationships. She spends time learning about each of her pupils on a personal level, which helps her to boost the youngsters' self-motivation. Additionally, she has an astute ability to maximize learning by implementing activities that are appropriate to her students' special requirements.

A strong love for teaching and her belief that she was meant to instruct children with special needs prompted Ms. Alexander to enter the field. "I always had big love for children," she states as she recalls her time as a babysitter and camp counselor. A transformational event in her life occurred when she entered the Peace Corps. It was the 1970s and she traversed to a foreign land, Micronesia, where she enriched students for three months while living with them on a school campus. In order to reach the children, she had to learn to speak a different language. "We had interpreters and a language course to bridge the gap," she remembers.

After the first semester, she remained in the Corps for more than two years, enduring the cultural and linguistic obstacles when others had left to return to their respective homes. The experience taught her to overcome adversity and gave her the strong "shell" she needed to properly handle difficult situations as they come up with her special needs students. In the near future, Ms. Alexander intends to continue "reaching and teaching" every student in her care.

Ms. Alexander received a Master of Arts from The University of Northern Colorado and a Bachelor of Arts from The University of Northern Colorado. She is a member of the National Education Association. In 2000, Ms. Alexander was a semi-finalist for the Lafayette Education Foundation's Middle School Teacher of the Year award. From 1989 to 1990, she was Carencro Middle School's Teacher of the Year and in 1989, she was a semi-finalist for Lafayette Parish School System's Middle School Teacher of the Year award.

Conversation with Ann Alexander

CAMBRIDGE WHO'S WHO: What would you like to promote most about yourself or your business?
ANN ALEXANDER: I've been teaching for 35 years and I'm still going strong. As long as I'm effective, I'm going to keep going. I'm only 58 years old; what else am I going to do?

Who have been your mentors or people who have greatly influenced you?
People who have greatly influenced me include Mary Virginia Winter, one of my previous supervisors; Beth Jantz, who was an assistant superintendent; and Bill Butcher, who was the principal at Carencro Middle School when I first got here.

Do you have a motto?
Love what you do and make a difference in the lives of your children every day.

What is the most rewarding aspect of your career?
When the kids finally get the concept you are teaching, such as math; when they learn how to read; or when they come back after they haven't seen me in 10 years and tell me that I've made a difference in their life.

What is your greatest professional accomplishment to date?
Teaching children at the school in Micronesia during my stint in the Peace Corps.

What are your short-term and long-term career goals?
My short-term goal is to make sure that the children succeed on the year-end tests that we have; also, that they do better than the year before. I am also dedicated to instilling a positive self-image and high self-esteem in them, because a lot of my kids come from a low socioeconomic status; they don't have a lot of self-confidence at all. My long-term goal has to do with when I finally retire: I want to be known as the teacher who really did care for these kids and didn't just show up for the paycheck. I don't do it for that.

What advice can you offer people aspiring to work in this profession?
You must really have a heart for the students and meet their entire needs – academic, social and behavioral.

What advice can you offer fellow members who work in your industry?
They have to step back and look at what they're doing. If they're not effective anymore, then they should retire. At that point, if they still want to do it, then be positive every day with the kids. Look deep into them and see what they're going through.

On what topic(s) do you consider yourself to be an expert?
Children with learning disabilities in the area of math, and children with emotional and behavior problems, because I [worked with them] for about 18 years. Most teachers burn out within three years.

What is the most difficult obstacle or challenge you have faced in pursuit of your goals?
When some of the emotionally disturbed children would "go off" or get out of hand, it was hard to get them refocused because they really didn't have substantial thinking or coping skills. Then, the parents would come and they would blame me for him or her going off and [the parents] wouldn't have any coping skills.

You have to overcome the environment; also, the parents' lack of social skills. It's very hard not to [judge them as parents]. For example, right now it's very cold and some kids are here in shorts and they don't have coats. I've purchased many coats for the kids, and I have a hard time when the parents let them go out like that.

What are you passionate about?
I like to exercise. I love traveling and spending time with my friends. I also love tennis, racquetball and any sports.

What makes you a valuable resource in your industry?
My compassion and knowledge of the subject matter.

Educational Administration

VELMA ANSLEY-NELSON
Administrative Assistant (Retired)
Goose Creek Consolidated Independent School District
4544 E. Freeway
Baytown, TX 77521 USA
vjnelson25@yahoo.com
http://www.gccisd.net

"Life is fascinating," says Velma Ansley-Nelson, recalling her 50-year career where she discovered that there was always something new to learn. She finds joy in helping others, and although she is now retired from her position as an administrative assistant for the Goose Creek Consolidated Independent School District, Ms. Ansley-Nelson has maintained a philanthropic outlook. She currently serves on the local board of an oversight committee that raises funds to aid hurricane victims.

As an administrative assistant, Ms. Ansley-Nelson utilized her knowledge of educational management to complete her daily responsibilities, which included processing payroll, helping children and overseeing staff. The Goose Creek Consolidated Independent School District offers elementary, middle and high school education to residents of Baytown, Texas. The district also offers a special education program for children with disabilities, an alternative learning program, and a bilingual education/English as a second language program, as well as advanced academics and special services for students with dyslexia.

Ms. Ansley-Nelson found true satisfaction while working in the education field, and feels that if one wishes to pursue a career in education, they should realize how rewarding it can be and stay positive no matter what obstacles they may face. She identifies a lack of parental involvement as a significant issue that faces education today. Though Ms. Ansley-Nelson recalls that the parents of her students were always willing and ready to discuss their children's education, she remains adamant about encouraging parental involvement and parent-child interaction, as they can really improve a child's capacity to learn.

Ms. Ansley-Nelson is very thankful for her mother, and attributes her success to the support she received from her, and to her own dedication. She is particularly proud to have been the first woman selected as a town councilor in the 1960s; she was elected and served two terms. "Serving on the city council was a big eye-opener," she explains.

In 1949, Ms. Ansley-Nelson completed an Associate of Arts at Lee College. She is a member of the Texas PTA and the Teacher Retirement System of Texas. In her spare time, she enjoys cooking, solving crossword puzzles, watching sports and spending time at her church.

Conversation with Velma Ansley-Nelson

Cambridge Who's Who: On what topic(s) do you consider yourself to be an expert?
Velma Ansley-Nelson: Being successful in life and serving people.

What motivates you?
I love education and helping people.

What characteristics help to separate you from your competitors?
I like to give back and serve people as much as I can. I love everyone and I try not to cut anyone down.

What short-term and long-term career goals are you currently pursuing?
My main goal is to continue doing a lot of church work over the phone, because I am unable to drive.

What is the most difficult obstacle or challenge you have faced in pursuit of your goals?
One year we had more than 1,000 children at the school, and we had many scares because our school was built over a pipeline. It blew one day when I was there by myself and I had to call the superintendent. He told me to do a backwards fire drill and get all of those kids out the back door with their teachers and go over to Safeway [a grocery store] until he could give me clearance. It was scary.

What is the most significant issue facing your profession today?
The kids don't study; they have no home environment. Some of our parents are right there with us — all I needed to do was call them and there they were. It is the lack of morals and parent values that is an issue today. As a whole, we still have some of our good principles and morals; we still have parents who care.

Did you ever consider pursuing a different career path or another profession? If yes, how did you end up working in your current field?
I was the first woman ever to serve on the city council. It was really something,

and the man I ran against just recently passed away — he was precious to me. I had one gentleman from jail call me and say that they didn't have soap, so I took soap down to him.

What advice can you offer fellow members or others aspiring to work in your industry?
Stay with it. Don't give up, because it will bear fruit. Besides everything else, there really is self-satisfaction.

What advice would you give parents to become more involved in their child's education?
Be an active parent. Become a member of our PTO (parent-teacher organization). They need to be involved in their children's schoolwork and activities. Our parents, on the whole, are very active.

What lessons have you learned as a professional in your field for the past 50 years?
We have to keep our parents informed.

Humanities Education

David S. Britton
1) Teacher, Head of Humanities Department (Retired)
2) Local Councillor and Group Leader
1) The Skinners' Company's School for Girls
2) Lewisham Conservative Group
117 Stamford Hill
London, United Kingdom N165RS
david.britton17@hotmail.com

David S. Britton is a local councillor and group leader for the Lewisham Conservative Group. He is also a retired teacher and head of The Skinners' Company's School for Girls Department of Humanities. Mr. Britton's expertise includes religious education and Islamic culture. While employed by The Skinners' Company's School for Girls, he supervised the humanities education department, managed a handful of employees, taught religious studies, and prepared students for public exams in the areas of history, economics, sociology and world religions. The most gratifying aspect of his career in education is having prepared so many students for university life by helping them to achieve successful exam results.

Mr. Britton underwent arduous priest training and religious education to become an expert in his field. After he completed his research studies thesis on religious tolerance and commitment regarding Islam and Christianity, he spent 20 years as an authority on Islam teachings. He educated others as part of an overseas development ministry program for six years in the 1970s and early 1980s in Zambia and Nigeria, where he met his wife. Mr. Britton has also been an interviewee on BBC TV, and quoted in London newspapers. He attributes his success to his dedication, determination, educational background and organizational skills.

In 1996, Mr. Britton received a master's degree in philosophy, and in 1993, he received a Master of Arts in Comparative Religion and Ethics from Lancaster University. Since 1983, he has been a certified teacher of English as a foreign language instructor. In 1973, he completed the Church of England ordination examinations at Salisbury University. He earned a postgraduate degree in education in 1969 and a Bachelor of Arts in Christian Theology, cum laude, in 1968 from Durham University. From 1990 to 2009, Mr. Britton served as the senior branch official and school representative of the Association of Teachers and Lecturers in Hackney, N. London. He attended and spoke at many annual conferences of the ATL and was interviewed by press and television in the United Kingdom. He is a member of Mensa International Limited, the International Reading Association and the Conservative Councillors' Association.

In his free time, Mr. Britton enjoys reading fantasy books, listening to music, writing, and researching the Spanish conquest of Peru, a topic on which he is due to publish a novel under the title "We Thought They Were Gods" in late 2010.

CONVERSATION WITH DAVID S. BRITTON

CAMBRIDGE WHO'S WHO: What are you passionate about?
DAVID S. BRITTON: I am passionate about all the things that I do, including education and religion; also, being a local councillor and party group leader.

What advice can you offer people aspiring to work in this profession?
Be sure that you want to do it before you start training. Then, keep on despite the difficulties. The children we teach are the reasons for our doing so, and we must always hold on to that.

Who have been your mentors or people who have greatly influenced you?
The most important person was Professor C.K. Barrett, who was my personal tutor at Durham University. I have also been motivated to continue to struggle by considering the examples of Martin Luther King Jr., Kenneth Kaunda and Nelson Mandela. My politics have been influenced by Harold MacMillan.

Do you have any weblogs, websites or links to articles you would like listed?
You can go to www.mensa.org and go to politics to find articles written by me. I am publishing in the next few weeks a book on United Kingdom education called "My Life in Education." I have written articles for the Mensa political newsletter and the Conservative Councillors' Association.

What are your short-term and long-term career goals?
My short-term goals are trying to get my educational book published and then getting on to writing my novel on the Spanish conquest of Peru. I would also like to be re-elected in May 2010, together with an increased number of counselors in my group, at the end of Gordon Brown's government.

And what specific steps have you taken toward achieving these goals?
I went back to Lancaster University to take an [additional] degree and I have campaigned in elections since 1964. I am also researching for my novel.

What would you like to promote most about yourself or your business?
I care for and about people. I have spent my life in the service of others and I intend to continue to do so.

What is your greatest professional accomplishment to date?
Getting so many students on their way to a university by helping them obtain successful exam results.

What is the most rewarding aspect of your career?
Seeing others succeed because of something I may have said or done.

What is the most difficult obstacle or challenge you have faced in pursuit of your goals?
It depends on the objective. Politically, it is the national British political situation, which has now changed but has blocked our electoral prospects. Educationally, it has been meeting my own high personal targets.

On what topic(s) do you consider yourself to be an expert?
Religion, especially Islam and Christianity, and education, especially as it applies to secondary school.

How do you remain current in your profession?
I do a lot of reading. I also talk to a lot of people.

What makes you a valuable resource in your industry?
My knowledge and determination.

What is the most significant issue facing your profession today?
Raising the standards and turning back the state.

COMPUTER AND OFFICE TECHNOLOGY

DEBBIE M. BURKE
Teacher
Knox Community High School
1 Redskin Trail
Knox, IN 46534 USA
burkede@knox.k12.in.us

As a seasoned educator with more than 14 years of experience, Debbie M. Burke has been in enough classrooms to know that it's impossible to have the same impact on everybody, as idealistic as the notion seems. With a realistic outlook, she strives to help at least one at-risk student a year. Her track record has been positive because typically, she ends up connecting with five to 10 students per year. "I am there for them and mentor them," she shares. "They probably would not graduate otherwise." As a department head and teacher at Knox Community High School, Ms. Burke applies her talents across the student body spectrum and enriches the top 10 most gifted pupils.

A lifelong desire to be a high school teacher prompted Ms. Burke to leave her former profession as a successful restaurant manager in search of greener chalkboards. With all those years of experience in management, she chose to obtain a business education degree so she could teach computer classes. Her classes deal with Microsoft Office and other computer applications, where students learn about a variety of software tools that they can use to enhance their lives. Each week, on average she teaches 100 students, in a variety of subjects. Additionally, she oversees private and after-school tutoring and hosts computer club competitions. The most gratifying aspect of her career is seeing her students walk across the stage at graduation, because it validates all the dedication and hard work she puts into her career.

Ms. Burke received a Bachelor of Science in Business Education from Bethel College and an Associate of Science in Business Administration from Ancilla College. She holds a vocational license from Ball State University, certification in CTA and certification in Microsoft Office. From 2002 to 2003, 2004 to 2005, 2008 to 2009 and 2009 to 2010, Ms. Burke was honored with the Most Inspiring Teacher award, as voted upon by Knox Community High School students.

In her spare time, Ms. Burke enjoys gardening, reading, needlework and interior design.

Conversation with Debbie M. Burke

Cambridge Who's Who: What would you like to promote most about yourself or your business?
Debbie M. Burke: I put children first.

What is the most rewarding aspect of your career?
When a student who has graduated comes back to say thank you, even after 10 years. They call, text and e-mail me, and come over my house. Even after all the time passes, I don't forget them.

What is your greatest professional accomplishment to date?
Being honored as Most Inspirational Teacher four different times.

What are your short-term and long-term career goals?
I want to stay in education – this is where I want to be. I have a background in business administration, as I ran a $30 million restaurant prior to becoming a teacher. When I came into education, the first thing they did was ask me if I had aspirations of becoming an administrator. I said, "The last thing I want to do is be an administrator – I've had enough of that." I like to tell my children that I made my millions and now I can afford to become a educator.

What made you become an educator after having this restaurant?
It was time for me to move on from being an administrator and I always wanted to be a teacher. I decided it was time to go back, get my degree in teaching and do what I wanted to do.

On what topic(s) do you consider yourself to be an expert?
Office procedures and computer programming, since I pursued certifications in business education and technology.

How do you remain current in your profession?
I'm taking two courses right now, one on virtuality and another on wikis and blogs.

What makes you a valuable resource in your industry?
My willingness to anticipate the changes that technology brings. I am a department head here as well. When I look at my counterparts, who are

lifetime teachers in my department, I notice that they just don't embrace technology at all.

What is the most significant issue facing your profession today?
Funding – for instance, they just cut my department budget in half.

What advice can you offer fellow members who work in your industry?
Remain current with education issues and technology. Always put the child first – they have bad days and need to be considered just as we do.

What are you passionate about?
Children are my passion.

Who have been your mentors?
Michael Matsey, who was my business teacher in college when I was going to get my business administration degree.

Do you have a motto or principle that guides your work?
Put others before yourself.

Business Education

Kathleen M. Busarsky, M.Ed.
Business Teacher (Retired)
Arroyo High School
4921 Cedar Avenue
El Monte, CA 91732 USA
kbusarsky@emuhsd.k12.ca.us
http://www.ahs.emuhsd.k12.ca.us

Teaching is the one profession that lays the foundation for a lifetime of enrichment, where students learn invaluable information about the world in which they live. For more than three decades, Kathleen M. Busarsky, with an extensive background in business, was an educator for Arroyo High School in El Monte, Calif. Her perseverance made her a valuable resource to both students and faculty alike, but as of June 17, 2010, she retired from her position. Her dedication to her students and enthusiasm for both business and education will make it a bittersweet farewell.

Throughout her 36-year career, Ms. Busarsky most desired to spread positivity to her students, so that she could witness firsthand the successes that many of them would go on to attain. The reward for her was not the paychecks she received, but rather the knowledge that she inspired a young man or woman to go into the field of business. In addition to teaching ninth- through 12th-grade students, she also taught a legal assistant night class. Several of the students that took that class went on to stay local and work at a legal firm in the area, a feat of which she is very proud. Additionally, she once had the parent of a former student tell her how influential she was in his daughter's life and that his daughter was now running the front office of his business. A couple of her former students have successfully remained employed at the district headquarters office for the past 10 years.

Even with her busy schedule, Ms. Busarsky finds the time to tutor high school students after school three times a week in the Personal, Recreational and Educational Progress (PREP) program. This is an academic enrichment program that offers tutoring in various subjects, including English, computers, science, and social studies, and is designed to inspire students to pursue higher education. The PREP program collaborates with the existing school organizations and helps to form new clubs according to the student's interests.

Being diagnosed with cancer, Ms. Busarsky was faced with the obstacle of addressing the life-threatening health issue, but she still never missed a day of class. She was required to undergo radiation treatment, so it was understood that she might want to take time off from teaching. However, she didn't let anything stop her from coming to school. "I grew up with my parents telling me how important it was to go to school every day," explains Ms. Busarsky. It was important to her to be present every day for her students. She was motivated by them and even through her trials, she stayed persistent and devoted.

Ms. Busarsky received a Bachelor of Science in Business Education followed by a master's degree in business education, both from Wayne State University. She holds certification in cross-cultural language and academic development and maintains memberships with several affiliations, including the California Teachers Association and the National Education Association.

Conversation with Kathleen M. Busarsky, M.Ed.

Cambridge Who's Who: Did you always know that you wanted to be a teacher?
Kathleen M. Busarsky: No – I was going to go into business, but that was over 30 years ago and at that time, it was a hard field for women. I thought that to become successful, I was going to have to be way above the men. I then decided that I should go into a field where it didn't matter whether you were a man or a woman. I started thinking slowly about teaching and it just evolved from there.

On what topic(s) do you consider yourself to be an expert?
I consider myself an expert in teaching ninth- through 12th-grade students in various subjects including office technology, shorthand, business law, mathematics, computers and English.

What characteristics help to separate you from your competitors?
My persistence. I am a cancer survivor and when I was diagnosed I came to school even through the radiation. My dad was a God-send to me and used to pick me up from school and take me to my radiation; I would come right back to school the next day. I didn't take any time off, whereas others who have been diagnosed may have taken off half a year.

What motivates you?
My mother was a hardworking woman of German ancestry and her motto was "Do it, get it over with and move on to the next thing!" She had an old-school way of thinking and it just rubbed off on me.

What lessons have you learned as a professional in your field for the past 36 years?
Be persistent, enjoy the kids and whatever their daily problems are, deal with it and get to the meat of the matter, which is the lesson that you are trying to get them to learn at hand. Glorify their successes.

What short-term and long-term career goals are you currently pursuing?
My goal is to retire in June and move into the home I recently purchased in the San Diego area.

What is the most difficult obstacle or challenge you have faced in pursuit of your goals?
My sickness.

What is the most significant issue facing your profession today?
The issues with funding; also, students coming in who are not proficient with the English language, which is why a lot of them are failing out of school. They don't know the language and are at a disadvantage. Some of them put forth the effort, but some do not.

Who have been your mentors or people who have greatly influenced you?
One of my English teachers when I was in high school influenced me; my mother and father have been my rocks.

What changes have you observed in your industry/field since you started?
There have been a lot of changes, good and bad. I love computers, but when they go down, it's misery. The computers go down so often [at our school] and it's very frustrating, not only for the teachers, but also for the students because they are not able to do their work.

How do you see these changes affecting the future of your industry?
If we could have more funding to have proper up-to-date equipment and keep it running, then things will be good. However, if that doesn't happen, it will be dreadful.

What do you find to be the most rewarding about your profession?
Knowing that students are becoming effective members of our society.

What is your favorite or least-favorite work-related task to do and why?
Grading is my least favorite part.

What advice can you offer fellow members or others aspiring to work in your industry?
I was speaking with a young woman recently and she was about to go to college. One of her choices was teaching. I told her that it is a good profession, where she can have off some of the summer to get herself reorganized and rested. In business, you don't have that.

PHYSICS AND SCIENCE INSTRUCTION

ELIZABETH B. CHESICK
Chairwoman, Physics Teacher (Retired)
The Baldwin School
701 Montgomery Avenue
Bryn Mawr, PA 19010 USA
echesick@aol.com

Elizabeth B. Chesick is a retired physics teacher who instructed students at The Baldwin School, a private girls preparatory school providing kindergarten through 12th-grade education. For more than 36 years, she held this post, teaching physics, physical science and high-energy particle physics, shaping and revising the curriculum as needed and demonstrating laboratory experiments to students.

Ms. Chesick comes from a lineage of educators, including her father, Moffatt Grier Boyce, who was a mathematics professor. Aside from her effectiveness as a teacher, she has also been a tireless advocate for education, serving on the board of the Philanthropic Educational Organization, which is a women's society that raises money for women's education and offers five different scholarships. Additionally, she is on the board of the American Association of Physics Teachers as the high school representative. It is an elected position and she has one more year in her three-year term, campaigning for ninth-grade physics education. "The AAPT is working to better prepare teachers via a number of undergraduate programs," she explains. Additionally, teaching physics to ninth-graders means that students take the course before they become concerned that enrolling in difficult courses closer to graduation may lower their grade point averages.

Ms. Chesick obtained a Master of Arts in Physics in 1958 from Tufts University and a Bachelor of Arts in Physics in 1956 from Wellesley College. In 1974, she received certification as a physics teacher though Villanova University. She is a member of the National Science Teachers Association, the Southeastern Pennsylvania Chapter of the American Association of Physics Teachers and the Interfaith Hospitality Network. Due to her more than 45 years of contributions to the physics education field, Ms. Chesick has received numerous accolades, including a Recognition Plaque for Service to Southeastern Pennsylvania in 2005 from the American Association of Physics Teachers; the Rosamond Cross Chair for Excellence in Teaching in 1997 from The Baldwin School; the Tandy Technology Scholarship in 1992; the Presidential Award for Excellence in Science and Mathematics Teaching for

Pennsylvania in 1988; and the Agnes and Sophie Dallas Irwin Grant for Study in 1980.

Since she retired, Ms. Chesick has enjoyed hiking, camping, creative writing, reading and traveling. She has also become involved with the Interface Hospitality Network — one of four networks in the Philadelphia area, comprised of 12 churches and synagogues, which helps needy mothers with children to improve the quality of their lives.

CONVERSATION WITH ELIZABETH B. CHESICK

CAMBRIDGE WHO'S WHO: What is your greatest professional accomplishment to date?
ELIZABETH B. CHESICK: Being able to teach physics to ninth-grade students, which I did a little bit differently; for instance, I may have used algebra and a tiny bit of geometry. It's all conceptual – things that they can observe in life. It's much more related to what they see every day. Teaching physics to ninth-graders was a wonderful experience and a lot of fun.

What would you like to promote most about yourself or your business?
I would like to raise awareness of my work on the board of Interface Hospitality Network. It's affiliated with an organization out of New Jersey called Family Promise, which assists homeless and/or single mothers and children. We usually deal with three families at a time. Karen Olsen, who started this about 20 years ago, thought that our churches and synagogues have rooms which they use only on the weekends and are vacant during the week, so why can't they be used to house homeless people during the week? So the network was born. Each family is screened; each mother works on getting a GED or high school diploma, a job and a place to live. She has goals that she has to meet every week. They are usually in the program for about four months and by the end of that, they usually have what they need.

On what topic(s) do you consider yourself to be an expert?
Teaching physics; also, my experience with the nonprofit work.

What are your short-term and long-term career goals?
My short-term goal is to read a bunch of books! There are some trips that I would like to take, including down the Nile in Egypt and on a Silk Road trip. I would also like to promote ninth-grade physics education. Long term, I'm writing memories of my father and I would like to get that finished. I'm also writing up stories that I used to tell in my classroom.

And what specific steps have you taken toward achieving these goals?
I have begun writing my booklet and I am currently the high school representative to the executive board of the American Association of Physics Teachers, where I am attempting to be an effective advocate for the subject.

What is the most difficult obstacle or challenge you have faced in pursuit of your goals?

Getting the money to go to college and then graduate was an obstacle. When I was searching for my first job, I heard there was a position for a chemistry teacher and I applied for it, even though I was not a chemist. My husband was a chemist, so I talked my way into getting hired. I do not at any point feel any discrimination against me because I was a woman and I never felt I would ever have any discrimination. I took my challenges and made them positive.

What advice can you offer people aspiring to work in this profession?

You really have to want to do it. It's enough work and drudgery that if you don't think you're going to like teaching, you really shouldn't [work in this profession]. You need to like the subject matter that you are teaching. If you are teaching something that you don't like, it makes it more difficult. You have to be willing to put in numerous hours outside of the classroom, including a lot of preparation for the next day. Also, you don't want to be too much of a good friend to the students; you have to have a little bit of distance. There's a fine line between being the authority figure and being able to talk to them. Teaching will keep you young!

What advice can you offer fellow members who work in your industry?

Don't retire! If you like your job, you should continue teaching as long as you can. I think if you enjoy what you're doing, then you should keep on doing it. It's nice to keep some connection to your subject.

Who have been your mentors or people who have greatly influenced you?

My father Moffatt Grier Boyce, who was a math professor at Vanderbilt University, influenced me to become a teacher. Others who have influenced me include Phyllis Fleming, a physics professor at Wellesley College; Jack Schnepps, a physics professor at Tufts University; Jim Nelson, a physics resource teaching director; John Layman, the director of the Woodrow Wilson Foundation Physics Teacher Institute; and my fellow recipients of the Presidential Award for Excellence in Science and Math Teaching.

How do you remain current in your profession?

I read the journals Physics Today and The Physics Teacher. I also attend national meetings of the American Association of Physics Teachers and the Southwest Pennsylvania Section of AAPT Networking with local physics teachers.

What makes you a valuable resource in your industry?

My experience that I gained from 45 years of teaching physics to high school students.

What is the most significant issue facing your profession today?
The United States is behind other countries with regards to the number of trained physicists and we are often in the position of having to employ physicists educated in other countries. This situation may be due to students considering physics too difficult to study. Another cause may be poorly prepared teachers – in subject matter and content. Having all students take physics would do wonders to increase the number of students opting to pursue careers involving physics.

Do you have a motto or principle that guides your work?
Don't worry about it; it will all work out in the end.

What are you passionate about?
I believe that all students should be exposed to some physics, even if on an elementary level. Knowing some physics makes it possible to appreciate everyday experiences and understand how the world works.

Elementary and Secondary Education

Hilda J. Cosby
1) Teacher (Retired) 2) Curator
1) Henrico County Public Schools 2) Museum In Memory Of Virginia
E. Randolph
2200 Mountain Road
Glen Allen, VA 23060 USA

As they say, "Once a teacher, always a teacher," and at the ripe age of 82, Hilda J. Cosby – a former elementary and secondary school educator – refuses to sit back in her rocking chair. Instead, she continues to enrich others as a curator at the Museum In Memory Of Virginia E. Randolph. Ms. Cosby became involved in her profession when her husband, who was a curator for 27 years, passed away. She was offered the unique chance to adopt his position and jumped at the opportunity. Housed in a home economics building built in 1937, the museum boasts a comprehensive collection of vocational education artifacts and information that is available for perusing by the public. As curator, Ms. Cosby is responsible for the general maintenance of the museum and for hosting informative seminars and tours.

After accruing many years of experience in elementary and secondary education, Ms. Cosby has learned the importance of understanding and tolerance toward one another. "My way is not your way, and yet if we disagree, we should be able to compromise for the good of the cause," she says. As she receives communications about the way business and government groups are thinking today, she has gotten the impression that people tend not to listen to each other's concerns. She voices that the best way for groups to work is to come together, discuss and determine a winning perspective without becoming angry because of their differences. Ultimately, she hopes that justice will prevail.

With a lifetime of success behind her, Ms. Cosby has her parents, who were educators, to thank for instilling in her good values. She is also thankful for the people who came into her life when she least expected it, in order to give her a helping hand, lead her on and encourage her. Ms. Cosby is a God-fearing woman, who acknowledges that without the Lord in which she believes, she is nothing. "I use stumbling blocks as stepping stones," she says. "Whenever I am faced with a dilemma or problem, I take it to God – you'd be surprised at how a means that you had never thought of will come your way and keep you going." Her spirituality has enabled her to gain the strength she needs, rather than point a finger or hold a grudge.

Ms. Cosby received a Bachelor of Science in Education from Saint Paul College. She is a member of the United Teachers Association, Northwest Business for Culture and the Arts, and the Virginia Association for Teachers. In whatever spare time this busy bee has, she enjoys working with local church groups, reading and traveling. She also donates to the March of Dimes and the American Cancer Society.

Conversation with Hilda J. Cosby

Cambridge Who's Who: What would you like to promote most about yourself or your business?
Hilda J. Cosby: In whatever I endeavor, I try my best. Currently, I am a curator at the Museum In Memory Of Virginia E. Randolph, which pays tribute to the pioneer in vocational education and training. When I give tours, or am approached by students who are doing research about her, I provide them with adequate information to maintain their interest. They go away with a lot more information about this educator's significance. I'm working on numerous projects at the museum, which keep me busy. Regardless of the extent in which I involved, I do my best to promote it. This helps me so I don't get lonely.

What is the most rewarding aspect of your career?
As a teacher, the most rewarding aspect of my career was educating others in such a manner where my students learned, wanted to learn more and continue to find education enjoyable, rather than something that wasn't satisfying. I felt rewarded knowing that they would learn about things that would help them to succeed as an individual in life.

What is your greatest professional accomplishment to date?
Being able to help people. For the past two years, I have been helping an individual who was in serious danger of not getting his life together and on track – he was really in a pickle. I continue to hope for him and I can see that things are gradually changing. I don't keep records of my accomplishments. People will come and thank me and I've forgotten about the act of what it was.

What is the most difficult obstacle or challenge you have faced in pursuit of your goals?
I've found that whenever I tried something new, one of my greatest obstacles was fear, as in whether or not I could accomplish the task. You need to overcome that fear and you'll be surprised. You can really get in your own way – in other words, you worry about something that you shouldn't be worried about at all.

On what topic(s) do you consider yourself to be an expert?
Elementary school education, which covers all of the subjects, and childhood development. The lowest grade that I taught was the third grade, which was

one of my favorite grades because of the children's age; they were eager to learn. You are dealing with all areas in the development of the child. You didn't have [that many] disciplinary problems there, because the students wanted to do their best for their teacher.

How do you remain current in your profession?
I do a lot of reading of books, articles and magazines. I attend meetings and conferences. Television is a source of communication and education if you watch the right programming.

What is the most significant issue facing your profession today?
Parents not being able to discipline their children affects how they learn and what they do in school. I wouldn't dare do the things that I see these children doing when their parents aren't around.

What advice can you offer fellow members who work in your industry?
Teachers (as well as parents) need to listen to their children to hear what they need and what they are experiencing. Most of the things children say, they have learned by listening to others. Teachers can learn a lot about their students if they listened to their vernacular language.

What are you passionate about?
I am passionate about teaching. I try to put my best foot forward. Even when I go out into the public I do this, because you never know who is watching you. I ask the Lord to guide my thoughts, speech and actions. I know that without him, I wouldn't be who I am.

Communications and Theater Education

Rebecca Kay Dean, Ph.D.
Professor, Founder
Northampton Community College
3835 Green Pond Road
Bethlehem, PA 18020 USA
rdean@northampton.edu
http://www.northampton.edu

Dr. Rebecca Kay Dean is a professor and founder of the communications and theater department (now communication studies) at Northampton Community College, within their humanities and social sciences division. She is considered by her peers to be a gifted spoken word instructor, who teaches film studies, film analysis, theory of film, cultural studies, speech communication, public speaking, and intercultural communication to students, and has just finished a new film course entitled "Intercultural Film Studies." With more than 20 years of professional experience, she has also written a course at Lafayette College called "History of American Political Rhetoric."

Dr. Dean believes that "kismet" — Turkish for the predestined course of events that comprises a person's life — led her to a flourishing career in academics. Born in West Virginia as the only child of two college professors, she was intrigued by the unique style of worship and inspired Pentecostal preaching inherent to the area. She went on to study multiculturalism as part of her doctorate-level studies, conducting a cultural analysis of southern Appalachia; additionally, she gathered transcripts of entire Appalachian Pentecostal radio program sermons to uncover what the preachers were trying to say. Her study was also cross-cultural as she examined not only sermon content, but also the deep division and separation of classes in the South that were especially exemplified by way of religious denomination.

"The practice of radio preaching is a means of cultural specificity," she describes. "They use the sermons to vent about their ordinary lives." The more she uncovered, the more she related this information to her upbringing, in an area where the rural members of "preacher culture" or descendents of the original settlers of the 18th Century are regularly called "hillbillies," a derogatory term for the rural and mountainous dwellers of the United States. In her dissertation, she discussed the reason "hillbillies" refuse to go mainstream; also, why there are so many little churches within these communities. "The people who live in these areas keep the congregations small to maintain a familial experience," she explains. "In this situation, the pastor or priest knows every single person by name."

With a proper understanding of the demographic, she hopes to educate and help others discern reality from the misconstrued. Today, she remains dedicated to spreading knowledge and understanding about multiculturalism. Additionally, she is working to ensure people gain a level of tolerance and respect, using her classroom as a culturally diverse place to share information and enrich others, while also working with the Southern Poverty Center's Program, "Teaching Tolerance."

Dr. Dean received a Ph.D. in English Cultural Studies in 1998, a dual master's degree in English and communications in 1984, and a bachelor's degree in English and Slavic studies in 1981 from the University of Pittsburgh. She is a moderator for the City Council and School Board, as well as a member of the American Association of University Women, the League of Women Voters, the Clean Water Institute, and the National Organization for Women. She also volunteers her time to several independent film societies in the Lehigh Valley, Pa., including Easton's Movies at the Mill, Bethlehem's Southside Film Society, and Allentown's 19th Street Theatre.

Conversation with Rebecca Kay Dean, Ph.D.

Cambridge Who's Who: How did you become involved in education?
Rebecca Kay Dean: My parents are professors. We call the doctorate our union card.

What would you like to promote most about yourself or your business?
The community college in which I teach is dedicated to multiculturalism and the fact that the 21st century is a global village. We have more than 30 countries represented by our students. I have had students from Yemen, the Ukraine and the Ivory Coast (Cote d'Ivoire). In one class, we counted 10 different languages; we had ten different words for cow.

What are your short-term and long-term career goals?
My long-term goal is to remain as effective in the classroom for as many years as I possibly can because teaching is my absolute joy.

And what specific steps have you taken toward achieving these goals?
I've already started talking to a woman in my school, whose specialty is to help students find their majors. We are talking about spotlighting my recognition in Cambridge Who's Who when we apply for a grant through our college.

What is your greatest professional accomplishment to date?
My greatest professional accomplishment is dignifying my culture through my dissertation.

On what topic(s) do you consider yourself to be an expert?
I consider myself to be an expert on myths in culture. Within all myths is a kernel of truth. I also consider myself an expert on linguistics. I love to be able to nail a southern accent because there is not just one. I also consider myself an expert on linguistic anthropology. We have learned that digging things up can only take us so far back, but taking it back to the great mother of all languages, the Indo-European family, helps us to uncover great waves of immigration — that's where you uncover myths and the origins of the different languages. There were languages before the Indo-Europeans arrived there. You can use language to trace migration and determine how hard a culture put up a fight to maintain its own language, because language is culture.

How do you remain current in your profession?
The American Communications Association [ACA] has a website, where I find journals and keep updated.

What is the most significant issue facing your profession today?
One issue facing my profession today is the No Child Left Behind Act. There are many Americans who cannot think critically. Furthermore, they are terrified when they are expected to think critically on their own. I refuse to give objective tests at all; instead, my students write for me, with the intention to develop their critical-thinking skills.

What advice can you offer people aspiring to work in this profession?
Learn everything you possibly can. Be someone who wants to learn everything you can. It is curiosity that has been killed.

Who have been your mentors or people who have greatly influenced you?
My whole family influenced me.

Pediatric Cardiology Instruction

Peter L. Ferrer, MD, FACC, FAIUM

Professor of Pediatrics (Cardiology), Radiology and Obstetrics
University of Miami
Pediatric Cardiology (R-76)
P.O. Box 16960
Miami, FL 33101 USA
robbferr@aol.com

Dr. Peter L. Ferrer, a gifted and dedicated medical professional, worked as an adult cardiologist for 10 years. For 42 years, he has been practicing and teaching pediatric cardiology. Presently, he is a professor of pediatrics (cardiology), radiology and obstetrics at the University of Miami Miller School of Medicine, where he teaches the ins and outs of congenital heart disease, ultrasound techniques and clinical pediatric cardiology to young doctors who are selected for the program. He finds it very gratifying to be able to educate students about heart disease, for they will go on to improve the lives of others. In 1983, he organized a fetal cardiology program, and in 1990, a program for adults with congenital heart disease.

Dr. Ferrer has experienced many highlights and great moments in his career over the years, from saving twins with fetal hydrops and atria tachycardia, a lethal disease of the heart, to seeing babies with congenital heart disease grow to become healthy adults, with many even becoming mothers themselves.

From 2004 to 2007, Dr. Ferrer served as the president of the Latin Society of Pediatric Cardiology and Cardiovascular Surgery. While presiding over the organization, which includes members from 27 countries around the world, he created a system in which scientific research could be done on a transnational level. As a result of the collaborative efforts of doctors of different nationalities, papers are being published, which will undoubtedly raise awareness about new developments in the field.

Dr. Ferrer received an MD from the University of Chile. He completed a residency in internal medicine and a fellowship in adult cardiology. He was a W.K. Kellogg Fellow and completed a fellowship in pediatric cardiology at Harvard and Yale universities. He is a member of the American Heart Association, a Fellow of the American Institute of Ultrasound in Medicine, a Fellow of the American College of Cardiology, and a member and honorary member of many international societies of cardiology. He has taught pediatric cardiology to 121 fellows, 58 of them international, and has helped them with research.

He has given more than 250 invited lectures, many at international meetings, and published 12 book chapters and 223 abstracts and papers with colleagues.

In his spare time, Dr. Ferrer enjoys photography, listening to classical music, reading, appreciating paintings and sculptures, and sharing his life with his wife, Debra, and his five sons.

Conversation with Peter L. Ferrer, MD, FACC, FAIUM

Cambridge Who's Who: What would you like to promote most about yourself or your business?
Peter L. Ferrer: I would like to emphasize the educational aspect of the work I do. Educating young doctors about health care ultimately helps many children, particularly in the treatment of childhood heart disease. At the university, we have a team of cardiologists, each one with expertise in a particular area of pediatric heart disease. We treat the fetus, the newborn and the young person who has congenital heart disease. Pediatric cardiology is a very complex but important field of medicine, and I am proud to be able to teach others and pass on to my students the benefit of my experience and research. Heart disease in children is not as widespread and does not grab as much attention as some other diseases that kill children, but it is an important disease and must be addressed.

What is the most rewarding aspect of your career?
Without a doubt, it is the gratitude I receive – the smiles I see on the faces of my patients; nothing replaces that. All of us who are in a profession helping people know this reward.

What is the most difficult obstacle or challenge you have faced in pursuit of your goals?
Due to my age and the number of years of experience I've had, I practically achieved the goals that I set for myself years ago – this is in terms of innovations, organizing specific cardiovascular laboratories and setting standards of care. Accomplishing what I have in my career was definitely a challenge. In the years to come, I would like to continue as an innovator and also preserve what I have created.

What is the most significant issue facing your profession today?
Providing quality health care to those in need is extremely important. Health care reform will take time to get right, and there will be painful issues to resolve, but I hope someday we will achieve greater equality in delivering health care to our entire population.

What are you passionate about?
My job and my career. I get up every day and feel the same motivation. It's a continuous passion, not something that goes up and down. That passion is channeled through the university, as the institution allows me to teach, do research and provide service – hence my loyalty. At the same time, the university provides me with a decent salary, which allows me to devote myself entirely to my field.

Who have been your mentors or people who have greatly influenced you?
My main mentor was the late Dr. Alexander Nadas. Dr. Nadas was a professor at Harvard and was one of the founding fathers of pediatric cardiology. I was at Harvard from 1968 to 1972. The people who influenced me were Dr. Richard Van Praagh and his wife, the late Dr. Stella Van Praagh. They were professors of pathology at Harvard and had a huge influence in contributing to my knowledge. I still have a very nice relationship with Dr. Richard Van Praagh.

Do you have a motto?
Not exactly, but "Smile and try to make people happy" would come close.

What is your greatest professional accomplishment to date?
It is hard to name only one. Certainly my greatest accomplishments would have to be my five sons. Having five occurred by chance because I didn't intend to marry twice, but things happen. I have to continue doing the best I can for the two younger ones.

Professionally, back in the 1960s, I started a new program in pediatric cardiology at the University of Chile. At that time, I worked with people who would continue my efforts. I eventually left there, but the program continues today. And I continue helping to improve the knowledge in that field. I have had approximately 58 young doctors from all over the world who have worked with me in fetal and pediatric cardiac ultrasound. I have also helped train another 63 fellows who entered the pediatric cardiology program at the University of Miami.

Also, I created two additional laboratories that I am very proud of: one at the University of Miami and another at Jackson Memorial Hospital in Miami – they are now very large. Through the years, I have improved them and incorporated new technology as it came along. I have created new programs as well. One is related to the diagnosis and management of fetuses with heart disease, which did not exist at the university prior to 1983. In 1990, I organized the congenital heart disease in the adult programs. So many more children survive today, and these patients must be followed and taken care of as adults. My idea has been to create a bridge between pediatric and adult care and to continue the care for these patients beyond the age of 21.

Accounting Instruction

Myrna L. Fischman, Ph.D., CPA
Chairwoman
Department of Accounting, Taxation and Law
Long Island University
1 University Plaza, H-700 Building
Brooklyn, NY 11201 USA
myrna.fischman@liu.edu
http://www.liu.edu

With 34 years of experience in accounting, Myrna L. Fischman considers herself lucky to have found a job in the field for which she has utmost passion. "I love what I do and I feel that it's one of the things that keeps me alive," she says. As chairwoman of the department of accounting, taxation and law for Long Island University, Ms. Fischman oversees administrative duties and is an advisor for a program where students work with the IRS to complete tax returns for individuals with low-level incomes at no charge.

Ms. Fischman entered her field because she always had an affinity for mathematics and business. As she gained valuable industry experience, she jumped at an opportunity to teach these subjects to others. After years in the educator's seat, Ms. Fischman has learned that it is necessary to know your field and genuinely enjoy it if you expect to be an effective teacher. Her philosophy is simple: you can't just learn from a book, you have to get out there and become involved in it. To those wanting to pursue a career in accounting instruction, Ms. Fischman warns, "If you don't love it, you shouldn't do it." There are many different facets to accounting therefore, she also recommends gaining as much experience as you can beforehand.

Without a sense of humor, Ms. Fischman believes she wouldn't have made it so far. "My intelligence and ability to laugh, even in critical situations, always helped me to get through something that was uncomfortable," she says. There were many people who helped her along the way. She believes that she didn't encounter any major obstacles in life, mostly because there was always someone there to help her through. She thanks her parents, Sally and Isadore Fischman, for being a great inspiration and only wanting her to do something that she loved. She dedicates her "Top 101 Industry Experts" chapter in memory of them.

A member on the board of directors of the New York State Society of Certified Public Accountants, Ms. Fischman received her Ph.D. in Accounting in 1977 from New York University. The highlights of her career were becoming a certified public accountant and receiving the Educator of the Year award. In her spare time she enjoys exploring mysteries, swimming, dancing, and reading.

Conversation with Myrna L. Fischman, Ph.D., CPA

Cambridge Who's Who: What is the most significant issue facing your profession today?
Myrna L. Fischman: Many people who currently go into teaching accounting have never practiced accounting. It's a clinical profession; if you don't do it, how can you teach it? You need more than book learning. You can't really learn it from a book, you have to do it. The universities are looking more for people who hold a Ph.D. rather than CPAs or those with a master's degree, who may have more experience. Anyone who is teaching in the business discipline should have done it because the books only go so far. The books are theory; practical application is very important. Life is not from a textbook.

What are your short-term and long-term career goals?
I want to live long and healthy. I'm where I want to be and comfortable with where I am; also, what I'm doing. I'm not looking for any more mountains to climb. I'm happy with making other people happy – that's really what I'm all about. I feel very fortunate that I'm happy with what I do.

Who have been your mentors or people who have greatly influenced you?
No one gets to where they are without help along the way. It first started with my own parents who said to me, "You can do whatever you want, but you better want to do it." Al Johnson was a man who helped me in my career. People pushed me forward all the time. It's the little things that people do for you. When I worked for the publishing house, Viking Press, a man in human resources made me better in terms of my speech. I was very fortunate along the way with the support and guidance that I received.

On what topic(s) do you consider yourself to be an expert?
Life – I've lived through so much and I've learned so much. There's a great deal of common sense that I have, more so than just specific knowledge and information. I share this with my students, for instance, when I help them to find a job.

How do you remain current in your profession?
I'm active in the professional organizations and I also read the literature as it

comes out. If you're teaching, you're learning because everything you do is in the textbooks. We have to be aware of the things that are changing.

What would you like to promote most about yourself or your business?
What we've been doing for the students at the university is running a volunteer tax assistance program. We've been doing this for more than 30 years and I am one of the advisors. We work with the IRS and they train the students to prepare free tax returns for low-income people. We also run the Agent Project with the IRS where the students work a whole day with an IRS agent and get some training. This is the second year that we've done that partnership. We run seminars as well and I run the tax seminar that we have at the university. The university is very involved with the community and is very supportive of the students.

What makes you a valuable resource in your industry?
I have a sense of humor and I only speak about things I know. If I don't know something, I admit it and I find out the answer.

What is the most difficult obstacle or challenge you have faced in pursuit of your goals?
Whenever there was a problem, there was always somebody around to help. I don't mind learning and challenging myself. I always consider myself to be fortunate.

What advice can you offer fellow members who work in your industry?
You need to take it one day at a time.

Do you have a favorite quote?
"He who fights and runs away lives to fight another day."

Career and Technical Education

Debbie C. Gordon

Chairwoman, Cooperative Education Internship Coordinator
Hayfield Secondary School
7630 Telegraph Road
Alexandria, VA 22315 USA
debbie.gordon@fcps.edu
http://www.fcps.edu

Debbie C. Gordon, chairwoman and cooperative education internship coordinator in the career and technical education department of Hayfield Secondary School, serves 21 middle and high school staff members in the disciplines of auto technology, business, cosmetology, family and consumer sciences, marketing, JROTC, technology education, and health and medical sciences. She teaches education programs, executes state-level training and outlines classroom curricula. Additionally, she counsels on career decision-making, job skills and workplace safety, handles ethical issues, coordinates cooperative internships with employers, and fosters partnerships within the business community.

Ms. Gordon, who reads Middle School Journal, Edutopia and Instructor to remain aware of the latest developments in her field, attributes her success to the personal and mutually respectful connections she has developed with her peers, and more importantly, her students. In 2004, Ms. Gordon was the recipient of the Teacher of the Year award from the Fairfax County Family and Consumer Sciences Education Association. That same year, the Crystal City Pentagon Rotary Club bestowed to her the Outstanding High School Teacher Award. In 1997 and 2004, she was a two-time nominee for The Washington Post's Teacher of the Year award. A definite highlight of her 34-year career was being selected as one of three state trainers for the Teachers for Tomorrow program through the Virginia Department of Education in Richmond. The pre-collegiate education curriculum is for select high school juniors and seniors who are interested in pursuing a teaching endorsement in college.

A longtime desire to be a teacher, combined with the inspiration she received from her family members who were educators prompted Ms. Gordon to pursue a career in education. The icing on the cake was a scholarship she received, which enabled her to pursue an undergraduate education in family and consumer sciences. Ms. Gordon received a master's degree in education with a concentration in curriculum and instruction in 1998 from Virginia Polytechnic Institute and State University and a Bachelor of Science in Family and Consumer Sciences in 1976 from James Madison University. She was nominated for the Virginia Exemplary Standard Program Review, which was awarded by Governor Bob McDonnell in June 2010.

In her spare time, Ms. Gordon enjoys traveling, exercising, skiing, ice skating, and snowmobiling.

Conversation with Debbie C. Gordon

Cambridge Who's Who: What would you like to promote most about yourself or your business?
Debbie C. Gordon: As an educator and role model for young people, I take extreme pride in my profession; students are my number one priority. The leadership roles I've held (career and technical education department chair, family and consumer sciences lead teacher, mentor, and school representative to the superintendent's advisory committee) help define me, but come after my students' needs.

What is the most rewarding aspect of your career?
The most rewarding aspect of my career is [having] the ability to transform the lives of others and see the personal and professional growth of my students during their high school career, including those "ah-ha" moments. For example, I was teaching how to read a W-2 and complete a 1040 EZ Federal Tax Return to my Education for Employment students and at the end of the lesson, one student said, "You're an awesome teacher." I asked him what made him say that statement and he said, "You even make taxes fun." Those kinds of moments make it rewarding.

What are your short-term and long-term career goals?
My short-term goal is to maintain strong student enrollment and provide quality instruction in Hayfield Secondary School's various career and technical departments. Those disciplines include auto technology, business, cosmetology, family and consumer sciences, health and medical sciences, junior ROTC, marketing and technology education. I want to keep a really strong department – not just in student numbers, but also in the quality of the staff that are hired to provide relevant academic knowledge and technical skills to prepare individuals for the world of work.

My long-term goal is to make a career switch and become involved in the teacher-mentor and collaboration services for Fairfax County Public Schools. I have to wait a year after I retire, and then I can be a teacher-mentor. I also plan to continue my role as a state trainer in the Virginia Teachers for Tomorrow program (with the Department of Education) and even be an adjunct professor, teaching foundations of education courses at local colleges and universities. I want to stay in education and make a difference.

What is the most difficult obstacle or challenge you have faced in pursuit of your goals?

Budget cuts across the state trickling down to the county level have reduced our career and technical education teaching contracts by four to 15 days within a two-year phase. It is challenging to keep the department members positive as each individual has to decide their personal level of commitment, based on a salary step and cost of living freeze for a second year, and now a contract reduction.

On what topic(s) do you consider yourself to be an expert?

Work readiness skills, cooperative education internships, Virginia Teachers for Tomorrow, and the family and consumer sciences curriculum in the state of Virginia.

How do you remain current in your profession?

By [reading] professional journals, being involved in professional organizations, mentoring others as they complete their observations and practicum, attending county and state trainings, developing and revising the career and technical education curriculum, assuming leadership roles at the school, county and state levels, and constantly networking with teachers.

What makes you a valuable resource in your industry?

I have extensive knowledge of curriculum and instruction related to various program areas within career and technical education.

What is the most significant issue facing your profession today?

The shortage of teachers and qualified educators in the current "critical needs" areas of special education, mathematics, science, reading, foreign language, career and technical education, English as a second language, English and library media. It is projected that in the next 10 years we will need between 2.2 and 2.4 million teachers nationally, while the current college pipeline will be producing only half that number.

What advice can you offer fellow members who work in your industry?

If you teach with a passion and have a sense of humor, every day you and your students will find some reward in what you've done.

What are you passionate about?

My passions are my students and the creativity that teaching allows, because [I am able] to develop relevant and real learning experiences in my lesson plans.

Who have been your mentors or people who have greatly influenced you?
Marlene Free, who is the former Hayfield Secondary School's department chair and Education for Employment instructor, has been my mentor; she has been most influential in my professional career. We are not just colleagues; we are friends and shared professional and life lessons during the 20 plus years that we taught together. She is a veteran teacher of 40 years. I admire her futuristic vision for family and consumer sciences and her endless dedication to our profession. She is currently retired in Georgia, but is actively involved in education and service learning around the world.

What is your favorite quote?
A quote from Forest E. Witcraft: "One hundred years from now, it will not matter what my bank account was, how big my house was, or what kind of car I drove, but the world may be a little better because I was important in the life of a child."

PHYSICAL EDUCATION

JACKIE M. HALL
Teacher, Coach
West Bourbon Elementary School
602 Fifth Street
Uniontown, KS 66779 USA
jhall@uniontown235.org

Coming from a lineage of athletes and educators, it was only natural for Jackie M. Hall to become a teacher and sports coach for West Bourbon Elementary School. She takes the enrichment of her students very seriously and not only provides them with a substantial instruction in the classroom, but also makes sure to enliven them with quality recreational activity. Through this combined approach, Ms. Hall is helping students to get the most out of their school days.

As a physical education teacher, Ms. Hall advocates healthy lifestyle behaviors. She coaches volleyball in the fall, and in the spring she coaches junior high and high school track and field. She is able to help each of her individual players work on their skills, providing them with honest criticism so they can improve their standing. She is also the junior high school's athletic director, responsible for the scheduling of sporting events.

Through her 28 years as an educator, Ms. Hall has become an effective networker, oftentimes reaching out to others who have been in the profession for many years. She finds this to be a very good way to improve her knowledge of the field. She has learned that love and devotion are key ingredients to any teacher's success. "Jobs are hard to come by nationwide so you need to be passionate about what you do," declares Ms. Hall. She makes it a point to always learn new teaching strategies by attending workshops and seminars. She also reads industry-related journals and newspapers.

Ms. Hall received a Bachelor of Education in 1982 and a Master of Education, with a concentration in physical education, in 1989 from Pittsburg State University. She is a member of the Kansas Volleyball Association, the Kansas National Education Association and the National Education Association. She was the recipient of the Outstanding Young Educator Award from Pittsburg State University.

CONVERSATION WITH JACKIE M. HALL

CAMBRIDGE WHO'S WHO: On what topics do you consider yourself to be an expert?
JACKIE M. HALL: Coaching, education, volleyball, and physical education.

What characteristics help to separate you from your competitors?
I feel I am constantly learning, attending workshops and reading information on my areas of interest. I feel that keeps me on top.

What motivates you?
My kids, volleyball, the track team, coaching and seeing the children progress.

What short-term and long-term career goals are you currently pursuing?
I love what I am doing and don't want to retire anytime soon.

How do you plan to achieve these goals?
My parents instilled in me the impetus to continue growing and reading, and to always take knowledge wherever I can get it.

What is the most difficult obstacle or challenge you have faced in pursuit of your goals?
When I started in Uniontown they had never had any physical education teachers, so in 1982 I started the PE program.

What is the most significant issue facing your profession today?
Financial budget cuts.

Did you ever consider pursuing a different career path or another profession? If yes, how did you end up working in your current field?
No, I always wanted to be an educator and coach.

What do you find to be the most rewarding about your profession?
I love having fun and enjoy what I do. I enjoy working with my students and seeing them progress.

What advice can you offer fellow members or others looking to become involved in your industry?
You need to network, talk to other people and ask questions. Talk to veterans and see how they have developed and evolved.

Who have been your mentors or people who have greatly influenced you?
My parents; they were both in education and my dad was also a coach. Athletics has always been in my family.

What changes have you observed in your industry/field since you started?
The technology and financial budget cuts. I really have to look at what I'm purchasing: is it necessary or can I (we) get along without it. I am also looking at other ways of obtaining money for my program through fundraising and grants.

How do you see these changes affecting the future of your industry?
I will always continue to look for ways to fund my program. I will do what is best for my kids.

SPECIAL EDUCATION

TAMMY JO HOLCOMB
Special Education Teacher
Jefferson Elementary School
1994 215th Street
Muscatine, IA 52761 USA
tjholcom@muscatine.k12.ia.us

Tammy Jo Holcomb has thoroughly enjoyed a fulfilling career as an educator for nearly 20 years. Currently a special education teacher at Jefferson Elementary School, Ms. Holcomb displays an intense passion for her work when teaching students with various learning disabilities, behavioral disorders and handicaps. Coming from a family that has experienced multiple learning disorders, she became involved in her profession as a way to offer hope and equal opportunities to students whom many may have felt were unable to be helped. Autism and attention-deficit hyperactivity disorder are among the challenges she faces in the classroom every day, but she is not deterred by their presence. Rather, these limitations motivate her to encourage excellence and challenge her students to aim higher.

Rote material delivery is not readily welcome in Ms. Holcomb's classroom. Instead, she chooses to employ innovative teaching methods that stress student interaction and the use of alternative resources, including her very own dog. As a trainer of a therapy dog, she and her canine work together to keep children engaged and interested in the curriculum. Though their various disabilities may incite outlandish or disrespectful behavior, each student is given specialized attention and treated as an individual with valid concerns and feelings. However, she is very careful not to baby them, stating "I'm very honest with the kids. When we're here to do reading, we don't have time to cry." In a profession that is often far-removed from the limelight, Ms. Holcomb enjoys the gratification she receives by helping children reach their tremendous potential.

The recipient of a Bachelor of Arts in Special Education from Western Illinois University, Ms. Holcomb is currently pursuing a master's degree in educational leadership at Morningside College to further her qualifications and gain more knowledge in her field. As a member of the Muscatine Education Association, she networks with other educational professionals and attends conferences to remain updated on the latest developments and advancements. For professional excellence, Ms. Holcomb was named a VIP of the Year by Cambridge Who's Who for the 2008 to 2009 year and selected as an outstanding professional representing special education.

CONVERSATION WITH TAMMY JO HOLCOMB

CAMBRIDGE WHO'S WHO: What would you like to promote most about yourself or your business?
TAMMY JO HOLCOMB: How important getting a decent education is – kids really need to know that they need to work for it. A lot of times people say, "I didn't get a good education because I had bad teachers." No, you had a bad education because you didn't put forth the effort to work with your teachers.

I also do something out of the ordinary by taking my dog to school for therapy. The kids are amazing with him and he's just as needy as they are some days. The kids I have will go talk to him and pet him, and there is no more misbehavior [from either party].

What is the most rewarding aspect of your career?
The job I'm doing right now. I'm actually holding a girl in my lap while talking to you and she's accepting that.

What is your greatest professional accomplishment to date?
Keeping kids in school who would have dropped out. Truthfully, I've had children as young as in the third grade who've quit school. If I can reel them in for another couple of years, I've done my job. A girl came up to me yesterday and hugged me. I had no idea who she was; I hadn't seen her since the third grade and today she's a beautiful eighth grader. She said to me, "I remember you. You talked to me in the hall one day when I was crying." I had not a clue that I had done that – she was not one of my students and not in special education, but I almost started crying because she remembered what I had done for her five years ago.

What are your short-term and long-term career goals?
My short-term goal is to go back to college for my master's degree. My long-term goal is to get my dog fully trained to come to school with me – that's a two-year project. Actually, if I had a true dream, I would want to open a school somewhere for special children whom people don't think may succeed.

And what steps have you taken toward achieving those goals?
I've started obedience classes with my dog. I took him to his first dog evaluation class and he was absolutely out of control. He bit the instructor and acted naughtily while I broke down and started crying. We went home and had a long talk, and now he's like a totally different dog with the techniques I'm doing.

What is the most difficult obstacle or challenge you have faced in pursuit of your goals?
The most difficult obstacle is trying not to get too close [to the work]. When you go home at night, you still dream about things [in the classroom]. I'm not a parent, not a friend – I'm their teacher.

On what topics do you consider yourself to be an expert?
I love behavior techniques and alternative teaching, such as teaching with dogs and manipulatives. Manipulatives include the use of calculators at an early age, computer technology, counters, charts, graphs, visual pictures, cheat cards, books on CD or tape, computer games, real life practice and so on.

How do you remain current in your profession?
I go to a lot of seminars on autism and oppositional children. One thing I'm really working on this year is trying to listen to the parents. We take a lot of blame in our business, but sometimes if you just listen, you realize that parents are upset too. A lot of times people say, "You don't understand, you're not a parent," and I say, "But I do take [the children's issues] home with me."

What makes you a valuable resource in your industry?
I think teachers and parents trust me, because they know their children have problems. They leave those problems at the door some days because as much as they want to hide it, they can't.

What is the most significant issue facing your profession today?
The lack of resources and trying to get my hands on the good stuff, things with validity and truthfulness. Some needed resources are the correct types of assessment tools, a curriculum that will show the students' growth, and easier types of data collection that are more parent-friendly. Also, additional information that will enable students to set and follow their own goals.

What advice can you offer to others in your profession?
Be true to the kids and be there for them. That's hard, because when a child spits on you, you don't want to be their friend in 10 minutes.

What are you passionate about?
I am very passionate about teaching alternative ways and getting real life back into our schools with old-fashioned drills. Let's not rush our kids. Kids need time to understand and explain their learning. They need time to like learning, and they need the passion to see beyond their home or community.

Do you have any advice for people aspiring to become involved in this profession?
You're going to feel like quitting every day, but stick with it. Love yourself, love your job and do not be afraid to love the kids.

Who have been your mentors or people who have greatly influenced you?
My mother Bonnie went back to school as an adult learner. She's been my inspiration and so are the kids.

Information Technology Enrichment

Janice E. Johnson

Chairwoman
Department of Business Administration
Shawnee State University
940 Second Street
Portsmouth, OH 45662 USA
ravencatt@verizon.net
http://www.ravencatt.com

Janice E. Johnson is an assistant professor and chairwoman of the business administration department of Shawnee State University. She has more than 19 years of experience in education and specializes in managing information systems and teaching IT applications, such as e-commerce and website design. Some highlights of her career include developing an e-commerce path for business administration students taking information systems management courses and creating a series of courses to help students achieve successful careers in e-business.

Ms. Johnson became involved in her profession because she enjoys working with computers, especially in e-commerce areas such as virtual worlds and website design. Fueled by her passion for IT, she penned the "Online E-commerce, HTML, and JavaScript Tutorials," an online resource covering Internet basics and the use of these respective programming languages. She and her colleagues, Dovel Myers and Dr. Michael Barnhart, created the SSU Cyber Center. The facility helps students and displaced workers in southern Ohio learn IT and interactive digital technology skills, and pursue careers in information technology. The center is funded by a Department of Labor grant, Shawnee State University, other grants and private sources.

Ms. Johnson received a Master of Business Administration from Morehead State University. She is a certified computer professional and a member of the HTML Writers Guild, the Faculty Senate of Shawnee State University, the Association of Virtual Worlds and the International Webmasters Association. Ms. Johnson is the assistant director of the Shawnee State University Cyber Center and director of the Shawnee State University Interactive Digital Technology Applications Center.

In her spare time, Ms. Johnson enjoys gardening and writing creative works. Since 1984, she has penned numerous poems and short stories, and written two novels. For a complete listing of her authored works, please visit her personal website at http://www.ravencatt-forum.com. She has her parents,

James and Gwendolin Johnson to thank for teaching her the value of education, and for showing her through their example that obstacles can be overcome and dreams can be achieved.

Conversation with Janice E. Johnson

Cambridge Who's Who: What first brought you into education?
Janice E. Johnson: I had never thought I would get into this. I started working as a tutor and a lab assistant, helping professors; it just went from there. They needed someone to cover one of the introductory computer classes and they drafted me for it. I never would have thought of myself as a teacher until I actually got into the classroom and found that I enjoyed it. I received good evaluations and this looked like something in which I could excel. It kept going, from being a part-time teacher to a temporary full-time position. I finally got hired full time and worked my way up, to assistant professor and then to chair of the department.

What is the most rewarding aspect of your career?
To be able to work with students and help them learn something; also, to see their eyes light up when they get it. When they start to make those connections on their own, it's wonderful. It's great to be able to sit and say that I helped a student get to where he or she wants to be.

What advice can you offer people aspiring to work in this profession?
They need to know that they are never going to be able to stop learning and it is never boring — things are always changing. It's a wonderful area in which to work, as long as you understand that it's not going to be a situation where once you get your degree, you can sit down and take it easy.

What advice can you offer fellow members who work in your industry?
Always keep in mind: the bottom line is that everything should revolve around the students. What we're here for is to provide the tools and environment for the student to be able to achieve not only their degree, but also the career in which they want to go. If you work to support the students, then everything else falls into place.

On what topic(s) do you consider yourself to be an expert?
I consider myself to be an expert on the technical things that I teach, with which I actually have experience. I like subjects where I'm able to talk with and engage the audience — it's give and take, and sharing information.

What is the most difficult obstacle or challenge you have faced in pursuit of your goals?
People look at me and think that there is a problem with females in the IT

field. I'm working with our tech prep in other areas to help the girls in the schools know that this is an option. I've never gone by tradition anyways. My parents, James and Gwendolin Johnson, were farmers. We had guidance counselors telling us not to think about college because they thought that we couldn't afford it. But my parents had the money saved for us. They taught us that there are things that happen, but you find other ways to handle them. Everything happens for a reason.

What are your short-term and long-term career goals?
My short-term goals are to come up with a strategy for the business department and determine which programs need to be upgraded. I'm looking at how to position ourselves to provide what our students will need when they come in here. On the personal level, we started the Johnson Family Scholarship and the first one was awarded in May 2008. When we started saving for this, my father nearly cried because education is very important to him – not just for his children, but also for everyone. He never got to finish high school. I purchased the 10 acres that my parents owned, so my long-term goal is to always maintain their home and farm. Eventually, I'm hoping to work with one of the conservation groups to place the land into a trust for a wildlife habitat.

What would you like to promote most about yourself or your business?
Shawnee State is a small university, but that means you will never be lost in the crowd. Students are on first name basis with their instructors. Our business faculty not only have the formal education, but all have some business experience outside education. They present not just what the textbooks say, but what real life experiences have taught.

What is your greatest professional accomplishment to date?
Creating the classes and curriculum for the Web design portion of our information systems management degree here at Shawnee State University. Prior to that, we had only been doing programming languages. But then the Web started to become a very important aspect, so I designed the classes so that students would be prepared to go from here and get jobs as webmasters.

How do you remain current in your profession?
I read magazines and books, I am a member of various groups and I get e-mails. I go to some conferences in my own region and we discuss the new changes. I watch the news online.

What is the most significant issue facing your profession today?
With education and technology, it is a question of "How do we get the kids to want to learn?" There's so much going on with technology, which changes

fast. They're going to have to find solutions to handling a truly global economy. When we hit the wall, the whole world hits the wall. There's so much that they have to learn and so much for which we have to prepare them.

Academic Administration

Cindy K. Knott

Dean
Grand Canyon University
College of Education
3300 W. Camelback Road
Phoenix, AZ 85017 USA
cknott@gcu.edu

Dr. Cindy K. Knott is currently the dean of the College of Education at Grand Canyon University, where she is dedicated to inspiring excellence in people to learn, lead and serve for a brighter future. A true leader, she provides oversight and direction for faculty, staff and students across the College of Education and Grand Canyon University to include training, support and mentorship assuring the highest academic integrity and ethical standards. Dr. Knott engages a diverse and global community of learners in the pursuit of finding their purpose.

Dr. Knott has been in the education field for more than 25 years. She has been a classroom teacher and assistant director in the public and private school systems, primarily in the area of special education. She has also served as an administrator, principal, full-time faculty member, and subsequently, dean. Prior to joining GCU, Dr. Knott held the position of director of academic affairs/regional assistant dean for the College of Education at University of Phoenix. She has received numerous awards for her exemplary performance as an educator.

Dr. Knott earned a Bachelor of Arts in Elementary Education and Special Education and a Master of Education from Arizona State University. She holds an administrative certificate from the University of Phoenix, and earned an Ed.D. in educational leadership from Nova Southeastern University, where her dissertation was titled "Inclusion Relationships: Collaboration in the Individualized Education Plan (IEP) Process."

In addition to Dr. Knott's lifelong education interests, she is an active community member and has traveled abroad. She participates and presents at many local, state and national conferences and organizations. Her professional goals include, but are not limited to, promoting servant leadership and lifelong learning in educational communities.

CONVERSATION WITH CINDY K. KNOTT

CAMBRIDGE WHO'S WHO: What would you like to promote most about yourself or your business?
CINDY K. KNOTT: I would like to promote Grand Canyon University's vision in preparing learners to become global citizens, critical thinkers, effective communicators and responsible leaders by providing an academically challenging, values-based curriculum from the context of our Christian heritage.

What is the most rewarding aspect of your career?
The most rewarding aspect of my career has been serving and developing the faculty, staff, and students in the College of Education.

What is your greatest professional accomplishment to date?
My greatest professional accomplishment to date was the development of the company's first teacher education online licensing program; also, the establishing of a placement office in an effort to address the shortage of quality teachers across the nation.

What are your short-term and long-term career goals?
My short-term goal is to collaborate with the university to build a local educational community. A long-term goal that I have set for myself is to publish a book supporting women in leadership roles.

And what specific steps have you taken toward achieving these goals?
With regard to my short-term goal, the community project is in the initial stages of development. My long-term goal is an integral part of my personal development. I have made it a priority to become a more visible leader by presenting at various conferences and publishing more articles.

What is the most difficult obstacle or challenge you have faced in pursuit of your goals?
A current challenge facing the field of education is remaining current and managing ongoing change regarding policy and procedure implementation.

On what topics do you consider yourself to be an expert?
As dean of the College of Education, I feel that online teacher preparation, domestic and international field experience, special education and higher education administration are my areas of expertise.

How do you stay current in your profession?
As a lifelong learner, it is important to participate in ongoing professional development, read professional journals and publications, and network with local and national education and leadership organizations.

What makes you a valuable resource in your industry?
As an educational leader, my wide range of teaching and leadership experience has proved to be a valuable resource in the industry.

What is the most significant issue facing your profession today?
A significant issue currently facing the field of education is recruiting, preparing and retaining highly qualified and effective teachers who are innovative and reflective in their profession.

What advice can you offer fellow members who work in your industry?
I would encourage fellow members who work in the industry to collaborate with each other, stay current with policy implementations, and engage themselves in the educational community.

What advice can you offer people aspiring to work in this profession?
As an experienced professional in the industry, my advice to aspiring educators would be to continue professional development and build relationships with the ultimate goal of maximizing student achievement.

What are you passionate about?
I am most passionate about upholding the integrity and academic rigor in teacher preparation programs with the focus of developing highly qualified and effective teachers throughout the competitive teaching field.

Who have been your mentors or people who have greatly influenced you?
Throughout my professional career, I have viewed all situations as a learning opportunity. However, my family and past and present executive leadership have provided support and encouraged me to continue on my professional path and finding my purpose.

Do you have a motto?
Inspiring excellence by learning, leading and serving for a brighter future.

Early Childhood Education

Joseph Noland, Ed.D.
Teacher
Northwest Elementary School
Coweta Public Schools
P.O. Box 830
Wagoner, OK 74477 USA
josephnoland@live.com
http://www.drjosephnoland.com

Few educators have the gusto, understanding or zest for the profession as does Dr. Joseph Noland, an early childhood education teacher at Northwest Elementary School, part of Coweta Public Schools. He teaches all core subjects and specializes in reading instruction; he also utilizes (and custom creates) educational tools using SMART Boards and computers to motivate students to learn. While many people would not have the patience to deal with kids, Dr. Noland is the exact opposite; he makes sure the youngsters are interested and involved. "They've got to love your class," he states, "and every single day, when they come out, they've got to be cheerful and happy, and tell their parents the wonderful things that they did."

While this may sound like an amazing feat, considering how difficult children can be, Dr. Noland's caring nature has helped him to win over many students — and steer them in the right direction toward lifelong success. Since he was 16 years old, Dr. Noland has worked with youth, beginning at summer camp. That year, he had written a letter to Lance B. Latham, the founder of the Awana Youth Association, asking if he could take out the trash for them. Mr. Latham wrote back and asked him to be a leader, which meant being in charge of 10 children, ages 8 to 10, in a cabin. "I was amazed," he remembers, of the first time he started working with kids. Dr. Noland didn't see it coming; he didn't know he could, but Doc Latham's vote of confidence made him the exemplary leader he is today.

Dr. Noland received a Doctor of Education in Curriculum and Instruction with concentrations in reading and special education, magna cum laude, in 1996; and a master's degree in reading in 1993 from Oklahoma State University. He is a member of the Council for Learning Disabilities, the Association for Supervision and Curriculum Development, the Council for Exceptional Children, the Council for Elementary Science International, the American Educational Research Association, the American Association on Intellectual and Developmental Disability, the National Council of Teachers of Mathematics, the National

Association for the Education of Young Children, the National Council for the Social Studies, the National Council of Teachers of English, the International Society for Technology in Education, the International Reading Association, the Association for Childhood Education International, and Phi Kappa Phi.

When he is not making the schools and communities of Oklahoma a better place, in his spare time Dr. Noland enjoys caring for his pets, camping and hiking. He volunteers for the American Red Cross, Boys & Girls Clubs of America, YMCA Youth Sports, and the Awana Youth Association.

CONVERSATION WITH JOSEPH NOLAND, ED.D.

CAMBRIDGE WHO'S WHO: What would you like to promote most about yourself or your business?

JOSEPH NOLAND: I've been teaching for 26 years and this is the first year I'll be teaching kindergarten. Kindergarten is a big deal now, and both the public and educators have a lot of interest in it. Nowadays, kindergarten is more like first grade. My school wanted me to take the position because of my knowledge of first grade. All of my relatives are delighted because they know I can do it. Some men don't know how to teach little kids. You have to have a lot of action, a lot of interest, and you have to be really animated with the kids. You have to teach like that the whole time, which I enjoy. You have to want to do it that way.

What is the most rewarding aspect of your career?

It's enjoying the children and seeing the difference you can make in a child's life. The teacher makes the difference; we are in the driver's seat.

What are your short-term and long-term career goals?

My short-term goal is to design an excellent-quality kindergarten program that prepares the students better, so that they will do well in first grade. I would also like to do a program geared toward 4-year-olds. I want to create a TV or internet program that would be similar to what Fred Rogers did with "Mister Rogers' Neighborhood." I would do it at the kindergarten level with 30-minute shows, using real kids and a live audience; I would have the kids participate in the program.

And what specific steps have you taken toward achieving these goals?

I've spent a lot of time researching kindergarten, especially the new trends, techniques and excellence that's required of first grade. I visit the other states, and look at other websites and teachers. I like to study the top schools in the nation and see what they are doing. I go to the top school district in Oklahoma and observe what the teachers are doing there. I look at the experts, the ones who are doing the training, writing the books, and/or been doing this for 35 years, and see what they're doing.

What is the most difficult obstacle or challenge you have faced in pursuit of your goals?
The most difficult challenge was going back to the university and getting a master's degree in reading and a Doctor of Education while I was already teaching. I had to keep my teaching job, but I wanted to get those degrees, so I took night classes. I would sometimes have classes until 9 p.m.

On what topic(s) do you consider yourself to be an expert?
I'm an expert in reading because my doctorate is a double major in reading and special education. Due to my experience as a reading specialist, I am an expert in helping children who are having reading difficulties. I have three certificates: elementary education, early childhood education, and reading specialist – all from the state of Oklahoma.

What makes you a valuable resource in your industry?
The main thing is that I understand the children. I believe you can't just teach material out of a workbook; you have to teach to the children. It's very obvious, but people miss that. You really can't teach "curriculum," you have to teach the children.

What is the most significant issue facing your profession today?
It's definitely readiness and preparing kindergarten students for the first grade. First grade is harder now and they have to be ready for the more challenging material. Some children are not quite ready for first grade, and you have to ease them in slowly.

What advice can you offer fellow members who work in your industry?
They have to enjoy the children and the parents. You have to smile, laugh and take pleasure in what they're doing. You can't be too hard; you have to lighten up and promote the kids.

What advice can you offer people aspiring to work in this profession?
They have to really study and understand what the new demands are on teachers. Teachers have to do everything right and be professional. They need to build up their professional skills, attitude and way of life.

What are you passionate about?
If I want the children to enjoy school, I need them to understand that learning is fun, going to school can be enjoyable, and it is a great way to become what they want to in life. School is a doorway to success, but I want them to enjoy it.

Who have been your mentors or people who have greatly influenced you?
Doc Lance B. Latham, founder of the Awana Youth Association, believed in me enough to make me a cabin leader of 10 boys at Camp Awana when I was only 16 years old.

Do you have a motto?
"Enjoy the children." That's what I tell the new teachers and substitutes. If you don't like the kids, then do something else.

SCHOOL ADMINISTRATION

KEITH M. PFEIFER, ED.D.
Superintendent
Grantham School District
P.O. Box 287, Suite 75
Grantham, NH 03753 USA
kpfeifer@sau75.org
http://www.sau17.org

One Classical Greek philosopher has been quoted as saying, "I cannot teach anybody anything; I can only make them think." Considered by many to be one of the greatest thinkers of the Western world, Socrates knew that in order to influence the intellectual capacities of others, he would need to change not what they knew, but how they came about knowing it. Keith M. Pfeifer believes wholeheartedly in a similar principle as superintendent of the Grantham School District. The district, which serves approximately 750 students, consists of elementary, middle and high schools accredited by the New England Association of Schools and Colleges according to peer-reviewed best practices dedicated to continuous improvement.

Mr. Pfeifer has been an educator for nearly 40 years, impressing upon the supple minds of students the importance of self-sufficiency guided by qualified, diligent teachers. He has always felt that in order to truly impact the future of a generation, it is necessary to first train its students to become independent thinkers and leaders who will use public education as a conduit for expression, cooperation and positive expansion. As a board member of New Hampshire Partners in Education, NEASC's Commission on Public Secondary Schools, and the Home Education Advisory Council of the New Hampshire Department of Education, he is instrumental in making decisions that affect policies and programs across his district and the state. Additionally, his memberships in the American Association of School Administrators and the Association for Supervision and Curriculum Development have been beneficial in forging relationships with other professionals of his rank who share similar goals and visions.

A self-proclaimed continuous adult learner, Mr. Pfeifer earned a doctorate in educational administration and organization from The Pennsylvania State University, a master's degree in special education from the University of Northern Colorado, and a Bachelor of Arts in Political Science and History from Hiram College. He frequently attends conferences hosted by his professional associations to exchange ideas on new developments within the public school system, and avers that "education will continue to make this nation great."

CONVERSATION WITH KEITH M. PFEIFER, ED.D.

CAMBRIDGE WHO'S WHO: How did you become involved in education?
KEITH M. PFEIFER: A long time ago, I served in Vietnam, where I lost friends and peers. Since they were not able to go on with life and share their skills and abilities, I thought the best way to share their legacy was to become an educator. I carry that with me every day.

What are your short-term and long-term career goals?
To continue to educate and guide each successive generation of students in my charge in order to prepare them for the complex and global world they will enter; to support my staff in providing the best quality education that we can offer; to continue my own professional development so that I keep abreast of the changes in education; to support and assist my school board in making decisions that will positively affect the children of this community; to support professional associations of school leaders in continuing the quality of education provided in this state and nation; and to provide service to the New England Association of Schools and Colleges, New Hampshire Partners in Education and New Hampshire Destination ImagiNation.

What specific steps have you taken toward achieving these goals?
I work daily to ensure that we, in the Grantham School District, are providing students with a solid foundation for the development of critical thinking and problem-solving skills. I support my school board to make decisions that will positively affect the school district and the education of students. I also serve on several New Hampshire Department of Education committees relative to the quality and delivery of education in New Hampshire.

On what topics do you consider yourself to be an expert?
On a daily basis, I work on curriculum, instruction, student assessment and writing, school finances, and operating schools as organizations.

How do you remain current in your profession?
I attend state, regional and national conferences related to education, read articles and research in my field constantly, speak with members of my profession whom I consider mentors, and listen to the views of other educators.

What makes you a valuable resource in your industry?

I have the experience and knowledge gained by my 37 years in public education. I have served in central office administration for 22 years and have had the benefit of working with multiple superintendents. Over the years, I have developed a willingness to learn and listen, and to share what I have learned.

What is the most significant issue facing your profession today?

This generation of children will enter an increasingly complex world; we must ensure they have the knowledge and skills to compete in it. Correspondingly, the needs of the students are more complex, as we have a more heterogeneous and multinational student population. We are in a trying economic time and thus faced with the challenge of trying to do more with less, in the form of decreasing local, state and federal fiscal resources.

What advice can you offer fellow professionals in your industry?

Listen before you speak. Share what you know and be open to learning what you don't. Have a vision and always keep the education of the students in mind.

What advice can you offer people aspiring to get into the profession?

Warehouse each experience you have and remember that public education is for all students. Singularly, public education is the most important thing in the world. We hold the competitiveness of this country in our hands daily. We can teach our students not only to know more and develop their skills to the best of their abilities, but we also need to teach them to solve problems and conduct complex higher-order thinking activities.

What are you passionate about?

Teachers and staff who are on the front line — we are the difference makers.

Who have been your mentors or people who have greatly influenced you?

The many teachers and staff with whom I have worked who took the time to share their profession and guide a young educator; the graduate school educators who were patient with me and helped fuel my curiosity; my family, who were patient while I was educating other people's children or away from home at all hours of the day; and Colonel Chamberlin, Maine Civil War soldier and leader, later of Bowdoin College as a professor of humanities and president of the college, who said, "When you are short on resources, CHARGE!"

Elementary-Level Mathematics

Vicki Keene Tackett
Mathematics Teacher (Retired)
Pikeville Elementary School
105 Bailey Boulevard
Pikeville, KY 41501 USA
applewood2@bellsouth.net

Vicki Keene Tackett is a former fifth-grade mathematics teacher at Pikeville Elementary School. On May 29, 2009, she retired from a 29-year career in education. The most gratifying aspect of her career was working closely with children and helping them to understand mathematics and science, so that they may advance to the next level in their academic careers. She has been acknowledged by her former students as a caring and compassionate teacher who providing them with a balanced education.

As the proud owner of a horse stable named Applewood Paso Fino Farm (along with 18 horses), Ms. Tackett enjoys riding on the trails around her home. When she started the farm several years ago, she had to purchase horses from other people, but that has since changed. She has done enough breeding so that every single horse she owns, which compete in the show rings, is hers – born and bred in eastern Kentucky. Ms. Tackett has someone on hand to help show the horses to prospective owners, who in turn enter them into national competitions.

Describing the horses she owns, known as Paso Fino Horses, Ms. Tackett says they are slightly smaller than normal horses, but not by much; also, they have a very quick gait. "Christopher Columbus brought the Paso Fino horse to America on his second voyage," she states. "They're nickname is the 'newest oldest breed,' although in English, Paso Fino means 'fine step.'" Considered a popular animal for trail riding, the Paso Fino comes in any color, just like a regular horse.

Ms. Tackett received a fifth-year degree in elementary education from Morehead State University and a bachelor's degree in elementary education from Pikeville College. She is a three-time nominee recommended by her students for recognition by Who's Who Among American Teachers. She is a member of the Paso Fino Horse Association, the Kentucky Education Association, the National Education Association and the National Council of Teachers of Mathematics.

Ms. Tackett enjoys spending quality time with her granddaughter.

Conversation with Vicki Keene Tackett

Cambridge Who's Who: What is the most rewarding aspect of your career?
Vicki Keene Tackett: The most rewarding aspect of my career is being remembered by students. I had a student say that I was their favorite teacher of all time.

What is your greatest professional accomplishment to date?
We are a very small farm on the very tip of eastern Kentucky and we have several national champion horses.

What are your short-term and long-term career goals?
The next step is to continue what we are doing and building the name of the farm, Applewood Paso Fino Farm, so that it is bigger and more reputable.

And what specific steps have you taken toward achieving these goals?
It takes dedication. It's just like with teaching – you don't get into it for the money; you get into it for the love. You have to stay dedicated and stick with it because in either scenario, teaching or with the horses, it doesn't come overnight.

What is the most difficult obstacle or challenge you have faced in pursuit of your goals?
The most difficult challenge has been gaining recognition. When you first start teaching, parents tend to ride you harder as if you don't know what you're doing. As you continue through your years (and you deliver consistent quality), they see that you do know what you're doing, and turn from watching you with an evil eye to respecting you.

As for horse breeding, when we started out, nobody knew who we were. We grew little by little and became members of the Kentucky Paso Fino Horse Association, which helped people become more familiar with us. Nowadays, we hear things from the crowds, who know us by sight. People talk to me and they call me by my first name.

On what topics do you consider yourself to be an expert?
With regards to education, I consider myself an expert on reaching out to and engaging children.

How do you remain current in your profession?
I still read the National Education Association newsletter and the retired teachers send me a bulletin each month. I have a couple of teachers at school

who have approached me about students who are weak in certain subject areas. They asked me if I would come back and work specifically them. I have agreed to do this, although not yet.

What makes you a valuable resource in your industry?
It has to do with how I care about the child, put them first and know that what I say to them or the way I treat them may be the best that they get all day long.

What is the most significant issue facing your profession today?
I think that American education is falling, rather than rising. I think they are trying to find one thing that is going to work for everyone. What I was taught when I went through my training is that there is not one thing for every single child out there. If they don't learn by lecture, you don't do lecture only. A teacher's approach to teaching the child is just as important as the quality of the subject material.

What advice can you offer fellow members who work in your industry?
Regardless of what is new out there, stick to the basics: reading, writing and arithmetic. If they don't get those, they're going to be lost.

What advice can you offer people aspiring to work in this profession?
Don't come into it for the money. You have to love kids.

What are you passionate about?
I'm passionate about becoming a bigger and better name in the horse industry. With regards to children, I would love to see education in the United States improve.

Who have been your mentors or people who have greatly influenced you?
Chester Bailey, who was a principal at Pikeville Elementary when I was in college; I had to go into the school and work under certain teachers. He had such love for those kids and the school at that time had about 600-700 of them. He would call every single student he met by their first name. I don't know how, but he did. I wrote a tribute for Mr. Bailey that got him an award.

Is there a motto or saying that reflects your professional philosophy?
There are a thousand and one ways to do it.

Counseling and Academic Administration

James J. Ungvarsky, Psy.D., MPA
Ranked Faculty
Regis University
College for Professional Studies
7450 Campus Drive, Suite 100, P-4
Colorado Springs, CO 80920 USA
jungvars@regis.edu
http://www.regis.edu
http://coloradomft.com

James J. Ungvarsky is a professor at Regis University in the College for Professional Studies, School of Education and Counseling. He instructs graduate students in counseling, and marriage and family therapy. Dr. Ungvarsky was instrumental in developing a post-master's certificate program in counseling military families. Previously, Dr. Ungvarsky was on the core faculty at the University of the Rockies, where he served as department chair of professional psychology, the director of communications, senior vice president/chief operating officer, and was selected as interim president. He is considered a leading lecturer in the areas of statistics and research design, psychology practice, marriage and family therapy, counseling military families, and organizational leadership and development. Dr. Ungvarsky formerly hosted an hour-long talk radio show on a local station where he would speak on topics concerning emerging trends in the field of psychology and on psychological factors of leadership. His prior experience as a certified financial planner and tax instructor has established his reputation as a solid administrator.

Dr. Ungvarsky attributes his success to his abilities to listen to the perspectives of his colleagues, accept others and their worldviews, and share his ideas with people in a respectful manner. His regular stints as a public speaker afford him the opportunity to reach people in his hometown as well as faraway locales. In March 2009, he provided students and faculty with insights about Western research history and methods during a two-week lecture series in China and Singapore. In October 2009, at the Third Annual Society for Humanistic Psychotherapy Conference, he presented a seminar titled "The Day I Made a Holy Man Swear: The Psychology of Self-Deception." And in January 2010, he presented a seminar titled "Self-Deception in Therapy" at the 36th Annual Advanced International Winter Symposium, where professionals in the addictions, mental health, and behavioral health fields convene to share ideas. Dr. Ungvarsky was invited to return to Hong Kong and

China in the spring of 2010, where he presented a lecture series on humanistic approaches to marriage and family therapy, existential approaches to substance abuse treatment, and emotional intelligence and self-deception in therapy. At The First International Conference on Existential Psychology in Nanjing, China, he again presented on self-deception in therapy in addition to supervision in integrative existential psychotherapy. In 2011, Dr. Ungvarsky will present at several conferences on counseling military families.

Dr. Ungvarsky received a Doctor of Psychology from the Colorado School of Professional Psychology (now University of the Rockies), a master's degree in public administration from San José State University, a Master of Psychology from Chapman University and a bachelor's degree in psychology from Cleveland State University. He is a member of the American Psychology Association, the American Counseling Association, the American Association for Marriage and Family Therapy, the National Latina/Latino Psychological Association, and the Psychological Society of the Pikes Peak Region. He is currently on the board of trustees for Leadership Pike Peak. He is a former president of the board of directors of Mental Health America (Pikes Peak Region) and a former member of the Crime Stoppers board of directors.

In his spare time, Dr. Ungvarsky enjoys practicing martial arts as a black belt in Kempo Karate and performing magic shows for children and adults alike.

CONVERSATION WITH JAMES J. UNGVARSKY, PSY.D., MPA

CAMBRIDGE WHO'S WHO: What would you like to promote most about yourself or your business?
JAMES J. UNGVARSKY: The fields of psychotherapy, counseling and higher education are constantly changing. Keeping up with the changes is challenging, so I consider myself to be a lifelong learner. To that end, I have started a new website that, in part, encourages others to become educated in those areas.

What is the most rewarding aspect of your career?
The most rewarding aspect of my career is seeing the students that I work with become well-respected professionals in the field.

On what topics do you consider yourself to be an expert?
Others may consider me to be an expert on statistics and research, self-deception in therapy, cultural issues in family therapy, and the psychological factors of leadership. However, I find myself often inspired by the works and thoughts of others.

What is your greatest professional accomplishment to date?
My greatest professional accomplishment involves the presentations that I have given in Singapore and China; also, being selected to be the interim president of the University of the Rockies.

How do you remain current in your profession?
I read publications and I am involved in presenting and setting up conferences. Right now, I am in the process of writing a couple of books. One is a graduate-level statistics textbook and the other is a book on deception.

What are your short-term and long-term career goals?
My short-term goals are to finish writing my books, expand my speaking engagements and explore the possibilities of instructing at other institutions. My long-term goal is to continue doing this well into my 80s.

What is the most significant issue facing your profession today?
Since my specialization is in the field of psychology, a significant issue is

getting enough qualified graduates from schools (in general) to meet the psychological health needs of the citizens of the United States. In the field of academia, it's getting people to endorse a lifestyle of lifelong learning.

What is the most difficult obstacle or challenge you have faced in pursuit of your goals?
The most difficult obstacle is defining what my goals are because oftentimes, there are so many things that I would like to do, but I don't have the time to do it all. It is basically [about] prioritizing those goals. Another obstacle has been maintaining a balance between my professional life and my family life.

What advice can you offer fellow members who work in your industry?
Stay fresh in your field, which means going out and being a life-long learner yourself. You need to keep growing and learning new things that aren't necessarily in your field of expertise. Also, challenge yourself to argue a stance on a topic that is opposite what you believe. Doing so will give you a fresh perspective and sharpen your critical thinking skills.

What are you passionate about?
What I am most passionate about is working within local communities to make sure that the people who don't have a voice for themselves receive the services and the things that they need in order to have a healthier or more fulfilling life.

Do you have a motto or favorite quote?
"Remember, a dead fish can float downstream, but it takes a live one to swim upstream." — W. C. Fields

Leadership in Higher Education

Maryann K. Vaca, Ed.D.
Doctoral Enrollment Counselor
Nova Southeastern University
1750 N.E. 167th Street
North Miami Beach, FL 33162 USA
drmvaca@bellsouth.net
http://www.fischlerschool.nova.edu/home.htm

Educators and health care workers are known to be some of the most selfless and inspirational professionals, both working to improve individual lives and the greater good of society. Dr. Maryann K. Vaca has worked in both industries, in entry-level and managerial positions that gave her valuable insight as to how she could most effectively utilize her leadership skills and knowledge of the nursing profession. With previous roles overseeing ten health care programs as associate dean of health professions in a community college, staff nurse, and hospital vice president of patient care services to her credit, she joined the Fischler School of Education and Human Services at Nova Southeastern University. Currently, Dr. Vaca is a doctoral enrollment counselor advising doctor of education (Ed.D.) students.

In the past, she implemented nursing courses for students at Elgin Community College as the associate dean of health professions, which prepared her for her critical role as the associate dean of Nova's doctoral program for one year. She also formed affiliations with local health care institutions to provide clinical learning experiences for students in the health professions. As a nursing instructor and associate director/director of hospital-based nursing diploma programs, Dr. Vaca drew from her experiences in direct patient care to enact policy changes that not only affected the educational system, but improved the overall quality of treatment delivered. Her ability to motivate others while providing support and helpful mentoring opportunities has distinguished her as invaluable to the nursing community and any educational institutions with which she is affiliated.

In 1967, Dr. Vaca received a Bachelor of Science in Nursing before earning a Master of Education, a Master of Arts in Nursing, and a Doctor of Education in Higher Education Leadership. She formerly served on the board of directors for the Visiting Nurse Associations of Fox Valley from 1995 to 2003, and is a former member of Sigma Theta Tau International, The Chair Academy, and Aurora University's nursing advisory committee. Currently, she hopes to continue her work at the university before retiring and enjoying more time with her loved ones.

Conversation with Maryann K. Vaca, Ed.D.

Cambridge Who's Who: What would you like to promote most about yourself or your business?
Maryann K. Vaca: What has been my greatest motivation throughout my career, because I have always worked with students, was being a student advocate and attempting to do things that would promote good. My focus was always on appropriate service to clientele. That is what has driven me, being an advocate and working to obtain the best that I could for the programs and students with whom I was affiliated.

What is the most rewarding aspect of your career?
I have been known as a definite change agent. One of my old bosses said to me, "I don't know how you do it, but you really are able to get people to change." Ultimately in getting people to change, I was always able to meet the goal I was attempting to achieve. If it meant going to the governing boards and advocating for a program change, I was always focused on what was going to be the best for the students and the institution as a whole.

On what topics do you consider yourself to be an expert?
I am an advocator, a motivator, and a facilitator. Those are what I have always felt were my strengths.

What is your greatest professional accomplishment to date?
I was asked to change the diploma program from a three-year program to a two-year program and to develop an affiliation with the local community college, so that our students at the hospital-based school of nursing would concurrently receive a diploma in nursing from our hospital and an associate degree from Cuyahoga Community College. I had to deal with the nursing faculty at our institution, who were adamantly opposed to changing the program from three to two years. I had to work with the community college to accept the fact that they would award an associate degree to our hospital-based diploma program students. I also had to go before the Ohio Board of Regents. Some of my peers said that several directors had tried and they didn't think I would be able to achieve it.

I believe in timing and at that time, enrollment at the community college was down. Showing them that our students' enrollment in general education and science courses meant financial gain for the college played a major role in the college administration's acceptance. It was a win-win situation. That was almost 30 years ago and the program is still in existence the way it was originally proposed, and is one of the few hospital-based programs still operating in the United States.

How do you remain current in your profession?

I read the Chronicle of Higher Education and other professional publications related to higher education, health care education, and student advising. I also participate in continuing education offerings for university employees.

What are your short-term and long-term career goals?

I would like to stay five more years [at the university], or as long as they are willing to have me. I don't want to change positions — I love what I do. Believe me, it's a challenge; every time I answer the phone or open an e-mail, I don't know what's contained in there. It's a challenge to be able to "bring students down from the rafters." I think that my background in health care has helped me because of my caring attitude and knowledge of how to deal with difficult patients or situations — I transferred it over to the education field. It's what I enjoy, so I'm not planning to look for another position.

What is the most significant issue facing your profession today?

I think the major issue is recruitment and once we get the students in, it's focusing on retention. You have to continually work toward having satisfied, successful students and that is not easy to do. Maintaining a quality educational program in today's economic times and dealing with the changing needs of the students who are enrolling in your programs is a major challenge facing us today.

What is the most difficult obstacle or challenge you have faced in pursuit of your goals?

The major obstacle has been dealing with people who are resistant to change. They will go out of their way to put up road blocks — that's where the challenge is. Then comes your personal satisfaction when you're able to overcome those obstacles.

What advice can you offer fellow members who work in your industry?

The greatest challenge for people is not to let little obstacles get in their way and always keep their final goal in mind. Ask yourself, "Why am I doing this?" and don't let people dissuade you from moving forward and attempting to make changes that will keep your clientele satisfied. Don't be afraid of opposition and negative situations; work around them. You have to get your soldiers, the people who are in your favor. Work with them first and eventually the majority of people are going to come around.

What are you passionate about?

I am most passionate about my family and foremost my husband, who has always been a tremendous support. I'm passionate about my professional career and I think having the support of my spouse has been one of the most important things. When you have a professional career and a family, you really have to determine how you are going to spend your time. You have to look at how you are best going to be able to meet the needs of your family and your career.

Do you have a motto?
"One day at a time," and "Carpe diem," — Latin for "Seize the day."

MUSIC EDUCATION FOR YOUTH AND ADULTS

JANE L. WILSON
President
Keyme Music
1280 Sebastian Lakes Drive
Sebastian, FL 32958 USA
janmusic@comcast.net

Jane L. Wilson, president of Keyme Music, is an advocate for the equal empowerment of youth and adult communities through musical education and performance. Her company has made waves in her community, as she helps one student at a time achieve advancement in their musical abilities. One such student, Thomas Ingui, is a 14-year-old child prodigy who plays the organ. Through Thomas, Ms. Wilson has been able to receive a tremendous amount of positive feedback, validating her efforts and enabling her to encourage more students than ever before. A highlight of her career was being featured in a six-page layout of Vero Beach Magazine, along with one of her students.

In addition to her ownership of Keyme Music, Ms. Wilson also functions as a substitute teacher in Indiana River County and plays the organ in her church. She attributes her success to her perseverance and love for her profession, which was instilled in her by her father. Music flows strongly in her veins, as she was a dulcimer player and singer from 1992 to 2002 for the Alpha Delta Kappa International Honorary Sorority Convention for Educators in Miami, Fla., San Francisco, Calif., and Toronto, Canada. She was the alma mater composer in 1987 for Jose Marti Middle School in Hialeah, Fla., and the composer of the "Excellence In the Eighties School Song" in 1985 for Monroe County, Fla. Ever the explorer of new musical techniques, she aspires to someday complete studio work in Pompei, Italy.

Ms. Wilson received certification in art in 1986 from Florida International University. She earned a master's degree in music education with a concentration in conducting choral and instrumental music in 1979 from West Virginia University, and a Bachelor of Arts in Music Education with a concentration in piano and minor in voice in 1972 from West Liberty State College. She is a licensed Realtor in the state of Florida and a registered music teacher.

Conversation with Jane L. Wilson

Cambridge Who's Who: What would you like to promote about your business?
Jane L. Wilson: I have perseverance and I absolutely love what I'm doing. It started as a career change and it's flourishing. I teach music and give rewards to the students for practicing. They don't usually like to practice, but I give them sheets to fill out with the minutes they practice. At the end of the day, for every 200 minutes they have practiced, they get to pick a prize from the Dollar Store. I am a little selfish here, because I do it all for my own enlightenment and enrichment.

How do you remain current in your profession?
I belong to a professional singers group, which keeps my knowledge current. I'm also a church organist. I strive to keep up with my competitors and continue to learn and enrich my life with music – this translates to delivering quality instruction to my students.

What lessons have you learned as a professional in your field?
One thing in particular is if they have animals and I go to their home, I acknowledge the animals when I go in. Then, they'll go off and lie down – otherwise, they want to be acknowledged and will absolutely interfere with the lesson. This has to do with an authentic love for the animals; they are a part of the family, after all. I get a great welcoming when I tend to the children and animals.

What are some questions that an individual interested in your services can ask to ensure a more productive relationship?
They would probably want to know a little about my background, as in my education and teaching experience, but usually I don't get a whole lot of questioning. One thing I explain to them is that they learn a lot faster at 8 years old than they would at 6 – unless they are especially gifted.

What is your least favorite work-related task and why?
My least favorite thing is collecting the monies. I don't have a problem with it, but then I have to go to the bank and sign all the checks, it keeps me away from teaching.

Who have been your mentors or people who have greatly influenced you?
I've had a couple of counselors who have really helped me a lot with some problems that I had, in terms of getting my life on track. One counselor in particular helped me after I broke off a relationship. When I went to him, I told him I was up for Teacher of the Year. He told me, "Every teacher I have counseled has gone on to become Teacher of the Year." And by golly, I did!

That was the most rewarding thing I had in my career, knowing that I was doing my job to the best that I could and was appreciated. It wasn't for me – it comes down to my students. You don't do it on your own. It's the people whom you teach who achieve these things for you. For instance, I've received more acknowledgements for the protégé's playing than for most of the classes I've given.

Technical Drilling Operations

Ron J. Dirksen

Global Reservoir Solutions Manager
Halliburton
3000 N. Sam Houston Parkway E.
Houston, TX 77032 USA
ron.dirksen@halliburton.com

After obtaining a Bachelor of Science in Mining Engineering in the Netherlands, Ron J. Dirksen was in a unique position to pursue a career in energy straight out of college. He started working in the oil and gas exploration sector and gradually moved into new product and service development. He later branched into alternative energy resource research. As the global reservoir solutions manager for Halliburton's Sperry Drilling Services Division, Mr. Dirksen drives vital research and development efforts to not only address current issues in directional drilling and well construction; but also the rising global concern for the availability of future energy resources.

With extensive knowledge in reservoir discovery, evaluation, exploitation and maintenance, nonconventional hydrocarbon energy resource development and alternative energy research, Mr. Dirksen has become an authority in the oil and gas industry. His international travel experience has empowered him to become a leader in human resources and workflow for reservoir solutions and drilling optimization. While he presides over these important details, Mr. Dirksen is in a constant pursuit for the latest technical applications and improvements. This search for improved technology raises numerous challenges, in that he must determine the relevance of emerging applications; he must then convey the technical specifications to Halliburton's research and development and technology development departments.

Acknowledging a problem exists is half the battle, and in his 29 years of relevant experience, Mr. Dirksen has learned the importance of conducting extensive intelligence gathering. Through his efforts to improve his company's data and information collecting, his department is able to not only address new developments, but anticipate what might happen 10 to 20 years down the line. While the undertaking may sound daunting, in the near future, Mr. Dirksen hopes to head the company's technical division. With his successful track record, he may just be the best man for the job.

Mr. Dirksen is a member of the Society of Petroleum Engineers and the Society of Petrophysicists and Well Log Analysts. A revered authority in the field, Mr. Dirksen publishes papers and reports regularly; he is also a public speaker on his expertise.

In his spare time, Mr. Dirksen enjoys soccer, rugby and traveling.

Conversation with Ron J. Dirksen

Cambridge Who's Who: What would you like to promote most about yourself or your business?
Ron J. Dirksen: I have expertise in the planning, education and drilling of wells in the oil and gas industry. This includes all the aspects related to directional drilling, directional drilling parts, survey management, and geophysical and petrophysical interpretation.

What is your greatest professional accomplishment to date?
I managed a company's Asia-specific region for five years and grew the business from approximately a $10 million to a $200 million per year business.

What were some of the most difficult obstacles or challenges you have faced in pursuit of your goals?
Primarily, the most difficult obstacle I have faced in pursuit of my goals has to do with the disconnects between the planning cycle and the execution cycle, in terms of communicating the many technological improvements in a timely fashion so they are available at the time they are needed.

Could you explain how you were able to overcome that?
We have improved the process by which we gather intelligence on upcoming projects, including the challenges and proposed outcomes associated with them.

How did you become involved in your profession?
I graduated from college and started working in the field right away. I grew myself and the industry grew with me.

What are your short-term and long-term career goals?
Short term is to continue leading the development of some critical technologies and processes in the industry, also the implementation thereof. The longer-term goal is to provide guidance to the industry as a whole and pave the way for the upcoming, much more challenging prospects.

What is the most significant issue facing your profession today that will affect your industry in the future?
Maintaining a good balance between the supply and demand of hydrocarbon energy. We need a reliable forecast of what the demand will be and what suitable technologies we need to exploit, the resources of which we will be tapping to keep up with the growth and continued demand of hydrocarbon energy globally.

What specific steps have you taken toward achieving these goals?
We are heavily involved in intelligence gathering through our involvement with joint industry committees. We are working on projects to assess, first of all, from where we are going to collect hydrocarbon resources. From there, we are determining what we're going to need in the near future, in order to address technical challenges.

On what topic(s) do you consider yourself to be an expert?
Drilling, drilling fluids, petrochemical and geochemical interpretation, and general well construction.

How do you remain current in your profession?
I'm a member of several engineering organizations. I attend, conduct and organize many events that bring together the global industry experts to discuss these kinds of issues.

What advice can you offer fellow members who work in your industry?
Think strategically and engage in industry forums and organizations, where you have the ability to network and discuss issues with cross-functional people with a lot of backgrounds, to get a better balanced set of information on which to base your decisions and viewpoints.

What advice can you offer people aspiring to work in this profession?
Pursue an education at an institution that can give you a broad background in the different disciplines involved in the oil and gas industry before specializing in something. Particularly in Europe, they offer courses that are very broad-based initially, so you can get a good foundation. Not all the institutions in the U.S. have that general focus early in the education process.

What are you passionate about?
The main one, I guess, is the need for people to communicate without fear.

How does that apply to you?
Quite often, I am in conversations with people who are not forthcoming with ideas or details because they fear that if they are open, it will reduce their influence and ability to do their own and their company's work.

Military Service Administration

Cynthia L. Gardner
Administrative Officer
Office of the Secretary of Defense
1400 Defense Pentagon
Washington, DC 20301 USA
cingrdn7@netzero.net

For more than 25 years, Cynthia L. Gardner has worked for the federal government and is currently an administrative officer for the Office of the Assistant Secretary of Defense for Public Affairs (Administration and Management). Her current position affords her the opportunity to use her extensive expertise in civilian/military personnel matters, correspondence management, records management, payroll, and OPSEC/INFOSEC/PERSEC — operational security, information security and personnel security programs. With excellent communications skills and a detail-oriented nature, she has succeeded in all the inherent areas that comprise administrative management. Among the many highlights of her career, two especially stand out as being memorable: her selection in 2005 as the Defense Information Systems Agency's (DISA) Executive Officer of the Year; and the Secretary of Defense Correspondence Excellence Award for August 2010, which her department earned for correspondence management superior to that of about 16 other competitors.

An independent self-starter who takes initiative and effortlessly carries out her responsibilities, Ms. Gardner is humble when speaking of her accomplishments: "I have been able to shine because of the opportunities I was given by people in front of me." In both her personal and professional lives, she received support that encouraged her to pursue her dreams of having a thriving, fulfilling career. Although succeeding in her profession is important to Ms. Gardner, she would rather be defined by the accomplishments of her two adopted daughters, 16-year-old Kelsi from China and 9-year-old Kenzie from Cambodia. Described as "amazing and incredible girls" who have enriched her world 100-fold since they joined her family, Kelsi and Kenzie are her inspiration to go forward with life even through the toughest of times. Although the passing of her beloved husband, Bob, has left an indelible chasm in Ms. Gardner's life, she remembers him as a truly kindred spirit who believed in her implicitly and shared her dreams.

To broaden her knowledge in her field, Ms. Gardner took courses including Information Resource Management 101 and Acquisition 101 at the Defense Acquisition University, and a Fundamentals of Writing course at the

Defense Information Systems Agency. She also studied government administrative management at The Performance Institute and in 2001 took Management Accounting and Control at the USDA Graduate School. Ms. Gardner received the Cold War Medal and is a two-time recipient of both the Commander's Award for Civilian Service and the Achievement Medal from the U.S. Army.

CONVERSATION WITH CYNTHIA L. GARDNER

CAMBRIDGE WHO'S WHO: **On what topics do you consider yourself to be an expert?**
CYNTHIA L. GARDNER: Correspondence management including writing, formatting and editing; military personnel management including manpower management, position description development appraisals, awards; and scheduling and managing a senior executive/general officer's daily life.

What characteristics help to separate you from your competitors?
I am a versatile, poised and innovative administrator with excellent organizational and written/verbal communication skills. I also have the ability to perform multiple tasks in a fast-paced environment. With uncompromising attention to detail, organization and deadlines, I can operate independently and on team endeavors. I am able to manage complex tasks and achieve results. As a fast learner, I demonstrate the ability to use strong communication and interpersonal and facilitation skills to achieve consensus on a wide variety of issues. I also have the ability to think ahead and anticipate needs.

What lessons have you learned as a professional in your field for the past 26 years?
Always arrive before the boss or you will play catch-up all day. If you say you will do something, do it and always respond to e-mail.

What short-term and long-term goals are you currently pursuing?
I plan to retire from the federal government in April 2014, after 30 years of service. I'd like to devote more time to photography, traveling and my children.

How do you plan to achieve these goals?
Retiring is the easy part; I'm eligible in October 2013, but I'd like to stay for the full 30 years. Photography is a hobby and I'd like to devote time to learning how to take a good photo with my older brother, who is a professional photographer. I also want to spend more time with my children traveling, being more involved in their education — more time just to be a family.

What is the most difficult obstacle or challenge you have faced in pursuit of your goals?
Picking myself up after my husband took his own life. I wanted to crawl in a

shell and shield myself and my children from life, and the repercussions of their father's death. My faith in God, myself, my family and friends got me through the long ordeal and ultimately led to a decision to write an inspirational book about surviving. Another difficult obstacle concerns advancement and monetary compensation for the depth and breadth of my skills. Administrative professionals are notoriously underpaid and poorly rewarded. I managed to hook myself to a rising star and when he rose, I went along for the ride. I earned a reputation for being good at what I did and people sought me.

What are some questions that an individual interested in your services can ask to ensure a more productive relationship?
I work in a customer-oriented office. We provide services to the OASD (PA) staff. Our job entails answering questions and providing support for every aspect of travel, supplies, civilian/military personnel, payroll, security clearance management and verification, badging, access, and correspondence control.

Did you ever consider pursuing a different career path or another profession? If yes, how did you end up working in your current field?
Yes, I originally went to American University to study nursing, but discovered it wasn't the right fit for me. I divorced my first husband and moved home to live with my mother. She was a secretary at Woodward & Lothrop; I was hired as a secretary and later became an assistant buyer before moving to the federal government.

What do you find to be the most rewarding about your profession?
Being able to move from agency to agency and location to location, being inside the Pentagon and working alongside the military.

What is your favorite or least favorite work-related task? Why?
I hate filing; the federal records management rules are extremely strict and I'd rather file it in alphabetical order than by subject. My favorite is personnel management. I work with military personnel at my current job and I thoroughly enjoy every aspect of helping our military with their performance evaluations, security clearances, ceremonies and moves.

What advice can you offer fellow members aspiring to work in your industry?
Dress and behave properly, and leave your personal life at home. Learn to take criticism however distasteful [it may be]. Whatever you tackle, become the expert and always remain humble.

Who have been your mentors or people who have greatly influenced you?
My husband, Bob: he understood people and always provided me with sound and thoughtful advice. He was my best friend and my biggest fan. He pushed

when I need pushing and hugged me when I needed just to be loved. We shared the same dreams and helped each other achieve those dreams. My mother, Carolyn Bacheler, was also a mentor to me. She divorced my father when I was 16, put all her furniture in storage, moved from Florida to Virginia, and started her life over at 56 years old. She rented a room for the first year and when I moved in with her, we moved the furniture to Virginia and rented an apartment together. She was an inspiration. Also, Frank Holderness gave me an opportunity to grow and learn. Frank allowed me to expand my horizons and fed my insatiable appetite for learning everything about being a good executive officer.

What changes have you observed in your industry/field since you started?
The technology and vast amount of information available at your fingertips.

Have you contributed to any publications or research in your field?
I wrote a chapter on testing for the Defense Acquisition University's testing management textbook.

Do you do any public speaking?
Not at my present job, but in the past I have talked on a variety of administrative management issues. I love sharing our adoption story with families considering international adoption. My husband and I would talk at our daughter's middle school career day; he would talk about a military career and I would talk about federal service. I also delivered his eulogy, weaving a wonderful tapestry of his life.

Do you feel that working for the government has somehow molded or changed your opinion of it?
Yes and no. It [the government] changes every four or eight years depending on the administration and how far down the food chain you sit. I believe it's the best place to work — it's recession-proof. Advancement is easy and you can apply for and work anywhere in the world. You meet the most amazing people and anyone can find their niche.

Do you feel compelled to separate your personal views from your professional life? Why?
Sometimes, depending on the subject; politics and religion are neither good party conversation, nor are they good workplace conversations.

Aviation Logistics and Management

Eric Russell Lown
Aircraft Production Controller
Fleet Readiness Center Southeast
11611 Sedgemoore Drive S.
Jacksonville, FL 32223 USA
1stallion76@comcast.net

Eric Russell Lown is an aircraft production controller for the Fleet Readiness Center Southeast, which is one of eight such centers sanctioned by the U.S. Navy to perform extensive overhauls, repairs and modifications to aircraft as needed. With expertise in aviation logistics and business management, Mr. Lown maintains airborne vehicles used by the military (including hurricane hunters and weather chasers), ensures that parts are in good condition and manages logistics for the operation.

From 1978 to 1998, Mr. Lown served as an enlisted aviation warfare specialist for the U.S. Navy. There, he earned a substantial amount of skills, including that of motivating others to succeed in adverse situations. "When I hear someone say 'I can't,' I bring them on my team," he remarks. "Those are the type of people I want, because later on they will be able to tell others about the things that I taught them how to do."

After Mr. Lown went out in the community, he began helping his friend with his print shop, which he did for six months. In an effort to help his pal with the business management aspect, Mr. Lown went out to meetings with the Council of Better Business Bureaus, Inc. and spoke to people within the community, which enabled him to interact with a wide variety of people. During this time, he received a phone call from the Chief of Staff on the Navy base who advised him to apply for an aviation logistics job that would be opening up. He faxed in his resume and was shortly asked to come in for an interview. He was hired for the logistics job as a contractor for the Fleet Readiness Center and, a year and a half later, was hired as a full-time civil service employee, working with various aircrafts.

Mr. Lown received a Bachelor of Science in Business Management in 2007 from the University of Phoenix. He is the vice president of the Local 22, Jacksonville chapter of the International Federation of Professional and Technical Engineers. In his spare time, Mr. Lown enjoys boating.

Conversation with Eric Russell Lown

Cambridge Who's Who: What would you like to promote most about yourself or your business?
Eric Russell Lown: I am a self-motivator. I give my best shot and my only shot to make sure that things are done professionally where nobody gets stepped on. If I do something with a team, even if I was the one who planned it, I make sure that they get the credit first, before I do. That way, in the future, when it comes time for people to ask what [the team] thinks of me, they would say that I gave credit to them for something I may have done. They know that I took the second seat on it and that I made sure that they got acknowledged as well.

What is the most rewarding aspect of your career?
The experience I gained by joining the U.S. Navy in 1978 all the way through to 1998, when I retired. All of my work involved aviation logistics management.

On what topic(s) do you consider yourself to be an expert?
Aviation logistics and management.

What is the most difficult obstacle or challenge you have faced in pursuit of your goals?
The way that the organizational loop is situated in military management, there are some managers whom, when going through the hiring process, decide that they want to hire inbound relatives. They bring them in and give them the same knowledge and abilities, which they have no way of processing, and utilize them anyway. Then, the manager will say that they want to groom them and advance them up the ladder quickly. However, they have no experience whatsoever. They have to come back to one of us to save them when they have to go in front of a commanding officer or admiral and do a presentation. It hurts later on down the line when you have to work for someone with no experience.

What advice can you offer fellow members who work in your industry?
Get all the education you can and listen to somebody within your own work field. The guy may look like a comedian and joke all day long, but he may be the one to whom you need to go. Use your knowledge, skills and abilities to your full potential so that you can advance. Always get all the education that you can because you can't stop becoming educated, no matter what.

What advice can you offer people aspiring to work in this profession?
If you are under the age of 25, I highly suggest that you go into the military. This way, you will be educated on the field and gain the skills of a trade you

want to enter. Once you are in the military, you will need to earn a college education before you can advance. That's what the military's goals are — they want everyone to have an education.

What are your short-term and long-term career goals?
In the short term, I would like to advance into management as a government employee, which would mean that I would lose my union rights and would have to give up my vice president position. I would also like to run for a political office in local, state or federal government.

And what specific steps have you taken toward achieving these goals?
I have worked in [Washington] D.C. with the union in the House and the Senate, so I was able to rub elbows with a few politicians. But the man I really want to speak with is Senator Joe Lieberman. He takes the bull by the horns and knows what he's doing. Jacksonville is a big military town. As long as I push veteran affairs and government issues, I'm sure I could get the vote.

Who have been your mentors or people who have greatly influenced you?
Growing up, I wrote a lot of papers about two people, whom I used as guides because of how young they were and how they were able to advance. One was Jesse James, who I later found out rode with a family member of mine.

I was born overseas in Germany. My grandparents were Jewish, as well as my mother, but she and my father became Protestants. I did a lot of research on Adolf Hitler and how his mind worked — how at the age of 35, he formed his own government and had people believe that if they put their mind to it, they could do it. He conquered all of Germany. He had the knowledge, skills and abilities, but his techniques of how he was handling people just weren't [right].

He wasn't a mentor of mine, but I think that if his skills were applied properly, he probably would have gone down as a hero. He should have done things in a positive way instead of building that hatred toward the Jews, because he was of the Jewish faith — his parents were Jewish. I think he was mistreated by other Jewish children and by his parents, which may have led to his corruption.

What motivates you?
I am a self-motivator. I don't bounce off of anyone else; I work on my own.

What lessons have you learned as a professional in your field for the past 32 years?
I've learned that nobody is wrong; everybody's ideas are meant to be used.

Strategic Military Analysis

Richard A. Smith
Military Analyst II
Applied Systems Technologies
25653 Bejoal Street
Barstow, CA 92311 USA
rashleysmith@dslextreme.com
http://astusa.com

Growing up on a small family farm in New England, Richard A. Smith knew that tilling the land and tending to animals were not the greatest passions of his life — in fact, he almost dreaded them. Working seven days a week throughout the year with no vacations wasn't appealing in the least, so he decided to pursue a career in the military, which might prove to be more challenging and rewarding. In high school, it was determined that his family could not afford to send him to college, which further influenced his choice to enlist.

For 22 years, Mr. Smith served the United States Army as an active duty electronics specialist. Though he was not present on the battleground, his experience with technical systems made him an integral facet of tactical missions as soldiers were deployed to defend their country. Providing them with the necessary training to ensure safety, precision and the effectiveness of certain mechanisms was critical to his leadership role as a master sergeant with the rank of E-8, as were his skills in fire support initiatives. He also trained groups, reported on battle scenarios and managed indirect fire missions while troops actively engaged in combat. Before assuming his current post as a military analyst for Applied Systems Technologies — a software development firm serving companies in the staffing industry — Mr. Smith worked with agencies to procure government contracts for military operations and provide logistical support, by building databases to accurately monitor data.

Certified as an electronics technician and fire support specialist, Mr. Smith also holds certification in Six Sigma processes, which identify an individual's ability to facilitate organizational change and improvement. In the near future, he aspires to expand his horizons into the consulting field, utilizing his military background and technical expertise to assist businesses and individuals. Having spent much of his career abroad for various missions, Mr. Smith enjoys traveling within the United States on an occasional basis.

Conversation with Richard A. Smith

Cambridge Who's Who: What prompted you to work in government contracting after retiring from the military as an analyst specialist?
Richard A. Smith: I had a considerable background in electronic military equipment. After retiring from the military, I went into the government contracting side because they needed people who had experience with different types of electronic equipment. I've been working with government contractors ever since.

On what topics do you consider yourself to be an expert?
My area of expertise is the replication of fire support activities. Military training is simulated by computers, as if the soldiers are on the actual ground. We replicate what they do on the ground with computers and then the computers pretend to fire a round at the soldiers for them to get an idea of what the damage would be. The simulation gives assessment to soldiers at the end of training to figure out their weaknesses and strengths. I worked as a technician throughout my time in the military and when I went into government contracts from 1983 to 2000, I worked in administration and logistics.

What is the most rewarding aspect of your career?
Since I've moved on to the simulation system that we use out here, I think the tactics and techniques that are taught in the military have had an impact. I know it had a huge impact when we first went into the Middle East. We've spent a lot of time developing techniques and trying to receive feedback from what we put into the training and what's happening on the ground. If we hadn't gone in the direction to train these [soldiers] on counterinsurgency before sending them into other countries, I think we would have lost a lot more lives than we did. They teach not only counterinsurgency, but the counter IED (improvised explosive device) part. We tested a lot of the devices that the military is currently using to counter those explosives and made sure they were going to work before putting them out there.

Do you have a motto or principle that guides your work?
I lead by example.

What advice can you offer people aspiring to work in this profession?
I'm one of those people who likes to analyze things before I go into them, but once I've made my decision, I'm going to go for it and stick it out. Be prepared and educate yourself before making your decisions.

Plant Variety Protection

Janice Strachan
Senior Plant Variety Examiner
United States Department of Agriculture
1700 Pumphrey Lane
Silver Spring, MD 20905 USA
janice.strachan@ams.usda.gov

There are some commodities in life, such as fruits and vegetables, whose origin we seldom question. We don't take the time to consider how they all come because they are easily attained at our local grocery stores and supermarkets. Well, there is a lot of careful analysis, testing and cultivation that takes place before the goods arrive by the truckloads, and it all begins with people like Janice Strachan. She is a senior plant variety examiner for the United States Department of Agriculture, and her responsibilities, which include examining plants to determine whether or not they are new, distinct, uniform and stable, recommending marketing rights and training others, are crucial to the welfare of global agriculture.

Ms. Strachan was instrumental in the enforcement of the Plant Variety Protection Act, which provided plant cultivators with exclusive marketing rights for their breeds, in the United States for a certain amount of time. Somewhat similar to a patent, this helps market the variety and aids the company to recover their development costs, thereby perpetuating the system. "If this wasn't in place, there's a possibility that other people would take those seeds, reproduce them, independently and sell them in competition with the original breeder," she explains. "Then, they wouldn't be able to recoup their costs."

With more than 25 years of experience administering the PVP application process, examination, and documentation and tracking, Ms. Strachan continues to remain aware of new developments in the field. As of April 2010, her main crop responsibility was corn, which has been leaving the amount of work on her desk at an uncomfortable level she calls "out of control," because so much of it was coming in that season. In the near future, she hopes to travel around the globe and conduct international training.

Ms. Strachan received a master's degree in botany from The University of Montana and a Bachelor of Arts in Biology from Thomas More College. She is a member of the American Society for Horticultural Science (ASHS) and Sigma Xi, The Scientific Research Society. From 2007 to 2010, Ms. Strachan served as the chair on the selection committee for the American Society for Horticulture Science's Outstanding Industry Scientist Award.

Conversation with Janice Strachan

Cambridge Who's Who: What would you like to promote most about yourself or your business?
Janice Strachan: I have been training others on how to do things in our office. For example, we are like a patent office, so people apply to our office for obtaining intellectual property rights. In the last few years I have been familiarizing the users on how to file those applications, what code words to use to get them through faster, and what they definitely should not do. This training is fairly new for our office. It's a win-win situation for us because if people put in good applications, it's easier for us to examine them. They get their intellectual property rights faster and we have a lower processing time, which is one of the things on which we are rated.

What is the most rewarding aspect of your career?
It's very nice when I go to a nursery and see a seed packet that says "PVP Protected" on it, because I can say that I [was responsible for] that.

What is your greatest professional accomplishment to date?
We revived our regulations, which took a lot of time, but was worth it. Being involved in that rewriting process is time-consuming, difficult and a little confusing, but by the end we were able to streamline our application process so that they don't have to send the physical seeds to our office. They can go straight to a storage facility, which saves us processing time here. It also means that the seeds are put into long-term storage as quickly as possible, since they are handled in the best manner. Additionally, we are now able to use electronic filing instead of using paperwork. It was a big accomplishment to get that done and now we are in a position where we can move along with the future, and do things online and electronically.

What are your short-term and long-term career goals?
We are already in the middle of a business process re-engineering project, transitioning to an electronic situation where the applicants will prepare and submit the application online. There will be some checking that is done by the computer so that by the time it comes here, it is already in much better shape, with all of the correct questions answered. Things will be sped up just by having that online system in place. There is a lot ahead of us, but it looks like a great looking future.

What is the most difficult obstacle or challenge you have faced in pursuit of your goals?
Everything is constantly changing. The science behind the seed companies

has changed. The laws as to what they allow and don't allow have changed as well. You also have legal cases that impact the laws, so just keeping up with the changes in the industry and in the international community is a big deal. I'm also expecting that soon, we will have another upgrade to our international treaty. In order to allow for them, we will have to make changes to existing U.S. laws.

How do you remain current in your profession?
I read other people's research, journals and literature and keep up with what's happening in the industry. I think the best way to do that is to get out to scientific meetings, such as events presented by All-America Selections [a seed trial and testing organization that evaluates flowers, fruits and vegetables]. It's important to go out to meetings and talk to people to really learn about the industry. I don't think we should hide in an office and never talk to the outside world.

What makes you a valuable resource in your industry?
The knowledge I have and the fact that I have been in the industry for 25 years.

What is the most significant issue facing your profession today?
Keeping up with the changes and not being afraid to change when you need to — this is a challenge for anybody in any industry. We need to acknowledge that things don't always stay the same.

What advice can you offer fellow members who work in your industry?
The hard part of getting a government job is filling out those forms appropriately. You have to have that sense of public service, but the real hurdle is figuring how to fill in the blanks so that you get through the screening process to the interview. It's a completely different process than in the private industry.

What are you passionate about?
I believe that proper training, knowing your job, and continuing to keep up with your job and surroundings are all important. I don't think people should expect a promotion just because they have been sitting in the chair for a while. They need to keep up with the industry and their job, and constantly get better.

Who have been your mentors or people who have greatly influenced you?
When I worked for the forest service, I had a manager named Ron Sussott, whom I really respected. I liked the way he did his job and how he mentored me. He may not have realized that he was doing it, but I still think of him as the best manager I have ever had. He was very easygoing and recognized

when he had a weakness. He was very trusting of me and was willing to [bestow] some of his responsibilities to me.

Do you have a quote that you live by?
"Good, better, best. Never let it rest. Until your good is better and your better is best." — Tim Duncan

MILITARY GUIDED MISSILE SYSTEMS

GRAYSON D. TATE JR.

Major General (Retired)
United States Army
12008 Defender Drive S.E.
Huntsville, AL 35803 USA
gtate50@redvil.net

On June 6, 1950, Grayson D. Tate Jr. graduated from the United States Military Academy at West Point and received his commission as a 2nd Lt. [second lieutenant] in the Field Artillery (FA). In January 1951, he was wounded in action in Korea. From 1951 to 1955, 1st Lt. [first lieutenant] Tate was at Ft. Bliss, Texas beginning a 35-year career specializing in guided missiles (GM), research and development (R&D), nuclear weapons, and ballistic missile defense (BMD).

In 1954, Maj. Tate was commanding officer (CO) of a battery in the Army's first tactical GM battalion (BN). From 1958 to 1961, he was assigned to HQ [headquarters], Army Ordnance Missile Command at Redstone Arsenal, Ala., heading missile technical intelligence and research-planning activities. From 1962 to 1964, Maj. Tate was at HQ, U.S. Army Ryukyu Islands on Okinawa. He was the chief evaluator for Annual Service Practice concerning two Nike Hercules and two Hawk Air Defense Battalions.

From 1965 to 1967, Lt. Col. Tate was CO of a sergeant missile battalion at Fort Sill, Okla. He served on the Department of the Army Staff, in the office, chief of R&D as chief, Nike-X and Space Division. In 1969, Col. Tate moved to the Office of Assistant Secretary of the Army (R&D) as the assistant for missiles.

In 1971, Col. Tate was CO [chief officer], 4th U.S. Army Missile Command in Korea, with nuclear missile fire support responsibilities to the CG (commanding general), Eighth U.S. Army and the CG, First Republic of Korea Army. From 1972 to 1974, he was director of gunnery at the FA School, Fort Sill, Okla., responsible for cannon gunnery instruction and training FA personnel for Army missile and rocket battalions. In 1974 through 1976, he served as the Lance Missile System project manager at Army Missile Command (MICOM), Redstone Arsenal. In 1975, BG (brigadier general) Tate was named deputy commanding general at MICOM. In 1977, the Army split MICOM into two commands, and he became CG, Missile Research & Development Command (MIRADCOM).

BG Tate was CG, Field Command, Defense Nuclear Agency (FCDNA) from 1977 until 1979. He was responsible for conducting the DOD Underground

Nuclear Test Program at the Nevada Test Site and for the Nuclear Contamination Cleanup of the Pacific Nuclear Proving Ground, Enewetak Atoll. From 1979 to 1983, Maj. Gen. Tate served as the Army Ballistic Missile Defense Program Manager (BMDPM), with responsibility for developing a BMD System of Systems to provide defense of the United States homeland, particularly for U.S. ICBM sites. Concurrently, he was the national range commander for the Kwajalein Missile Test Range, Marshall Islands. His final assignment was as deputy director for Operations and Administration at HQ, Defense Nuclear Agency in Washington. On March 31, 1985, he retired.

CONVERSATION WITH GRAYSON D. TATE JR.

CAMBRIDGE WHO'S WHO: What would you like to promote most about yourself or your business?
GRAYSON D. TATE JR.: I have had a great deal of experience in four principal areas: guided missiles (GM), research and development (R&D), nuclear weapons, and ballistic missile defense (BMD).

What type of experience do you have in those fields?
I received extensive training on many missile systems and had command experience at all organizational levels. I "cut my teeth" and got my first experience as a first lieutenant in the 1st Guided Missile Group at Ft. Bliss, Texas in 1951 where we prepared and launched U.S. copies of the German V-1 Missile, (called the "Loon"). As a captain, in 1954 to 1955, I served as the commanding officer of a battery in the Army's first tactical (first-generation) surface-to-surface missile battalion, a nuclear-capable Corporal Missile Battalion. As a lieutenant colonel, I was the battalion commander of a nuclear-capable Sergeant Missile Battalion, the second-generation missile system that replaced the Corporal. Also, as a LTC, I served as the deputy commander for operations for the 9th Field Artillery Missile Group at Ft. Sill, Okla., when we were training nuclear-capable PERSHING Missile Battalions at the time they were being deployed to the U.S. Army, Europe. As a colonel, I was the project manager for the nuclear-capable Lance missile system (third generation) that replaced the sergeant. Also, as a COL, I was the commander of the U.S. Army 4th Missile Command in Korea, which included a Sergeant Missile BN and a nuclear-capable Honest John Rocket battalion. The 4th Missile Command had nuclear fire support responsibilities to the commanding general of the Eighth U.S. Army and to the CG, 1st Republic of Korea Army. Also, as a COL, when I was director of gunnery at Ft Sill, Okla., I was responsible for the training of officers and enlisted personnel for Sergeant, Lance, and PERSHING Battalions, and for Honest John rocket battalions. In 1962-1964, I was deeply involved in the air defense of Okinawa and was the chief evaluator for the 30th Air Defense Brigade Annual Service Practice for two years. I also had three years of experience in missile R&D activities while serving on the staff of the Army Ordnance Missile Command. During the four years that I served on the Department of the Army staff, I was involved in every Army missile system including Surface-to-Surface, Surface-

170

to-Air, Ballistic Missile Defense and Anti-Tank missile systems. In 1977, as the CG of MIRADCOM at Redstone Arsenal, I was responsible for all Army missile and rocket systems except Patriot and Ballistic Missile Defense. In 1974-1975, I served two years as the Army project manager for the Lance Missile System. The four years of 1979-1983 as the program manager for the Ballistic Missile Defense System (BMDPM) was the most challenging and difficult assignment of my career, but also the most frustrating because we were not able to achieve the deployment of a BMD system to provide for defense of the nation.

I had two assignments in the Defense Nuclear Agency, the first as CG, Field Command in Albuquerque, N.M., where my responsibilities included the conduct of the DOD [Department of Defense] Underground Nuclear Test Program at the Nevada Test Site. I was also responsible for the radiological cleanup of Enewetak Atoll in the South Pacific, a three-year effort involving about a thousand personnel from the U.S. Army, Navy, Air Force, Marines, the Department of Energy and the Department of the Interior. While at field command, I also served as the exercise director of the first Joint Nuclear Weapons Accident Exercise, which involved all responding organizations (Army, Navy, Air Force, Marines, and the Department of Energy) at the Nevada Test Site, and which included the use of real, live nuclear contaminants to emphasize realism.

What advice can you offer people aspiring to work in this profession?
My advice for a career similar to my own would not be significantly different than one that involves any major field of science and engineering. During their high school years, many people that I have known did not have a clue about what profession to choose for themselves as they considered where to work or what college to attend. At age 16, I knew I wanted to go to college, but had no specific profession to pursue it. Then, expectedly, my dad asked me if I had ever considered trying to get a congressional appointment to West Point. The thought had never entered my mind, but I did some research on the subject, took the physical and academic validating entrance exams and waited hopefully for my notification. Fortunately, I did receive that appointment and entered West Point at the age of 17 on July 1, 1946. A military career appealed more and more to me as I progressed through my four years there; it led to a very satisfying 35-year active duty career. I have talked to many young people who have changed their college majors — some more than once — before really making a decision on a career field.

My advice to them is to make that decision as early as you can, but keep an open mind if you find something else that really "tickles your fancy" and "turns you on." So, my advice to a young person includes: read as many books, pamphlets and other papers as you can on any career field you consider and start this process in your sophomore or junior year of high school. Talk to adults who may work in those fields. Ask them why they chose their career field. Ask them what subjects they would advise you to study in your high school and college years to prepare yourself for their career field. If you can, at your high school, try to take courses that will best prepare you for college, with emphasis on those that are pertinent to the careers you are considering (for instance, lots of math, physics and chemistry courses for a budding engineer). Pick a good college that is strong in your field of interest. Do not avoid the difficult subjects! Ask a lot of pertinent questions to your college professors. Join a campus organization that is devoted to your chosen line of work. A bachelor's degree is a great advantage in properly preparing yourself for successful employment — it is an absolute requirement for my chosen career field. When you find a job, develop conscientious work habits, ask questions, and always complete your assigned work. Try to bring the idea to mind for your supervisor — "How did I ever get along without this new employee?"

Begin work on a master's degree if you can do so. Try to be recognized as a conscientious worker who gets the job done and who is willing to help fellow employees when you can. Give some thought to "thinking outside the box." If you find a hole in your knowledge or education that is limiting your performance, find a way to fill that hole and go for it. If you have chosen the military as your career field, there are many good service schools to attend that can properly prepare you to succeed, whether you are considering a career in the officer or enlisted ranks. If you are thinking of working in the American industry and in the field I pursued, most of what I have advised is still golden.

What are you passionate about?
I feel strongly that the primary function of the federal government is to defend our nation and assure our liberty against the threat of any and all foreign powers. This means that the executive branch (president) must submit a budget to the U.S. Congress that is adequate to provide the necessary personnel, equipment and facilities for that task. The Congress must then approve funds adequate to assure that such national security can be attained. My experience over a 35-year career leads me to believe that at this time in history, the United States must, at all times, have done the homework and be able to deploy Ballistic Missile Defense and Air Defense capabilities rapidly enough to meet any threat that emerges. Those systems must be tested and able to competently and confidently protect our national interests from enemy missile threats, both now and in the future. At the present, that threat

is primarily from Russia and China. However, it could include North Korea and Iran if we are not successful in limiting their nuclear weapons development programs and long-range missile capabilities. Similarly, the United States must continue to pursue technology programs, including missile systems, which will give more and better protection to our deployed forces, including protection against aircraft, shorter-range missiles and artillery.

What is the most difficult obstacle or challenge you have faced in pursuit of your goals?
My personal goals were not all defined at the same time. As a first lieutenant, I was told that my Korean War wounds would likely limit my chances for success as a field artilleryman, so I applied to go to Ft. Bliss, Texas, in order to get involved in guided missiles. During those four years at Ft. Bliss, I actually worked in the Systems Test Division, White Sands Missile Range for about a year in an R&D environment, which I found to be quite fascinating. Then, my assignment to the Army's first tactical guided missile battalion — one with a nuclear capability — defined another environment which I liked and found to be very challenging. I realized that if I was to continue working in guided missiles, R&D, and nuclear weapons, I needed additional education. So, I applied for civil schooling and had the privilege of attending one of our finest engineering colleges, the Georgia Institute of Technology. During my two years there, I was able to earn both a Bachelor of Science and a Master of Science in Aeronautical Engineering. I was pleased that my master's degree thesis was published by the Army and provided at least a little support to our development of new helicopters. Fortunately, I had a wonderful succession of assignments, which allowed me to use more and more of the knowledge I had gained and eventually led me into project management at the Army Missile Command, into the Defense Nuclear Agency and finally into the ballistic missile defense arena. During all those years and my variety of assignments, the absolutely most difficult challenge was to try and keep up with the technology, particularly for missile and nuclear exploitation, the Army R&D "ways of doing business," and contract management; also, to understand the challenge and impact of our ongoing arms control negotiations, and the need to promote programs for which I had passion and enthusiasm and, fortunately, responsibility.

Who have been your mentors or people who have greatly influenced you?
First, I would name my dad, G.D. Tate. He was a wonderful Christian man who taught me the value of friendship, ethics, respect for others, and hard work. He was also my high school principal and mathematics teacher. My Congressman from Texas, George Mahon, provided my appointment to West Point, encouraged me during my years there. Frank Smith, my elementary school football coach, taught me a very tough lesson one day about "mouth control"

that I remember to this day. My high school football coach, Wilson Head, taught me the value of persistence and conditioning and the great value of "having a plan for success." My junior varsity football coach at West Point, Maj. (later Col.) Joel Stevens, gave me an unforgettable lesson about loyalty to his players. Capt. (later Col.) Don McConnell, my boss when I was a second lieutenant artillery forward observer in Korea in 1950-1951, who taught me so much and assured my survival more than once. Lt. Col. (later Col.) Paul Gray, my battalion commander in the Army's first tactical guided missile battalion, greatly inspired me to always do my best and "be all [I could] be." Col. Harry Griffith, my boss during much of my time on the Army staff in the Pentagon, taught me by example about mentoring, compassion, and decency to all associates. Lt. Gen. George Sammet selected me for duty as the Lance Project Manager, inspired me, and launched me into the career area I desired. Gen. John Vessey, who was the Army vice chief of staff, was my boss when I served as the BMD program manager. His professional advice and, at times, willingness to listen with patience, was greatly helpful and appreciated. And finally, the one person whose sacrifice, example and direction are the most valuable of all, is my savior, Jesus Christ. His example provides a great inspiration to me to try to be regarded as a willing and dedicated Christian soldier — whether on active duty or retired.

To whom or what do you attribute your success?
I have mentioned several individuals who greatly influenced me during my Army career. As it turned out, my personal decision, while a first lieutenant, to seek an assignment to Ft. Bliss, Texas after my lengthy hospitalization from Korean War injuries, was a most fortunate move. It steered me into the kind of assignments that I really enjoyed, which were very challenging. I had the good fortune to work for some really top-notch and inspirational officers and civilians, and learned much from them. I also had the good fortune to have some very capable people working for me who made my organization "look good." I tried to take advantage of every schooling opportunity in order to increase my knowledge base. That additional education turned out to be invaluable to me, including both my civil schooling at Georgia Tech and the succession of schools offered by the Department of Defense schooling system. Dedication and hard work were important to me and I tried to set an example for those who worked for me. In addition, there is always one other factor that always deserves to be mentioned, and that is just plain "good luck." Certainly, I had my share.

What is the most rewarding aspect of your career?
One of the most rewarding aspects would be the wonderful experience I had over my 35 years of active duty service, which includes my association with

professional military officers, enlisted men and civilians, and the contractor personnel with whom it was my privilege to work. I am very pleased to have had a very long and personal involvement with the Army; also, having been able to participate in and see the great progress made by the Army in the research, development, procurement, deployment and sustainment of guided missile systems of all types. When comparing first-generation systems to those now in the hands of our troops, it is most satisfying to have been a player on some of the development teams whose dedicated and professional work made that progress possible. I believe that most really knowledgeable people are convinced that the U.S. Armed Forces are the best in the world and have equipment that is "second to none." And, the most personally rewarding of all was the Army's decision to promote me to the rank of major general. That was never my primary professional goal and I was honored to have been able to serve the Army and the nation in assignments that would otherwise not have been possible.

What is your greatest professional accomplishment to date?

I would say that my greatest professional accomplishment during my career occurred during the time that I served at the Ballistic Missile Defense program manager. This was a time when there was a great deal of competition between the U.S. Army and the U.S. Air Force for R&D and the procurement of funds. Even within the Army, there was a considerable resistance to committing such a large budget to BMD. Some Army officials resented the pressure that the Office of the Secretary of Defense exerted to direct those funds. Also, there was a strong element in the Congress, in the Air Force and among several independent analysis firms that did not — and some still don't — believe in the value of Ballistic Missile Defense. Others were concerned that a BMD program could lead the Soviets to believe that the U.S. did not intend to continue to honor the ABM Treaty that had been painfully negotiated with the USSR and signed in May 1972. Incidentally, a portion of the BMDPM Charter from the secretary of the Army gave the BMD program manager the responsibility for ensuring that our BMD program did not violate any provisions of that ABM Treaty. Surely we must do all that we can to protect our population from nuclear weapon attacks. President Reagan's strong support for BMD was, of course, most helpful, particularly his celebrated "Star Wars" speech on March 23, 1983. A primary question that had emerged was whether or not our Intercontinental Ballistic Missiles (ICBMs) could survive without a BMD system to protect them from the Soviet ICBM threat at that time. This philosophical difference of opinion and the competition for funds made it very difficult to keep the BMD program funded and on schedule for each budget year. In fact, there were times when large parts of BMD funding were in great jeopardy. Those of us in the BMD business worked very diligently in our attempt to assure that we were developing the technology that would allow us to provide critical protection from Soviet attacks on our deployed ICBMs. Many in the Air Force simply did not believe defense was required to assure survival, and that survival could be attained by specific basing techniques. From 1982-1983, this became a particularly difficult problem during the days when the methods of deploying the MX Peacemaker ICBMs (deployed as Peacekeeper) were being formulated (e.g. multiple protective shelters or closely spaced basing) and when concurrent analysis was being done by U.S. Army BMD personnel and by the Air Force to assess ICBM survivability with and without BMD. In the Army, we believed defense was required, but the Air Force did not. Helping to keep the BMD program alive and well was an accomplishment of which I was quite proud.

What are your short-term and long-term career goals?
I am now fully retired and have no short-term or long-term goals other than enjoying life and giving my professional opinion when asked.

What makes you a valuable resource in your industry?
I am a valuable resource from the standpoint of my knowledge of the history of and my extensive participation in the four areas mentioned (guided missiles, R&D, nuclear weapons and ballistic missile defense). I have combined these experiences and labeled my field of expertise to be "Military Guided Missile Systems."

Orthopedic Surgery

Stephen R. Adcock, MD

Doctor
Satilla Regional Medical Center
2002 Alice Street
Waycross, GA 31501 USA
adcockmd@windstream.net
http://www.satilla.org

Dr. Stephen R. Adcock doesn't want to kill the dream for anyone who has ever aspired to become a doctor, but nonetheless, he is a realist through and through. He warns that for one to pursue a career in the medical field, they must first realize that it takes a high level of dedication and a substantial investment of time and resources. Dr. Adcock, a doctor in the Orthopedic Department of the Satilla Regional Medical Center, is still amazed that with many professions, not just in medicine, college students pick majors without having any idea what they'll entail. "No one in their family does it or they have never been onsite, such as in a classroom or an operating room," he elaborates. "You need to make the right choice."

Raised in a household with a minister/college professor father and English professor-turned-elementary schoolteacher mother, Dr. Adcock was the youngest of four children. He was fortunate enough that his three other siblings were accomplished: one brother an orthopedic surgeon, another, a retired dentist and lawyer, and a sister who is a teacher. But it was his orthopedic surgeon brother who became his mentor, taking him to the hospital to learn firsthand what the medical field entailed. Dr. Adcock was hooked.

Board certified by The American Board of Orthopedic Surgery, Dr. Adcock works alongside his wife Diane (who is a registered nurse) in the office and the operating room. He is responsible for visiting and treating patients with musculoskeletal issues including arthritis, trauma and congenital deformities; overseeing emergency care; performing reconstructive and microsurgery for hand, wrist and forearm trauma; tending to tumors, children's fractures and deformities; and caring for individuals suffering from arthritis, carpal tunnel syndrome, nerve and sports injuries, and paralysis of the upper extremity. Additionally, he administers care and reconstruction for old injuries, among other modalities.

Dr. Adcock completed his residency in orthopedics in 1983 at the University of Louisville. He received an MD in 1978 from The Medical University of South Carolina and a Bachelor of Science in Biology in 1974 from the University of

South Carolina. He is a member of the Medical Association of Georgia, the Southern Medical Association, the Georgia Orthopaedic Society, the Southern Orthopaedic Association, the American College of Forensic Examiners, the American Academy of Orthopedic Surgeons, and the American Mensa.

Conversation with Stephen R. Adcock, MD

Cambridge Who's Who: What would you like to promote most about yourself or your business?
Stephen R. Adcock: I am currently in private practice, which involves being tied up on weekends and holidays. But I would like to eventually leave private practice at some point and go elsewhere and still be using my expertise. I would certainly be interested in using my knowledge and experience to benefit others. For example, I have done some medical-legal work on the side. I was raised to be honest and fair and I think I could weigh things and use my area of expertise to say what is right or wrong.

What is the most rewarding aspect of your career?
Helping people through difficult physical issues.

What are your short-term and long-term career goals?
My short-term goal is to do the best job that I can. There is a reason why it is called a "practice" of medicine. We're never perfect, we never know everything and there are constant advances. The techniques that I learned 20 years ago may not be considered state-of-the-art. There is always this ongoing quest to keep up and get better. My long-term goal is to make some sort of transition, such as to go into arbitration or teaching — both of my parents were teachers.

And what specific steps have you taken toward achieving these goals?
I am continuing to learn and have to constantly keep up-to-date on the current issues.

What is the most difficult obstacle or challenge you have faced in pursuit of your goals?
The fact that there are too many variables to master. My desire to achieve perfection is a constant struggle — it's an impossible goal. It's very difficult to ever be completely satisfied. Even when the end result is perfect in a surgery, it annoys me when I have to do something twice.

How do you remain current in your profession?
I go to quite a few conferences. I subscribe to about 12 to 15 orthopedic journals. Someone in medicine would appreciate the fact that I'm recertified. I have to recertify every 10 years. Also, there are online updates that I view and with which I keep up.

On what topic(s) do you consider yourself to be an expert?
General orthopedic surgery, except on the neck and back.

What makes you a valuable resource in your industry?
Knowledge, experience and compassion. I think that compassion is important with medicine.

What is the most significant issue facing your profession today?
The current state of health care; also, where it's heading.

What advice can you offer people aspiring to work in this profession?
Anyone considering a career in medicine really needs to find a mentor, someone with whom they can spend time. There is an investment with time and money and once you're there, you can't afford the change. Stay committed to doing the best job possible as well as staying current on all procedures and technology.

What are you passionate about?
I strongly identify with my profession. I'm passionate about my family.

Who have been your mentors or people who have greatly influenced you?
My brother, who is 13 years older, was a great influence. He was a doctor while I was still young enough to decide. Through him, I gained some idea of what it meant to be an orthopedic surgeon. The chairman of my department, Dr. Harjess from the University of Louisville, was also an influence.

Geriatric Care and Psychiatry

Eugenia Ybanez Blomstrom, RN-CNS

1) Registered Nurse, Clinical Nurse Specialist, Psychiatric Mental
Health Nurse Practitioner 2) Assistant Professor
1) Vericare 2) University of Houston System
eblomstrom@aol.com
http://www.twu.edu

As an educator with substantial experience in clinical nursing, Eugenia Ybanez Blomstrom possesses both clinical and theoretical knowledge to train the health care practitioners of tomorrow. A clinical nurse specialist with proficiency in psychiatric and mental health care, Ms. Blomstrom has spent nearly 40 years focusing on the treatment of patients with psychological issues. Currently working as an assistant professor at the University of Houston's Sugar Land Campus, she collaborates with nearby nursing facilities to acquire learning opportunities for students to gain practical hands-on experience in their respective fields. She also deals specifically with the elderly population to provide specialized insight regarding mental and physical illnesses.

Ms. Blomstrom began her career in various hospital units, where she developed skills in an assortment of disciplines. She found that psychiatry, when used in conjunction with her practical nursing expertise, offered vast opportunities to examine patients at their most basic levels. In other words, she is able to treat the body as well as the mind, and to evaluate conditions to ensure that ethical decisions are made regarding their care. Another aspect of her clinical specialty is research centered in contemporary methods and discoveries regarding medicinal use. To prevent overmedication, she advises individuals and their families on healthy lifestyle practices that will eliminate the need for excessive chemical interference in their bodies.

A subscriber to the New England Journal of Medicine, Ms. Blomstrom remains updated on current issues within her field through her involvement with Texas Nurse Practitioners and the Gerontological Society of America. She is also pursuing a Ph.D. in Nursing at The University of Texas Medical Branch to complement the Master of Science in Nursing she earned at The University of Texas Health Science Center at Houston. She looks forward to assuming a more substantial role at the university, where she will be able to make an impact on the careers of students and the patients whose lives will depend on their training.

Conversation with Eugenia Ybanez Blomstrom, RN-CNS

Cambridge Who's Who: When did you decide you wanted to be a nurse? Did you always know you wanted to be a psychiatric nurse practitioner?
Eugenia Ybanez Blomstrom: I was in grade school and wasn't even interested in psychology. I worked as a coronary care nurse for a long time, which was my specialty. I worked in the emergency room because I liked the adrenaline rush, and in intensive care. Now I am a psychiatric nurse practitioner and a professor at a university.

What is the most rewarding aspect of your career?
For me, it's teaching. I like to teach things that will prevent people from having to go into the hospital or take medication. I believe in primary prevention. My area of interest is polypharmacy, or the use of multiple medications, because that makes people go to the hospital. I am actually going to be doing a presentation on polypharmacy with the elderly population in March [of 2010].

What is your greatest professional accomplishment to date?
Completing my dissertation was a great accomplishment. I currently have an article that is ready for publishing, which deals with polypharmacy. If it gets published, that will also be another accomplishment. We are a [drug-dependent] society and we need to get away from that. I actually just got a contract with the Veterans Administration Hospital so I will be able to put some students there for psychiatric studies. That usually takes a whole semester, but we did it a lot faster than that, which is great.

What are your short-term and long-term career goals?
My long-term goal is to be tenured here at the university. My short-term goal is to have my article and dissertation published.

What is the most difficult obstacle or challenge you have faced in pursuit of your goals?
Getting students into clinical sites because we have too many students and not enough sites for them.

On what topics do you consider yourself to be an expert?
My topic of expertise is mental health issues specific to the geriatric population.

How do you remain current in your profession?
I keep up with peer-reviewed journals and look on the computer to find out what's going on. I am a political activist, so when I see that all of the decisions are made in the political arena, I try to stay abreast of the current issues. I also write letters to my senators.

What makes you a valuable resource in your industry?
I am always on the cutting edge. Because I am in the academic world, I always have my hand in the latest developments and newest research. I am able to utilize my computer to tell me what's going on out there with the elderly or in the political industry in terms of medicine.

What is the most significant issue facing your profession today?
The health care [legislation] issue that is going back and forth in Congress. It does need to change, so we need to start somewhere. We haven't done anything in quite some time; our health care system is unstructured and needs to be fixed.

What advice can you offer fellow members who work in your industry?
Stay current with health care issues and always be an advocate for the patient.

What advice can you offer people aspiring to work in this profession?
You won't know unless you try. Allow yourself to be creative and dream your dream.

What are you passionate about?
I'm passionate about primary health care. I think people need to eat well from the beginning — if we take care of our bodies, our bodies will take care of us. We need to think positive thoughts and allow the younger generation to be creative. If they fall and stumble, so what?

Who have been your mentors or people who have greatly influenced you?
My parents, Jose and Sue, were wonderful to me. I grew up in a happy home and love my family, so I'm glad for that. My parents were married for 60 years until they passed. They were wonderful and let us try new things with the idea that if you fall, you fall — it's not a big deal.

Do you have a principle or philosophy that guides your work?
Be mentally and physically healthy and allow yourself to challenge life.

NURSE ANESTHESIOLOGY

MELBA L. BRAY
Certified Registered Nurse Anesthetist
South County Anesthesia Associates, Ltd.
348 Nantucket Drive
Ballwin, MO 63011 USA
lmbray30@att.net

If Melba L. Bray didn't take a moment to decide she would retire at the end of the year, chances are she would be in the nurse anesthesiology field for a very long time to come. She is presently a nurse anesthetist at South County Anesthesia Associates, Ltd., a private practice that provides anesthesia services for two surgery centers and St. Anthony's Hospital. Well-versed in her role, she performed obstetrical anesthesia for 16 years and then returned to general anesthesia. She attributes her longstanding success to her hard work, passion for her profession, ability to stay updated on current trends, and the support she receives from her superiors and family.

As a nurse anesthetist, Ms. Bray is responsible for caring for patients, assisting physicians in cardiac ablation, working with pacemakers and defibrillators, and teaching clinical anesthesia to postgraduate students. Since she has been in nursing for more than 47 years, Ms. Bray has seen the profession change tremendously. When she attended nursing school, for instance, it was a three-year program. Nowadays, candidates need a college degree, or even a Ph.D. "I've seen how it's advanced over the years and these students are going to be in school half their lives before they ever start!"

For the veteran nurse, one thing remains consistent though — the fact that there are so many opportunities in nursing, with a lot of different roles to fill. For this reason, Ms. Bray is an unabashed champion for the job, harnessing a tremendous amount of energy to motivate and mentor individuals who seek a rewarding yet challenging career. "I hope to become a positive influence to other young people entering the anesthesia profession," she states.

Ms. Bray received a certification in anesthesiology in 1983 from the American Association of Nurse Anesthetists, a diploma in nurse anesthesia in 1983 from Barnes Hospital, and a diploma in nursing in 1963 from St. Joseph's Hospital. She is a member of the Missouri Association of Nurse Anesthetists, the Missouri Nurses Association, the Missouri Association of Advanced Practice Nurses, the Choctaw Nation of Oklahoma and the American Association of Nurse Anesthetists.

CONVERSATION WITH MELBA L. BRAY

CAMBRIDGE WHO'S WHO: How did you become involved in the nursing industry?
MELBA L. BRAY: When I was thinking about what I wanted to do with my life, in those days, the boys went into medicine and the girls went into nursing. The profession appealed to me because I like science and biology. I had one aunt who was a nurse, and another aunt who was a [notable] in nursing, who helped to set up a VA hospital — they both influenced me. I took a class in nursing school taught by an anesthesiologist and I became totally fascinated by the concept of anesthesia. I knew that was what I wanted to do.

What is the most rewarding aspect of your career?
The satisfaction you get from helping someone feel better and helping to restore them back to health.

What is your greatest professional accomplishment to date?
The ability to do both, balance my family life and my career.

What are your short-term and long-term career goals?
My short-term goal is to retire at the end of this year. I would like to spend more time visiting with my daughter, grandson and other family members.

And what specific steps have you taken toward achieving these goals?
I am working two days a week now. Anesthesia has been a wonderful career. I hope to impart my knowledge, expertise and passion to the young people taking over.

What advice can you offer people aspiring to work in this profession?
It is such rewarding work. Be dedicated to your profession and work hard to improve it. Keep yourself well educated. You are going to have to battle and defend yourself in your profession and it's not always going to be easy.

What advice can you offer others who aspire to work in your industry?
Study hard in high school and college, especially in math and the sciences. The requirements are more demanding nowadays; soon, you will need a Ph.D. to work the entry level in nurse anesthesia.

What is the most significant issue facing your profession today?
Physicians need us — they wouldn't survive without nurses. While this is the reality, there is a nursing shortage. They have made the standards to get into nursing so high and the kids up here are having such a hard time getting into a university. They make getting into college for nursing so difficult, where you need a [very high] GPA. Nurses do so much, but they are still very poorly paid.

Another issue has to do with competing factors in the field. The anesthesiologists support anesthesia assistants today, but they are not trained as nurses. This poses a problem. Nurse anesthetists can work alone, but the anesthesia assistants can only work under the direct supervision of an anesthesiologist.

On what topic(s) do you consider yourself to be an expert?
Anesthesia care. Additionally, my talent was helping set up different departments in the hospital. For example, I opened a coronary care unit.

What is your favorite quote?
"God, grant me the strength to reach out for my dreams and see the world with understanding and love, and believe in the beauty of life and the dignity of mankind."

How do you remain current in your profession?
I have always attended anesthesia seminars throughout my career. Additionally, I read anesthesia journals.

What makes you a valuable resource in your industry?
My dedication and hard work.

What are you passionate about?
Supporting the nurse anesthesia profession and nursing in general. They are so needed in this society.

Who have been your mentors or people who have greatly influenced you?
Dr. John Schweiss, an anesthesiologist at St. Louis University; Dr. Robert Miller, an anesthesiologist at St. John's Hospital; Dr. Sally Schneider, an anesthesiologist at St. John's Hospital; Dr. Keith Kenimer, an anesthesiologist at St. John's Hospital; and the anesthesia staff of St. Anthony's Hospital. Sister Jeanette, a friend and teacher, and my mother were the greatest influences in my life. My husband and my family have been my greatest supporters.

RECONSTRUCTIVE AND COSMETIC SURGERY

DONALD J. CAMPBELL, MD
Plastic Surgeon
The Aesthetic Center of Gainesville
1296 Sims Street, Suite B
Gainesville, GA 30501 USA
djcampbell@negpsa.com
http://www.negpsa.com

"Treat every patient like they are your mother," says plastic surgeon Dr. Donald J. Campbell, who has 10 years of experience in his profession. He has been a part of the Aesthetic Center of Gainesville for the past two years, where he oversees business operations and performs cosmetic and reconstructive surgery. He also offers pro bono work through the facility, which provides cosmetic and plastic surgery to patients of all ages.

Dr. Campbell's focus is on breast reconstruction and his primary concern is the well-being of his patients. "You have to read your patient and figure out how best to treat them," he says. Prior to joining The Aesthetic Center of Gainesville, he served as the chief resident of surgery at the University of Tennessee College of Medicine Chattanooga, a graduate institution offering continuing medical education as well as rotations and internships for recent medical school alumni. Dr. Campbell fulfilled a residency in general surgery there before completing a fellowship in cosmetic surgery at Vanderbilt University in Nashville, Tenn. He earned a Doctor of Medicine from the Mercer University School of Medicine in 1999 and a Bachelor of Science in Biology at Appalachian State University, where he graduated cum laude. Additionally, he received postgraduate scholarships from The National Football Foundation and the National Collegiate Athletic Association.

A board-certified general surgeon, Dr. Campbell is a member of the Medical Association of Georgia, the American Medical Association, the Southeastern Surgical Congress, Alpha Omega Alpha Honor Medical Society, Beta Beta Beta National Biological Honor Society, and The National Football Foundation. He has received many awards, including distinction as an Academic All-American scholar athlete from the state of Georgia and an inductee into the Sports Hall of Fame at the Northeast Georgia History Center. In five years Dr. Campbell hopes to establish his own practice. He has two children named Hannah and Blevin and in his spare time, he enjoys golfing, traveling, watching football, and reading nonfiction and history books.

Conversation with Donald J. Campbell, MD

Cambridge Who's Who: What would you like to promote most about yourself or your business?
Donald J. Campbell: I perform mastectomies and breast reconstruction after breast cancer.

What is the most rewarding aspect of your career?
The most rewarding aspect of my career is trying to make women going through breast cancer actually feel like their breasts are improved after they have [overcome] the difficult process.

What is your greatest professional accomplishment to date?
The best thing that has happened to me is being accepted by the medical community at such a young age as a go-to person in the area for breast reconstruction.

What are your short-term and long-term career goals?
My long-term goals are to continue what I love doing, which is plastic surgery, and to enjoy life and my two children. We have been able to produce much more natural-appearing breasts. [We have] newer technologies with tissue expansion and newer-generation implants that are more natural coming into market, and once they are approved by the FDA, they will improve breast reconstruction.

What is the most difficult obstacle or challenge you have faced in pursuit of your goals?
The most difficult challenge is to get the implants approved and passed by the FDA. Some of the implants that are much more natural haven't been held up by them. That's one of the problems we are facing in the industry — they haven't approved them yet. They have only been placed in studies in the United States and [surgeons] have been using this same technology in Europe for a number of years.

How do you remain current in your profession?
I remain current in my profession by reading the Plastic and Reconstructive

Surgery journal. The American Society of Plastic Surgeons has meetings all the time that my partner and I attend to stay current. I also lecture locally.

What makes you a valuable resource in your industry?
I am a valuable resource in my industry because I have excellent training.

Who have been your mentors or people who have greatly influenced you?
I was fortunate enough to train at Vanderbilt, where I was working with a lot of surgeons who are at the cutting edge of the field, such as G. Patrick Maxwell. That has allowed me to come back to my area and actually be an expert.

On what topics do you consider yourself to be an expert?
I consider myself an expert on cosmetic and reconstruction surgery.

What are you passionate about?
I am passionate about being an adult self-learner. Every day I try to learn more about this field, and about life and the psychology of dealing with these patients. I try to make them feel better about the process they are going through. I think that this is one of those areas where you are trying new things with different patients, but you have to really be able to read the patients and find what they need.

Do you have a motto or principle that guides your work?
Always do more than expected.

HEALTH CARE OPERATIONS

MELISSA COLE, BSN, MSW

President, Chief Executive Officer
Cole Consulting LLC
New Mexico, USA
http://www.linkedin.com/in/melissacole

Melissa Cole was inspired by her mother, Sterling, to enter the field of health care, an action that has opened many doors. As a health care leader for more than 25 years, Ms. Cole has maintained a passion to leverage technology that increases patient safety, which has taken her on a journey across the country. Speaking nationally on best practice implementation of clinical electronic medical records while at Siemens, to presently providing education for physician leaders with the Institute for Medical Leadership, Ms. Cole continues to link today's leaders with best practice solutions.

As CEO of Cole Consulting LLC, Ms. Cole partners with experts across several industries, bringing best practice solutions to leaders and health care systems across the country. Services offered include: lean training for health care executive teams, physician leadership training, executive coaching, interim director/executive services, organizational cultural assessment, and change management solutions. Cole Consulting LLC also provides assessment and training for health care vendors in health care executive etiquette.

Drawing from her experience in hospital operations, change management, technology implementation, and best practice of clinical electronic medical records adoption, Ms. Cole is delighted to have found a profession where she is helping both patients and organizations. Her fervor for improving health care is ever-growing; she enjoys meeting and spending time with those who share her same vision.

The 2010 president-elect of the New Mexico Chapter of the American College of Healthcare Executives and an active member of the Healthcare Information and Management Systems Society, Ms. Cole received a Bachelor of Science in Nursing from Hope College in 1985 followed by a Master of Social Work from the University of Michigan in 1989. In recognition of her professional skills, she received the Certificate for Duty Above and Beyond from The University of New Mexico Hospital in 2000 and the Performance Award from Siemens in 2003 and 2005. She also supports the Center for Biological Diversity, Habitat for Humanity International, and the New Mexico Chapter of the United Way of America. In the future, Ms. Cole seeks to present internationally on leveraging technology to improve health care delivery and patient safety.

Ms. Cole lives in New Mexico with her spouse, Susan Oliver, a clinical social worker in the emergency department at The University of New Mexico Hospital. By participating in triathlons, Ms. Oliver inspires many via her dedication and focus to overcome any challenge. To balance their professional activities, both enjoy hikes in the mountains with their dogs.

Conversation with Melissa Cole, BSN, MSW

Cambridge Who's Who: On what topics do you consider yourself to be an expert?
Melissa Cole: Change management, workflow innovation, implementation of quality initiatives, and clinical adoption of technology in health care settings.

What characteristics help to separate you from your competitors?
I connect well with others; I find joy in discovering common interests when meeting new people. I appreciate the unique challenges organizations face and I'm skilled in discerning what the next best steps are based on organizational strengths. I am a visionary who realizes the solution may not even exist yet and appreciates the need to hold a space for it to enter.

What motivates you?
The knowledge that there is a better way to deliver care. I find it very rewarding to connect health care leaders with innovative solutions.

What lessons have you learned as a professional in your field for the past 25 years?
Stay focused on the possibilities instead of perceived road blocks. What we give focus to is what we create.

What short-term and long-term career goals are you currently pursuing?
In the near term, I would like to support hospitals in the adoption of wireless vital sign surveillance on general medical/surgical units and in the emergency department waiting areas. This alone improves emergency department throughput/in-patient capacity management, resulting in significant cost avoidance and improved patient safety. My long-term goal is to become an international speaker on leveraging technology to improve hospital operations and patient safety. Technology can be a wonderful tool, but without an understanding of change management and technology adoption, hospitals lose their investment and the momentum for the next technology project.

What is the most difficult obstacle or challenge you have faced in pursuit of your goals?
Self-perceived limitations.

Did you ever consider pursuing a different career path or another profession? If yes, how did you end up working in your current field?
Yes, I have many interests: music, travel and motion pictures, to name a few. Although I've worked in health care for over 25 years, I have had the opportunity to explore several fields. While an exchange student in Finland, I was asked by Chris Brubeck if I would be interested in auditioning as the bass player for Herbie Hancock. I house sat and booked summer holidays for a winter on a Greek Island, and was the producer on set for an independent film shot in Santa Fe. My varied experience has enhanced my contributions to health care. Hospital operations, change management and patient safety are my personal mission. Health care has afforded me many opportunities and wonderful experiences.

What do you find to be the most rewarding about your profession?
I enjoy helping systems shift and supporting others in that process. My personal mission is to improve patient safety by leveraging technology.

What advice can you offer fellow members or others aspiring to work in your industry?
Find your personal passion — run after it — and the money will follow.

What changes have you observed in your industry/field since you started?
Personal consumer technology adoption is moving at a faster rate than hospital adoption. Finding a balance — matching the technology with the clinicians and patient needs is a challenge for most facilities. This has sped up significantly since I started in health care in the 1980s.

How do you see these changes affecting the future of your industry?
Considering the diminishing resources in health care, it is crucial that we find ways to maximize technology to support the increasing health needs of our ageing population. Medical homes, innovations in chronic disease management, wellness incentives — how we view health care — needs to have a significant shift if we are to manage the challenge before us. I am compelled to play a part in overcoming this challenge.

What is the most significant issue facing your profession today?
The lack of resources to provide care delivery, along with a system in need of significant change, if it is to manage the growing aging population is the biggest issue.

Who have been your mentors or people who have greatly influenced you?
Linda Matern, president of C2MedPartners; Chris Van Gorder, president and

CEO of Scripps Healthcare (2010 ACHE Chair); and Dr. Susan Reynolds are the three that quickly come to mind. Linda has amazing vision and is able articulate and execute her vision. She always takes time to mentor others and is a great coach. When I heard Chris speak at a conference in 2009 I decided, "I want to support what he is doing!" — that lead me to become the president-elect of the ACHE chapter in New Mexico. Chris has wonderful energy and experience, which makes him a great leader and an inspiration for many. As the owner, president and CEO of the Institute for Medical Leadership, Dr. Susan Reynolds provides physician leadership education and executive coaching. The level of experience and talent of the faculty she has drawn for her programs is outstanding. Susan is able to quickly assess what an organization needs to excel and provide a plan for success to be actualized. She has been an incredible support to me, and inspires me to reach for my goals. All three of these people are experts in the field; they are generous with their time and knowledge and have provided significant contributions to innovations in health care.

Health Care Data Exchange Administration

Sylvia Endicott-Sullivan
Management Analyst
United States Department of Veterans Affairs
1335 E. West Highway, Third Floor
Silver Spring, MD 20910 USA
sylvia.endicott-sullivan@va.gov
http://www.va.gov

Sylvia Endicott-Sullivan has more than 28 years of project management experience. She is currently working with the Nationwide Health Information Network [NHIN] to promote the exchange of data between private health agencies and government entities. This critical consolidation of data will end up saving health care companies much money by eliminating the need for constant retesting — the information will be more readily available and there is potential to reduce the number of tests required, therefore reducing cost and providing better patient care.

Ms. Endicott-Sullivan became involved in her profession after being hired by the Veterans Administration Medical Center in Grand Island. She started out as an administrative assistant and then worked up the ranks to become a supervisory program assistant, a management systems analyst, and then a health systems specialist and implementation manager for the Veterans Health Administration. She attributes her success to her hard work, determination and dedication to improve the delivery of information and provide better care for veterans. Her expertise includes business process re-engineering, training and education as she manages clinical information technology projects and the development of technology solutions for transferring data.

In 2004, Ms. Endicott-Sullivan received a master's degree in project management from The George Washington University; in 1997, she received a bachelor's degree in public administration from Doane College. She is a member of the Project Management Institute, Inc., the Healthcare Information and Management Systems Society, the American College of Healthcare Executives and the National Healthcare Information Network. She is an Exalted Ruler of the Elks Lodge 994. In 2006, Ms. Endicott was the recipient of the Excellence in Government Award from the International Association for Computer and Information Science. From 1998 to 2000, she was honored with the Outstanding Award for Dedication and Devotion by the Government Computer-Based Patient Records Program Management Office.

In her spare time, Ms. Endicott-Sullivan enjoys reading, singing, distance running, hunting, and fishing.

CONVERSATION WITH SYLVIA ENDICOTT-SULLIVAN

CAMBRIDGE WHO'S WHO: What would you like to promote most about yourself or your business?
SYLVIA ENDICOTT-SULLIVAN: I have project management experience. I work with the U.S. Department of Defense and the U.S. Department of Veterans Affairs on an initiative involving the electronic transfer of clinical information. The test we are doing right now is with Kaiser-Permanente: they are exchanging information of people who have agreed to have their health data shared with all of their providers. This will lead to the ability to exchange information between the private sector and federal entities, allowing us to continue our commitment to provide the best possible health care to our nation's veterans.

The recent changes to health care legislation must be a big topic.
I would expect the changes in health care legislation to create an increase in the number of veterans who will make application for care within the Veterans Health Administration.

What is the most rewarding aspect of your career?
The opportunity to work with veterans and returning soldiers.

What is your greatest professional accomplishment to date?
My greatest professional accomplishment to date was obtaining a master's degree in project management from The George Washington University.

What are your short-term and long-term career goals?
Short term, I would like to be more closely involved in medical center management. Long term, after I retire, I would like to do project management consulting work.

And what specific steps have you taken toward achieving these goals?
I have maintained my Level III project management certification. I remain current in technology and electronic data exchange development efforts and requirements. I continue to act as a subject matter expert in health data and information exchange. I do speaking engagements and training sessions and updates on the status of electronic health information exchange between the Department

of Defense and VHA. I was recently accepted into the VHA's mentoring program, where I will mentor upcoming career-potential VA employees.

How do you remain current in your profession?
I continue to evolve through my professional affiliations. I am a member of the Project Management Institute and am affiliated with health care organizations such as the American College of Healthcare Executives. I continue to participate in professional networking and stay current by attending conferences and reading relevant periodicals.

What makes you a valuable resource in your industry?
My historical knowledge and ongoing educational accomplishments.

What is the most significant issue facing your profession today?
How do we effectively distribute the funding allocations we get from Washington? How do we provide care for all of the Iraqi and Afghan soldiers while also maintaining the care that's required by our now aging Vietnam veteran population? You can only do so much. There certainly needs to be a heightened awareness of what the needs are of our current veterans, particularly the trauma cases. People have no idea how much money it takes to care for a double or triple amputee or someone who has a traumatic brain or spinal cord injury — that's lifelong. They're certainly deserving of treatment and care, but it has to be budgeted in a way that we continue providing the care for them without taking away from somebody else.

What is the most difficult obstacle or challenge you have faced in pursuit of your goals?
The most difficult challenge for me was trying to maintain my career requirements and do the right thing for my job while my mother was dying of pancreatic cancer and my father had Alzheimer's disease. I was trying to fulfill my personal obligations, maintain my professional responsibilities and, at the same time, provide care for elderly parents.

My mom was sick for three months. It was like, "Boom, you've got cancer. Boom, you're dead." My dad had Alzheimer's for 10 years. He just died a year ago. That's why I am here in South Dakota and haven't been able to pursue some of my own long-term goals — I was the only person who was able to be here to help them with their own personal tragedies. Now is when I'm trying to get on with my career and advance myself before my retirement.

On what topic(s) do you consider yourself to be an expert?
Hospital administration, veterans' benefits, clinical information exchange, resource allocation, and project management.

What advice can you offer people aspiring to work in this profession?
Veterans Health Administration is a great place to work. The benefits and retirement plans are good. Again, it doesn't come without some sort of personal sacrifice. People, youth in particular, need to know that they have to continue their education. Some of them still don't see the need to finish high school. They don't understand that there's a big difference in income between a high school graduate and someone who has bachelor's degree. You get back what you put into your education and also prove to people that you're willing to make those kinds of commitments.

What are you passionate about?
I am passionate about doing what's right for the veteran population that I have made the commitment to serve. Personally, I studied classical music for eight years. I run multiple marathons. I am passionate about setting personal goals and being able to prove that you're committed enough to accomplish those goals.

Who have been your mentors or people who have greatly influenced you?
I've had some great bosses, including Peter Groen and Ken Swasey; some of my co-workers, which include Dale Givens and Dave Johnson; my parents Betty and Robert Endicott; and especially my husband, Lawrence Sullivan, who has offered ongoing support and understanding while I advanced my career and pursued educational opportunities.

Do you have a favorite quote or motto that you live your life by?
Every morning in Africa, a gazelle wakes up. It knows it must run faster than the fastest lion or it will be killed. Every morning a lion wakes up. It knows it must outrun the slowest gazelle or it will starve to death. It does not matter if you are a lion or a gazelle. When the sun comes up, you better be running.

Rehabilitation Nursing

Susan L. Fanska, RN
Charge Nurse
Truman Medical Center Lakewood
7900 Lees Summit Road
Kansas City, MO 64139 USA
sfanska1@comcast.net

A fervor for education, combined with a spirited dedication to helping people, brought Susan L. Fanska into the health care industry more than 35 years ago. Now a charge nurse for Truman Medical Center Lakewood, Ms. Fanska has made it a point to keep up with the ever-changing nursing field. With rising expectations of nurses (and more so of those in managerial positions) becoming a hot-button health care issue in recent years, Ms. Fanksa has not hindered; rather, she embraces the challenge and adjusts to meet whatever tasks she may face.

Ms. Fanska brings her expertise of medical rehabilitation and orthopedics to Truman Medical Center Lakewood, an academic health center serving the Kansas City community. As a charge nurse, she is responsible for caring for patients while supervising other nurses, which takes a lot of multitasking. Ms. Fanska strongly suggests that anyone going into the nursing field should become increasingly involved in the profession and diversify their knowledge. She also asserts that it is better to explore the various fields of nursing to be certain of the direction in which you wish to go. Since nursing can be a taxing occupation, she advises that it is wise to find a way to relax and relieve the stress. That way, the pressure doesn't build up inside you. "I think that people burn out because it is a very stressful job," she says. One way she likes to relax is by working on crossword puzzles with her family.

Ms. Fanksa's desire is to ensure that her patients get better through education and counseling. As a nurse, one can become emotionally attached to the patient, especially when they are the one with whom the patient may be seeking a connection. That emotional side becomes even more apparent in nursing when dealing with patients' problems, which Ms. Fanska admits can be difficult. Being able to master one's own emotions is one thing, but having to follow the emotions of another human being, along with your own, can be even more challenging.

In 1980, Ms. Fanska earned an Associate of Arts in Computer Programming from Penn Valley Community College, followed by a Bachelor of Arts in Psychology from Park University. A certified rehabilitation registered nurse since 1997, she holds memberships with the Association of Rehabilitation Nurses and Camp Fire USA, from which she received the Wohelo Award. In the future, Ms. Fanska hopes to learn more about behavioral health through continuing education and by attending seminars. This way, she will be able to establish a foothold in the psychiatric field.

Conversation with Susan L. Fanska, RN

Cambridge Who's Who: What is the most rewarding aspect of your career?
Susan L. Fanska: Seeing people get better, and educating and counseling patients.

What is your greatest professional accomplishment to date?
Becoming certified with The Association of Rehabilitation Nurses and receiving my CRRN [Certified Rehabilitation Registered Nurse] certification.

What is the most difficult obstacle or challenge you have faced in pursuit of your goals?
The personal, emotional aspect of nursing and the stress of trying to multitask and adjust to what's going on every day; also, having to adapt and deal with failures and the problems of patients.

How do you remain current in your profession?
I attend seminars and we have an online educational system for behavioral health personnel.

What makes you a valuable resource in your industry?
I have had such diverse experience that has given me adaptability. I also have very good computer skills.

What are you passionate about?
The Campfire Boys & Girls organization (now Camp Fire USA).

What advice can you offer people aspiring to work in this profession?
When you first get out of nursing school, go to a medical surgical unit to get practical experience before you choose a specific field to go into. It's totally different than being in nursing school.

Do you have a favorite quote?
"All the darkness in the world cannot put out the light of a single candle." — Hector Black

Who have been your mentors or people who have greatly influenced you?
My aunt Ruth and my mother.

On what topic(s) do you consider yourself to be an expert?
Medical rehabilitation and orthopedics.

What is the most significant issue facing your profession today?
Retention of nurses and the new health care bill. There are also a lot of nurses out there who are not working in the field.

What is your most memorable experience as a nurse?
Caring for patients after the Hyatt disaster in Kansas City, Mo., in July 1981.

What lessons have you learned as a professional in your field for the past 38 years?
I have learned to care for patients with spinal cord injuries and head injuries, including the possible complications with medications.

Has your position been affected by changes in health care? How?
Of course. It is like all other professions, where they ask you to do more within an eight-hour period of time. We have also been majorly impacted by computers. They have helped improve communication about a patient's history and provide easier access to information about disorders and medications.

What are your short-term and long-term career goals?
My short-term goal is to learn more about behavioral health. My long-term goal is to be more effective in team building.

And what specific steps have you taken toward achieving these goals?
I am trying to go to seminars and read about different diagnoses. I am also trying to learn to be more assertive and supportive.

Home Care and Medical-Surgical Nursing

Cheryl Gates-Beller, BSMNS, RN, BC
Registered Nurse, Case Manager
American Nursing Care
609 Gender Road
Canal Winchester, OH 43110 USA
ckbeller@bright.net

Cheryl Gates-Beller is the embodiment of the best of the nursing profession — a caring, impassioned and tireless individual who understands the dynamics of quality care as it pertains to different generations. As an independent health care provider and case manager for American Nursing Care, Ms. Gates-Beller ensures quality medical management services, including home care. Her expertise is in medical-surgical nursing, palliative care and wound care management, and she is quite proficient in overseeing hi-tech intravenous services. She is also an expert witness and a legal nurse consultant.

The nursing discipline courses strongly through the veins of Ms. Gates-Beller, who has more than 45 years of experience. Her mother-in-law was a nurse who wisely advised her to absorb everything she could in her early years, to use as a lifesaving reference later. Her way of doing things has less to do with greed for the almighty dollar, a problem that plagues the capitalist health care system surrounding her. Rather, she is a woman who believes that nursing is done from the heart and "if yours is not in it, then you shouldn't be there."

Ms. Gates-Beller, who attributes her success to her management and leadership skills, has her mother, Helen Martin, to thank for so many things. She says that the matriarch, who was a survivor of breast cancer, bestowed to her the gift of life twice. When doctors discovered that her mother had cancer, Cheryl was still in her 30s. At the time, routine mammograms were not the norm for women her age. On a whim, the doctor examined Cheryl. As they found her mother's cancer, they also found Cheryl's in situ and took care of it right away. "I know that's why I'm still here today," she reflects.

Ms. Gates-Beller, a registered nurse, received a Bachelor of Science in Management of Nursing Services in 1995 from the College of Mount St. Joseph. She holds certification in medical-surgical nursing from the American Nurses Credentialing Center. Ms. Gates-Beller is a member of the Ohio Nurses Association, the Alumni Association of the College of Mount St. Joseph, the Riverside-White Cross Alumni Association and the American Nurses Association.

In her spare time, she enjoys kickboxing, exercising, and doing yoga with her daughter.

Conversation with Cheryl Gates-Beller, BSMNS, RN, BC

Cambridge Who's Who: What are your short-term and long-term career goals?
Cheryl Gates-Beller: My short-term goals are the same as my long-term goals: I want to practice nursing for as long as I can and do as much as I can. I want to accomplish and compile what I can now and project it as far as I can. With my experience and my clinical knowledge, I don't think they are going to view my age as something that is stopping me, but I've got to keep an edge, which is my goal.

On what topic(s) do you consider yourself to be an expert?
I have certifications to back up my knowledge base. I am certified in medical surgical nursing and I've had extensive critical care and infusion training. I've been certified in chemotherapy and oncology nursing.

How do you remain current in your profession?
I take as many continuing education units as I can and I read six journals a month, including RN, Nursing2010, Palliative Care and Wounded Skin Care. I even read those books such as "NCLEX-RN for Dummies" and use them for teaching because it is putting nursing into a concept that the regular person can understand.

What is the most significant issue facing your profession today?
The nursing shortage is the most significant issue. People are getting out of the hospital quicker and they are sicker when they go home. The insurance companies are basically failing everybody, which leads up to more people requiring care in the homes. That's why I feel that my place now is in home care, because you've got to have somebody who can take up where the hospital stops and try to make up for what the hospital doesn't provide.

What advice can you offer people aspiring to work in this profession?
It's like what my mother-in-law said: "Get in everything you can," and try out every area. Maybe pediatrics isn't for you and you decide to move on to working with the elderly, but you will already have a pediatric base. Everything starts and ends someplace and you can derive knowledge from that. If you

are as interested as I am, when something comes up, you will go to the library or listen to the radio, because you've got to keep up with it. If you don't know something, you're not going to be any good for yourself or for your patient. Keep it an ongoing process.

Who have been your mentors or people who have greatly influenced you?
My mother and my brother both had cancer. I took care of both of them and they taught me how to live. They also taught me how to die with dignity, and they gave me the privilege and the honor to be there by their side and help them with that. That process is a whole different thing when you are on the other side of the sheets, taking care of somebody who means that much to you. I would have to say my dad, Hoyt Martin, is another mentor of mine. I was raised on a farm, so we had things that we had to do every day of the year — that is why I still live by that policy. He gave me a strong work ethic. I am still in an occupation that is 24-7 because health care doesn't take holidays.

What are you passionate about?
I haven't found a thing in nursing that isn't interesting to me. I always come back home to nursing because that's where my heart is. I'm very passionate about family as well.

What would you like to promote most about yourself or your business?
I serve homebound patients and am interested in doing consulting. I am also looking for ways to instruct, encourage or give advice to nurses online.

What is the most rewarding aspect of your career?
I have taken something from every patient that I have ever cared for. I try to take away their fear and give them back their self-esteem. I think it has enriched me and encouraged me. It's not just me helping them; they're helping me.

Do you have a motto?
"I'm keeping the caring in health care." "Nursing is a service to all mankind."

Nephrology

Herschel R. Harter, MD
1) Associate Professor 2) Physician
1) Louisiana State University 2) Northeast Louisiana Kidney Specialists
711 Wood Street
Monroe, LA 71201 USA
randy.lay@centurytel.net
http://www.totalkidneycare.com/index.html

Being almost 70 years old doesn't stop Dr. Herschel R. Harter from doing what he loves most: taking care of his patients. He enjoys keeping himself busy and doesn't plan on stopping anytime soon. For over three decades, Dr. Harter has been both an associate professor at Louisiana State University and a physician for Northeast Louisiana Kidney Specialists.

According to the American Society of Nephrology, "each year, more than 100,000 Americans are diagnosed with kidney failure. The most common cause for kidney failure is diabetes." The physicians at the Northeast Louisiana Kidney Specialists are dedicated to patient care and the research of this disease. This group offers services such as diagnostic laboratory testing, and outpatient dialysis facilities for those with peritoneal dialysis. Dr. Harter contributes his knowledge of nephrology, hypertension and lipid research to this facility as well as the School of Medicine at Louisiana State University.

Coming from a low-income background, achieving the education he did was an accomplishment, although he admits it was challenging because of the distance put between himself and his family. Dr. Harter received a Doctor of Medicine from Georgetown University and, as the oldest sibling, was first to go to college. He paved an educational road for his siblings to follow, and now his whole family has achieved that same distinction. Hoping to remain active in both capacities, he continues practicing medicine and teaching at the university, and maintains close relationships with many whom he has treated.

Dr. Harter is board-certified in nephrology and internal medicine and keeps himself up-to-date within his field by holding memberships with such organizations as the Louisiana State Medical Society, the American Society of Nephrology and the American Federation for Medical Research. He also pursues more understanding of his profession by reading The New England Journal of Medicine.

In his spare time, he enjoys working on his horse farm, fishing and hiking.

Conversation with Herschel R. Harter, MD

Cambridge Who's Who: On what topics do you consider yourself to be an expert?
Herschel R. Harter: Nephrology, hypertension, lipid metabolism and diabetes.

What characteristics help to separate you from your competitors?
I have completed a lot of research and published over 100 papers and several chapters in books. That's what gives you more understanding about what the field really is.

What motivates you?
I am almost 70 years old and I do this because I feel so close to my patients. At my age, most [of my colleagues] have retired but I am still healthy. I still go in and do a full day's work; I still teach at Louisiana State University and practice.

What lessons have you learned as a professional in your field for the past 34 years?
The most important thing is to be patient with the patients. Ultimately, they will tell you what's wrong with them.

What short-term and long-term career goals are you currently pursuing?
I'm trying to find a way to wind down while still keeping myself busy. You cannot, if your brain works, just quit. You have to have other things to do, so I have a horse farm that keeps me busy. I also plan to continue working at the practice, at least part time, to keep my brain active.

What is the most difficult obstacle or challenge you have faced in pursuit of your goals?
I came from a relatively poor family, so achieving the education I had was the biggest difficulty. I came from Alaska and went to Georgetown University; after I left home, I almost never went back except to work in the summertime. The biggest problem was being separated from my family.

What is the most significant issue facing your profession today?
The changing health care climate.

What are some questions that an individual interested in your services can ask to ensure a more productive relationship?
I see patients with specific problems such as kidney failure and hypertension. You have to be a compliant patient who is willing to follow the recommendations that we give. Otherwise what we do fails.

What do you find to be the most rewarding about your profession?
Having a patient survive an illness and become my friend for life.

What is your favorite or least-favorite work-related task to do and why?
The paperwork is cumbersome; it is hours and hours of [signing] papers.

Who have been your mentors or people who have greatly influenced you?
Dr. George Shriner, who [was a pioneer in] the field of nephrology and worked at Georgetown University, where I was a medical student, influenced me the most. He is the reason that I went into nephrology. The chief of medicine of Barnes Hospital when I officially got there, Carl V. Moore, was also a mentor. He was the father of hematology and one of the finest teachers I ever had. Dr. Sauloklahr, the chief of nephrology at Washington University in St. Louis also influenced me.

HEPATITIS C TREATMENT

TERRY JONES-COPELAND
Staff Nurse, Registered Nurse
John H. Stroger Jr. Hospital of Cook County
1901 W. Harrison Street
Chicago, IL 60612 USA
gvcpln@sbcglobal.net
http://www.mphci.com

When it comes to the provision of quality patient care, there are many reasons to praise Terry Jones-Copeland. She is a staff nurse in the ambulatory health care department of the John H. Stroger Jr. Hospital of Cook County, and is responsible for treating and educating patients within the specialty care division. As the medical facility gradually shifts its focus to patient education, Ms. Jones-Copeland has demonstrated great enthusiasm for stepping up and being an effective communicator. The outcome is more discerning patients who take greater responsibility in following his or her most appropriate course of treatment.

Ms. Jones-Copeland approaches her patients with profound compassion and an extensive knowledge foundation. Whether she is administering diagnostic tests, analyzing results, dispensing medications or maintaining patient records, she has proven over and over again to be a reliable individual capable of deploying exemplary nursing services. She derives great pleasure receiving countless thanks from her patients, who appreciate how she helps them understand their diagnoses, medications and side effects.

For a good part of her early life, Ms. Jones-Copeland dreamed about becoming a nurse to help the less fortunate and educate them so they could understand their health problems. Prior to her role as staff nurse at John H. Stroger Jr. Hospital of Cook County, Ms. Jones-Copeland served as a staff nurse and nurse coordinator at Bethany Hospital (1986-1989), a staff nurse at Woodlawn Hospital (1985) and a staff nurse at Asher Highland Home Health (1983-1984). In the near future, with retirement around the corner, Ms. Jones-Copeland would like to return to school, receive a bachelor's degree, and consult for pharmaceutical companies.

Ms. Jones-Copeland received an associate degree in nursing from Mississippi Valley State University. She is a certified nurse preceptor and holds certification in CPR and electrocardiography. In 2006, she was the recipient of the Outstanding Employee in Specialty Care award, as recognized by the John H. Stroger Jr. Hospital of Cook County.

Conversation with Terry Jones-Copeland

Cambridge Who's Who: What prompted you to pursue a career in nursing?
Terry Jones-Copeland: My family influenced me, especially my grandfather. When he got sick, I decided to take care of him. In tending to him, I felt that I could provide care for others.

How old were you at the time?
I was 16 years old.

What would you like to promote most about yourself or your business?
I participate in a lot of patient education, which is a major focus at our hospital.

What is the most rewarding aspect of your career?
Taking care of patients and seeing them get better.

What is your greatest professional accomplishment to date?
Becoming a nurse.

What are your short-term and long-term career goals?
My plan is to retire early and go back to school.

What are you trying to pursue?
I am looking to get a bachelor's degree in nursing so I can do consulting.

On what topic(s) do you consider yourself to be an expert?
The treatment of hepatitis C.

What are you passionate about?
Computers — there's a lot I don't know and a lot I want to know. I was just speaking to one of my colleagues about this. I told her I want to learn how to make bulletins with pictures in it. I know how to make bulletins, but I don't know how to crop the pictures. I can then make them more professional to help build my business.

What advice can you offer fellow members who work in your industry?
Study hard, stay focused and don't give up.

Mental Health Case Management

Ann N. Kalesnick
Case Manager Registered Nurse,
Qualified Mental Retardation Professional
Washington State Department of Social and Health Services
P.O. Box 200
Medical Lake, WA 99022 USA
kalesan@dshs.wa.gov

According to the American Nurses Association, Florence Nightingale, in her "Notes on Nursing: What It Is and What It Is Not," defined nursing as having "charge of the personal health of somebody...and what nursing has to do...is to put the patient in the best condition for nature to act upon him." Ann N. Kalesnick has exemplified this definition throughout her three decades as a registered nurse, the success of which can be attributed to her determination and caring nature. A registered nurse manager and qualified mental retardation professional for the Washington State Department of Social and Health Services, Ms. Kalesnick understands the philosophy of nursing as it pertains to the care of the patient instead of focusing solely on the sickness.

The mission of the Washington State Department of Social and Health Services is "to improve the safety and health of individuals, families and communities by providing leadership and establishing and participating in partnerships." Ms. Kalesnick personifies this statement and is open to the new adventures that each day brings as she takes care of mentally challenged individuals and assists physicians in diagnosing patients. Although a general perception is that nurses maintain lower status or less responsibility than doctors, the specialized education and commitment to excellence for each patient that nurses provide is certainly not to be overlooked or underrated. Following her intuition, Ms. Kalesnick has come to know that her instincts and strive to reach her goals are invaluable tools along the path to becoming the best health care provider she can be.

Ms. Kalesnick is certified in mental health nursing and in 1985 received an associate degree in nursing from Bakersfield College. She stays up-to-date on her industry through interactions with others in her community and her professional affiliations with the Washington State Nurses Association and The American Nurses Association, Inc. She enjoys reading and gardening in her spare time, and sells collectibles, gifts and various other items through a family-owned store called "Medical Lake Emporium."

Conversation with Ann N. Kalesnick

Cambridge Who's Who: What would you like to promote most about yourself or your business?
Ann N. Kalesnick: There's a real need in today's world for my profession. For example, there was a woman I knew, who was just a few years from retirement when I worked with her. From her late teenage years, she was a nurse. She said that when she first started, only the doctors could take blood pressure. Now all kinds of things come down to staff other than the doctor. We have physician assistants and RNs and those positions are becoming increasingly important. The nurse still has that holistic approach that is different from the physician assistants'.

What is the most rewarding aspect of your career?
Seeing that my intuition worked, I was right and that it has helped is a really good feeling.

What is your greatest professional accomplishment to date?
I don't take no for an answer because a lot of times, people say that I can't do it. If I see something I want to accomplish, I just go ahead and do it.

What are your short-term and long-term career goals?
My short-term goal is to get through the day. My long-term goal is to continue being productive because after you've worked at a position long enough and a lot of people have either retired or left, the things that the previous people did may not be what the new people have decided they want to do. You always have to be open for a challenge.

What is the most difficult obstacle or challenge you have faced in pursuit of your goals?
People who didn't want me to do [certain] things.

On what topics do you consider yourself to be an expert?
Being able to draw out the records and look at a person to see what their needs are.

How do you remain current in your profession?
Through my interactions among the community. We have people who go into the hospital or clinics and all of their paperwork comes back through me. I have a piece of everybody's discipline and I relate it to what I do. When I work

with the staff in other disciplines (such as in client rights), they bring all kinds of information with them. I interact with them and learn.

What is the most significant issue facing your profession today?
Recruitment and retention.

What advice can you offer fellow members who work in your industry?
You look for the cause and once you find the cause, you can find the solution; or somebody can help you find the solution.

What are you passionate about?
Keeping the records straight. If you don't have any organization to your records or your tasks, you just spin your wheels.

Who have been your mentors or people who have greatly influenced you?
Dr. Alesic, Lois Page, one of my instructors and an assistant superintendent to a California Hospital all influenced me.

Speech and Language Pathology

Sandra K. Lee
Director of Speech and Language Pathology
Amedisys
Biloxi, MS 39531 USA
sandralee52@yahoo.com

The one field that is too often underrepresented in its relevance to the health care industry may very well be the profession of speech pathology. Sandra K. Lee, now directing and developing the speech pathology program for Amedisys of Biloxi, Miss., may be one unofficial spokesperson. She firmly believes that the expertise derived from the unique professional training of a speech pathologist often becomes an essential link to the medical survival, cognitive enhancement, communicative rehabilitation or educational welfare of many patients.

Mrs. Lee bases much of her work on the recognition of brain plasticity and its ability to remediate — even after a lengthy duration of etiology onset. Neuroplasticity is the transformation of neurons and reorganization of neural networks, and their function, due to new and life-changing experiences. Recognition of brain plasticity has resulted in numerous patients experiencing productive therapeutic gains far beyond time restraints that once limited speech pathology intervention. Her work has been highly influenced by William Matteson, Ph.D., and includes traumatic brain injury, cerebrovascular accidents, anoxia, and additional diagnosis with a highly variable duration of etiology onset.

Early life experiences that included a mother blinded by Von Hippel–Lindau disease and brothers experiencing an array of disorders including deafness and cerebral palsy promoted her to leave an administrative position within a 220-bed facility to seek her current degree. Prior to her current position, Mrs. Lee developed and directed speech pathology programs for Regency Hospital, the Tom C. Maynor Rehabilitation Center, and Riley Hospital. Her work has also included additional acute care, rehabilitation, educational, outpatient, and long-term care facilities.

Her areas of expertise include tracheo-esophogeal prosthetics, tracheostomy/vent patient care, advanced studies in voice disorders, dysphagia intervention with extensive work in videofluoroscopy, cognitive rehabilitation, language disorders, speech disorders, and communicative disorders. She has initiated extensive work in The Listening Program created by Advanced Brain Technologies, and researched and designed many innovative programs, such as caloric concentration, natural viscosity options for dysphagia, thermal packing, and an airway protection program, which include applications to the cardiopulmonary and COPD (chronic obstructive pulmonary disease) patient. Mrs. Lee is currently writing and editing "The Quick Reference to Swallow," as well as an inspirational book entitled "Patient I Give You Beauty." She has spoken at conferences for radiology specialists, in educational settings (nursing and psychology departments), and for a diverse group of medical professionals.

Mrs. Lee received her degrees from the University of Southern Mississippi, graduating with highest honors upon receiving her bachelor's degree in speech and language sciences in 1988 and master's degree in speech pathology in 1989. She graduated as a Phi Kappa Phi scholar and has received additional awards for excellence and quality of patient care.

Conversation with Sandra K. Lee

Cambridge Who's Who: What would you like to promote most about yourself or your business?
Sandra K. Lee: Speech pathology provides the essential bridge to communication barriers and numerous unique medical interventions that are an essential link to effective medical care, while providing support and training to family and significant others.

What is the most rewarding aspect of your career?
My greatest reward definitely lies in the rehabilitative progress and improved quality of life that so greatly impacts the lives of my patients and their loved ones.

What is your greatest professional accomplishment to date?
There is no greater joy than to provide speech pathology services to many who have failed to meet their full rehabilitative potential years after the onset of their disability. My greatest patient experience happens to be Alexandria Jordan Thompson, my granddaughter. After surviving the impact of a large truck traveling 85 mph into her door, Alexandra was described as "a blank slate." Just a few of her injuries included global brain bleeding, left hemisphere skull compression, as well as two compressed regions of the frontal lobe, cerebral fluid loss from her left ear, corpus callosum destruction, and the blow of the shifting gear to her upper brain stem region. My years of experience in the amazing field of speech pathology, the firm belief in the neuroplasticity of the brain, and an unfailing faith in Alexandria's creator and her Lord and Savior, Jesus Christ, provided the strength and knowledge to exceed every boundary placed upon Alexandria's recovery. Educators doubted her ability to return to school, even with a special education placement. Today, Alexandria is a beautiful, 17-year-old blue-eyed blonde who scored junior college-level in math and English skills. She is not only school-bound; Alexandria is college-bound! My deepest thanks go to Abby Wells, the young college student who always believed in Andrea's neuroplasticity!

How do you remain current in your profession?
The process is unrelenting. A few of the resources include accessing the Amedisys Learning Lab. However, personal research includes the study of medical journals, medical websites, medical consults, and selected conferences.

What are your short-term and long-term career goals?
In the short term, my goal will be to keep my knowledge and training current, including the completion of a Ph.D., which was placed on hold after Alexandria's

recovery. In the long term, I will strive to develop the highest-quality speech pathology program for Amedisys of Biloxi, Miss., while continuing to develop innovative therapeutic interventions that prove beneficial to our patients.

What is the most difficult obstacle or challenge you have faced in pursuit of your goals?
The greatest challenge to date is to develop the highest-level speech pathology program for Amedisys of Biloxi, Miss. The establishment of such a program required educating all medical staff pertinent to the patient's care of the diverse etiology and symptomatology of dysphagia and cognitive disorders while building a strong team approach. Therapeutic outcomes are often related to the early onset of patient referral.

What is the most significant issue facing your profession today?
To continue and inform and educate the surrounding medical fields and patient community of the vital role speech pathology plays in the optimal health care of many patients. The diverse symptomatology and correlating primary diagnosis that warrant a speech pathology referral are too often overlooked before the exacerbation of dysphagia or cognitive/language deficits that thwart optimal outcomes. Possibly, the most under-referred patient will be the silent aspiration and/or the pulmonary/cardiopulmonary patient caseload.

If you could offer advice to fellow members who work in your industry, what would you say?
My advice would be to comprehend that their knowledge base and training is never complete. Seek out a mentor who evidences a vast array of skills, experience, and most of all, professional ethics. Without character and high ethical standards, the speech pathology care becomes a hollow resource for patient care.

Who have been your mentors or people who have greatly influenced you?
My greatest influence can be found in Psalms 119: 97-105. When once asked by Dr. Proli who my mentor was, my honest response was "My God and Savior Jesus Christ." Fortunately, he placed Dr. Etoile DuBard in my path. Her support was amazing, as it was with many other speech pathologists. The work of William Matteson has proved vital in patient care and the confidence to provide successful intervention to many who have long exceeded the norms of therapeutic referrals.

Do you have a motto or principle that guides your work?
Every patient is deserving of the highest-quality patient care and my utmost effort to provide that care with sincere respect and support.

Nursing and Clinical Management

Judith M. Lynch
Clinical Manager
Exempla Healthcare
1835 Franklin Street
Denver, CO 80218 USA
lynchj@exempla.org

Inspired by her mother, who was also a nurse, Judith M. Lynch has been developing her proficiency in patient safety within the health care industry for more than 40 years. Now the clinical manager for Saint Joseph Hospital (part of Exempla Healthcare), Ms. Lynch goes in to perform her job duties with grace and humility. Additionally, she seizes any opportunity to mentor new and upcoming nurses, preparing them for the challenging territory and constant changes the field of nursing brings.

Ever since Saint Joseph Hospital broke ground in 1961, it has been offering safe and efficient health care to the Denver, Colo., community and earned acknowledgement nationwide for offering top-tier care. Thrice it was ranked nationally as one of the Top 100 Teaching Hospitals by Mercer Management Consulting, Inc., and HICA, Inc. It is the leading heart hospital in Denver and performs more than 400 open-heart surgeries annually. The facility also delivers more babies than any other Colorado hospital, with nearly 5,000 births in 2009. Working at one of the largest nonprofit hospitals in the region, Ms. Lynch brings expertise in the care of post-surgical orthopedic and neurosurgical patients. She enjoys helping the people who come into her care and continually hopes to make a difference, for the better, in their lives.

As an avid coach and mentor to young nurses, Ms. Lynch takes great pleasure in helping others to comprehend what they can expect. "You really have to know what you're getting into," Ms. Lynch explains. "People's expectations are not always realistic." She feels that when someone becomes a nurse, it is truly a calling; you can't pursue it for the money.

The field of health care is ever-changing and the work is never-ending. However, Ms. Lynch is very thankful for her staff and as a manager with exceptional leadership skills, she always acknowledges a job well done. "I don't like to toot my own horn," she says. "I like to credit the people who really do the actual work. "I really feel that if it's the staff that did it, then they need to get the kudos."

A registered nurse, Ms. Lynch received a Bachelor of Science in Nursing from the University of St. Francis. She also obtained certification in medical-surgical nursing.

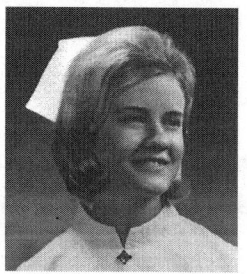

Conversation with Judith M. Lynch

Cambridge Who's Who: On what topics do you consider yourself to be an expert?
Judith M. Lynch: Mentoring and coaching, and new experiences and opportunities.

What do you find to be the most rewarding about your profession?
Making a difference in people's lives.

Did you ever consider pursuing a different career path or another profession? If yes, how did you end up working in your current field?
I actually wanted to be a nun while growing up. I also considered being an airline stewardess, but nursing was something I sort of fell into.

What is your favorite or least-favorite work-related task to do and why?
My most favorite is task giving out rewards and recognition. My least favorite is having to counsel my staff.

What advice can you offer fellow members or others aspiring to work in your industry?
You need to sit down with a person who is doing the job you want to do and have them tell you what they do from day to day. People tend to want jobs because of the money and that's not why people should become nurses or managers. It is a calling and you have to be a leader as well as a manager — there is a difference between the two.

If you could be an advocate or spokesperson for any major health issue, what would it be and why?
I am not for Obama's health care reform. I think that there are a lot of problems with what he wants to do; he has an altruistic attitude that everyone is entitled to health insurance. The fact is that not everybody wants health insurance and everybody can get health care if and when they need it. Nobody is ever denied the care. At my hospital, we never turn anybody away and we take care of patients for as long as it takes.

What short-term and long-term career goals are you currently pursuing?
My particular unit is going to make a move from where I am now to across

the street. We will be doing all of our surgeries over there — pre-operative and post-operative. That is a huge challenge because it is different from what we do now and it will probably take a year for that transition to be complete. Another goal is that we hope to increase our patient and staff satisfaction. My long-term goal is to retire in three years.

What is the most difficult obstacle or challenge you have faced in pursuit of your goals?
This particular field is ever-changing and nothing ever stays the same. If a nurse left the field for two or three years, she wouldn't know that it would be so different [when she returned]. The technology is different, the patients are more engaged and informed, and they ask more questions.

BLOOD BANK OPERATIONS

SANDRA ANTOINETTE MARTINEZ
Apheresis Manager
New York Blood Center
1200 Prospect Avenue
Westbury, NY 11590 USA
smartinez@nybloodcenter.org
http://www.nybloodcenter.org

Sandra Antoinette Martinez realizes that in order for life to flow smoothly in urban centers, blood banks must have a constant supply available to the public. As the apheresis manager for the New York Blood Center, she is in charge of overseeing the bank's operations, which includes training nurses and medical technicians to work with blood, communicating effectively with patients and donors, and enforcing best practices. With more than 36 years of professional experience, Ms. Martinez is most certainly an innovator, leader and facilitator for improvements at the NYBC. Recently, she has begun work to import a European process whereby additives are introduced to a blood solution to effectively carry platelets, which in turn will require less plasma. Once approved by the FDA, the Platelet Additive Solution, or PAS, will help to bring blood availability to more safe and desirable levels.

Ms. Martinez became involved in her profession because she thoroughly aspired to help people. Early in her career, she served as a nurse at the Long Island Jewish Medical Center for three years, where she transfused the products that she now provides through the NYBC. She readily admits that nursing as it relates to blood work has fulfilled her in many ways, least not because of the disciplinary aspects. She believes it to be a challenging field, which teaches health care professionals how to use inductive reasoning and anticipate patients' needs. "If I were to die tomorrow, I would say that I did the best I could to help as many people as possible," she beams.

An expert in the field of phlebotomy, Ms. Martinez has published three abstracts. Additionally, she moderates and presents forums on apheresis, transfusion practices and innovative technologies for the AABB (formerly the American Association of Blood Banks) and local medical organizations. She received a Master of Science in Nursing Informatics and Nursing Administration from Molloy College. She is a member of the American Association of Blood Banks, the American Sighthound Field Association, Sigma Theta Tau International and Psi Chi.

In her spare time, Ms. Martinez enjoys horseback riding, fishing and watching movies.

CONVERSATION WITH SANDRA ANTOINETTE MARTINEZ

CAMBRIDGE WHO'S WHO: What would you like to promote most about yourself or your business?
SANDRA ANTOINETTE MARTINEZ: In the last 36 years, I stayed at this job rather than go to a hospital because I'm working with donors who are the most wonderful people because they get nothing for their donation. I think what has kept me in this job is the people whom I have met, who have such good hearts. In discussing blood banking with the donors, we realize it's all about the patients in our community hospitals and that there is never enough blood. That supply has to be there.

What is the most rewarding aspect of your career?
When I first started nursing in 1967 at the Long Island Jewish Medical Center, I transfused this gentleman at night to keep him from hemorrhaging. After I left and became a registered nurse, I saw this man; it was years later, but I was at the other end, collecting blood for him.

What is your greatest professional accomplishment to date?
Understanding that nursing has many roles and faces and that nurses make a difference. This includes blood banking, where nurses can bring a certain level of professionalism and expertise. For instance, nurses can explain sterile techniques to technician, plus all of those things for which we have an education. I'm proud that I became a nurse because I had been diagnosed with a learning disability and I was told that I would only ever be a beautician. I proved them wrong. Not only did I do the sciences, but I also have a bachelor's degree in sociology, psychology and anthropology. I graduated with honors.

What are your short-term and long-term career goals?
My big goal is to make more platelets products so that this company can be more self- sufficient, where we don't have to buy out-of-state blood. We are the first in the nation to bring in the European way of platelet drawing. It would be a change by adding PAS, which is a big thing. They use less plasma, with an additive. In Europe they take less plasma from their donors and substitute it with a sugar saline solution, which keeps the platelets alive just as well as the plasma.

And what specific steps have you taken toward achieving these goals?
The federal corporation is in the process of trying to get clearance. This PAS solution is being used in Europe, so we gave all the information to the FDA and we are currently waiting for them to approve it. Then, we will attempt to replicate what they are doing in Europe. Studies will be done and then we will be working with hospitals to see if the patients do better with this product.

What is the most difficult obstacle or challenge you have faced in pursuit of your goals?
Besides getting the FDA approval for PAS, it's a matter of paper work. We will be the first in the nation, so there are validation protocols that must be met, which means additional, extensive research has to be done.

On what topic(s) do you consider yourself to be an expert?
My expertise is in working in conjunction with all the other disciplines to make this FDA approval happen. I work with my colleagues to help make this a reality.

How do you remain current in your profession?
I read a lot of the blood bank journals. I get daily updates from the American Association of Blood Banks on my computer. The American Association of Blood Banks is key for our industry. I read the American Blood Center newsletters and I try to stay as current as I can.

What makes you a valuable resource in your industry?
I think it is my experience because I was on both ends of the process, transfusing and collecting blood. One of the things that make a blood donor tick is, usually, that they have had family members who have had to use blood. They come in because they realize the importance of it. I've heard from my donors about what has happened in their family. Everyone has a really important story to tell.

What is the most significant issue facing your profession today?
The biggest thing is getting the word out for the New York Blood Center on how important it is to donate on a regular basis, to keep the supplies replenished for when we need them (we only have a donor basis of 8,000). A significant issue is getting the young people to donate blood, because we need every last one of them.

What advice can you offer people aspiring to work in this profession?
Blood work is probably the most rewarding thing you can do. People don't see what goes on in the background to make blood [transfusions] happen in the hospital. We need people to go into the sciences to become nurses and medical technicians who can analyze blood.

What are you passionate about?
I'm passionate about helping people.

Who have been your mentors or people who have greatly influenced you?
My mother, Rosemary, was a widow at 43 years old, with five kids. She greatly influenced me. Essentially, she picked up and kept the family going; she went back to school and received her degree in accounting.

I also learned my nursing skills from a woman named Jenrose Alfano, who brought me to another level. I worked with her in primary nursing, when it wasn't being used in any other part of the United States. She was a nurse with a master's degree and taught other nurses to think like doctors. She fought with doctors for patient care and was a phenomenal nurse educator. She made a very big difference in my life.

ARTHROSCOPY AND TOTAL JOINT ARTHROPLASTY

CARL EUGENE MCCULLOUGH

Orthopedic Resource Coordinator, Physician Assistant
Memorial Health Care System
3213 Harrison Pike
Chattanooga, TN 37406 USA
carl_mccullough@memorial.org
http://www.memorial.org

Carl Eugene McCullough, orthopedic resource coordinator and physician assistant for the Memorial Health Care System, has more than 32 years of experience in orthopedic services. For the past 10 years, he has assisted physicians as they conduct orthopedic, neuro, plastic and spinal fusion surgeries for the Memorial Health Care System. He also acts as a liaison between physicians and the hospital. Prior to starting a career in health care, Mr. McCullough worked in television for eight years, and was able to support his way through college. He began studying to become a dentist and then took a greater interest in orthopedics. As his career progressed, he became more of an expert in knee and hip arthroplasty. He has also taken on a role of orthopedic staff supervision.

Serving South Florida residents for more than 55 years, Memorial Health Care System has grown to become the fifth-largest health care organization of its kind in the United States. The company, which is comprised of the flagship Memorial Regional Hospital and several affiliate locations, provides exceptional medical and surgical services and has been honored by numerous publications (including Modern Healthcare and Florida Trend). Additionally, the American Hospital Association bestowed Memorial Health Care System with the Living the Vision Award and the Foster G. McGaw Award, which designates certain health care centers as national models for the improvement of community health.

Mr. McCullough, who attributes his success to the support he receives from his family, received a Bachelor of Science in Biology in 1985 from The University of North Alabama. In 1979, he received an associate degree in orthopedic physician assistant technology. He is a certified CPR instructor and teaches cardiopulmonary resuscitation to others. He is also a member of the Tennessee Society of Orthopaedic Physician's Assistants and the American Society of Orthopaedic Physician's Assistants.

In his free time, Mr. McCullough enjoys playing basketball and tennis, biking, and swimming.

CONVERSATION WITH CARL EUGENE MCCULLOUGH

CAMBRIDGE WHO'S WHO: What is the most rewarding aspect of your career?
CARL EUGENE MCCULLOUGH: Having the ability to help people in need.

Who have been your mentors or people who have greatly influenced you?
My father, Willard Jones, inspired me by being a good role model and showing me a good work ethic. Several male teachers during elementary and high school helped influence me as well.

What is your greatest professional accomplishment to date?
My greatest professional accomplishment to date has been my longevity and longstanding professionalism.

What are your short-term and long-term career goals?
My short-term goal is to keep up with the current technology because it's always changing, especially in orthopedics.

And what specific steps have you taken toward achieving these goals?
I am participating in continuing education and going to different meetings. I look at websites and attend conventions.

What is the most difficult obstacle or challenge you have faced in pursuit of your goals?
You have to keep the right attitude about certain things. Sometimes, financially, it can be tough when you're trying to do everything.

On what topic(s) do you consider yourself to be an expert?
Arthroscopy and total joint arthroplasty.

What makes you a valuable resource in your industry?
My years of experience.

What is the most significant issue facing your profession today?
It would be cost. With the health care industry the way it is, health care reform is very critical to the things that we do.

What advice can you offer fellow members who work in your industry?
Stay professional and current on whatever it is that you do. Be up on the latest technology and stay abreast.

What advice can you offer people aspiring to work in this profession?
Try to be associated with people who are go-getters, or with an institution that is progressive.

What are you passionate about?
Respect for patients.

Do you have a motto?
"Above all do no harm."

ADDICTION PSYCHIATRY

ARNOLD MECH
Physician
The Mech Center
7500 San Jacinto Place
Plano, TX 75024 USA
amy.mech@themechcenter.com
http://www.themechcenter.com

Dr. Arnold Mech doesn't readily consider himself to be a holistic practitioner, which, to some, may mean the use of incense instead of alternative treatments and self-generated techniques to treat medical issues. However, the approach he takes with patients who seek help with their various addictions is predicated upon a comprehensive view of the biological and psychological factors that affect a person's ability to understand and cope with their disorder. With certifications in child, adolescent, adult and addiction psychiatry, and a designation as an American Society of Addiction Medicine-certified addictionist, Dr. Mech brings more than 20 years of qualified experience to his work counseling patients at The Mech Center outpatient and research clinic. Overseeing a team of health care professionals whose mission is to provide personalized treatment options, he ensures that after an initial assessment, diagnosis and plan of action, his patients possess the keys necessary to unlock their greatest potential and transform their lives.

If medication has been prescribed for a patient, Dr. Mech and his clinical team manage the regimen to assist in the healing process and facilitate a return to healthy living. Every patient does not require a prescription, however, and Dr. Mech is adamant about reducing overmedication by considering numerous possibilities for a person's particular imbalance. He says, "You want to think outside the box and use a different frame of reference — look at all potential factors. Consider neurons in the brain; it's all interrelated and your interventions need to be very comprehensive." Rather than merely determining that a person has a symptomatic disorder, he helps them to make lifestyle changes and take a self-directed approach to managing their mental and overall health.

Beginning in 1974, Dr. Mech embarked on a lifelong journey of learning with a Bachelor of Science in Biology earned at Loyola University, followed by an MD from the Loyola School of Medicine and a psychiatric residency at the Loyola Medical Center. He then completed another psychiatric residency at the Karl Menninger School of Psychiatry and Mental Health Sciences before obtaining a fellowship in child psychiatry from the Menninger Foundation. Currently, Dr. Mech conducts field-related research in his specialty and proffers his findings in industry publications and professional meetings. He also interacts with other mental health care professionals as a member of the American Medical Association; the American Psychiatric Association; the American Academy of Child Adolescent Psychiatry; the American Academy of Addiction Psychiatry; the American Society of Addiction Medicine; and the International Association of Eating Disorder Professionals.

CONVERSATION WITH ARNOLD MECH

CAMBRIDGE WHO'S WHO: **What would you like to promote most about yourself or your practice?**

ARNOLD MECH: As an industry expert in addiction psychiatry, I'm passionate about the brain and looking at the interrelationship among some of the factors that may predispose people to develop substance [addictions] and other psychiatric disorders. It's important to think outside of the box and look for underlying, predisposing and perpetuating factors. Once those are addressed, it can lead to a reduced burden of symptoms that enhance a person's overall psychiatric wellness. I presented some original research in Istanbul for the European College of Neuropsychopharmacology in September 2009. The topic was "Possible Biomarker for Substance Use Disorder in ADHD Patients," subtitled "Managing Risk and Maximizing Benefits." For example, a person can have a vitamin D deficiency, which until the last few years, had not really been appreciated in psychiatry. Vitamin D is important for bone health, but a significant deficiency can contribute to a person's symptoms in addiction psychiatry. In the past year, we've been looking at patients who've had low or low-normal vitamin D levels and witnessed significant improvement in their conditions.

What is the most rewarding aspect of your career?

The most rewarding aspect is being able to take people where they are, partner with them, and get them to a point where they're doing as well as they should be doing. I always tell people I'm not a psychiatric apologist – I'm an apologetic psychiatrist because I get a lot of people that have been treated, but no one got passionately interested in them. They shouldn't have to get used to being depressed, or one step ahead of a relapse of whatever substance they've been using to self-medicate. I think it really helps to be able to join someone... [who may have lost grasp of hope]...and say, "Things can be better than this. It's not just about getting by." That's not an abundant expectation for their life; they should be able to have a lot more passion and excitement. If they don't live life with passion, it's not good.

What has been your greatest professional accomplishment to date?

I tell people I've been doing this for 30 years, I've got five certifications, I present original research internationally, and then I hold up my thumb and forefinger about two inches apart and say, "I know this much about the brain." Most of what I've learned has been from listening to patients, thinking with them and thinking about what's been missed so far. The greatest accomplishment I've achieved is listening to patients tell me how to treat them. I've studied the interrelationship between sleep, addiction, vulnerability and other disorders. It's really been my pleasure and privilege to have patients tell me about things they don't always want to share. They used to think in the 1970s that you were born with 100 billion brain cells, you lose some every day and then you die. The reality is that the brain is like a garden that grows. When you take people from miserable to half miserable, that's not really the goal. Instead, the goal is to treat their symptoms aggressively until completely remitted so they get to a full level of wellness; help to build their neural network so they become less vulnerable to relapse. Medication has become a stepping stone to not needing medicine. If they leave with more hope than they came with, I'm happy.

What are your short-term and long-term career goals?
My short-term goal is to present some of this vitamin D information at the European College of Neuropyschopharmacology's next meeting in Amsterdam. We've looked at well over 100 patients to see if they've had significant changes and measured their level of depression on some of the inventories I've authored, before and after the vitamin D intervention. We should have a way to think about some of these vitamin D levels – what does it do for your brain? What are some of the things we could do to assess and treat people for something as innocuous as vitamin D [deficiency]?

A long-term goal is to set up a nonprofit educational research foundation to be as comprehensive as possible in finding all of the things that relate to brain functioning, things we can control. We don't have control of what genetic predispositions we're given, but that doesn't mean it's a sentence you have to live out; you can look for the factors that you can influence and manage that predisposition.

What is the most difficult obstacle or challenge you have faced in pursuit of your goals?
Managed care — companies that come in and try to dictate to the patient and their physicians what medicines and doses are best. It's out of control!

On what topics do you consider yourself to be an expert?
Child and adolescent psychiatry — in fact I'm currently involved in a research trial looking at ADHD-associated insomnia, which has never been studied

before. The study looks to see if you can get kids to actually sleep as long as they need in the developmental point in their life, to help them focus better. It also looks at medicines that treat adults. I'm also an expert in sleep medicine and its relation to psychiatric disorders. We look at data from sleep studies to see why people have psychiatric symptoms during the waking hours and make interventions that will not only help symptoms, but improve people's sleep quality and continuity at night.

How do you remain current in your profession?
I attend and present at national and international conferences, conduct research, and write. I'm currently working on a book about some of my studies.

What makes you a valuable resource in your industry?
When I'm involved in a patient's care, I'm really a passionate advocate for a positive outcome for them. I'm not likely to accept that this is as good as it gets. When someone comes to me, I don't simply say, "OK you're on this medicine, which seems to be better than nothing; here's your prescription. See you in a month."

I feel like I'm a resource because my hopes for them are that they can do better than what they are. In the worst cases, we get accustomed to people having significant impairment in their functioning because of addiction and psychiatric disorders. For example, I was at a conference a couple of years ago and there was a room with maybe 400 addiction psychiatrists discussing treatment where the question was asked, "How many of you are successful at getting people off of buprenorphine?" I raised my hand because we probably get about 80 percent of our patients off buprenorphine in six to 12 months. I looked around and there were only about 15 to 20 hands.

Nursing Administration

Doris J. Parris
Registered Nurse, Supervisor
The Brooklyn Hospital Center
121 DeKalb Avenue
Brooklyn, NY 11201 USA
dparmat@aol.com

Doris J. Parris was a registered nurse at New York Methodist Hospital, where she had been employed for more than a decade. With over 24 years of expertise in nursing supervision, Ms. Parris ensured quality patient care through total quality management. Additionally, she oversaw such critical aspects of the hospital as medical strategies, nursing administration and ambulatory nursing. Currently Ms. Parris serves as a registered nurse and supervisor for the Nurse-Family Partnership (NFP) of The Brooklyn Hospital Center, a nurse home visitation program for low-income first-time parents and their offspring.

Ms. Parris reads RN and ADVANCE for Nurses (among other industry-related publications) to remain abreast of new trends and technologies. For as long as she could remember, she always desired to become a nurse. She attributes her success to her God-given talent of mercy and desire to help others. "I just love what I do and I have a spirit of caring and feeling for other individuals," she says.

The satisfaction she gains from making a positive difference in patients' lives is apparent, but none gives her a bigger smile than assisting someone to welcome the gift of new life. In the past when she helped her pregnant clients to give birth, to her delight they would sometimes bring the baby back to the facility where she worked — an experience she says is nothing short of wonderful. "I realize that I bring new life into the world," she explains, "and a little bit of me — sometimes, based on one or two words of advice of inspiration — helps prepare them for taking care of this new life."

In 1985, Ms. Parris received a Bachelor of Science in Nursing from Syracuse University. During her time off, she enjoys spending time at church. The Brooklyn Hospital Center is a 464-bed hospital providing a realm of high-quality inpatient, ambulatory and emergency services to the community of Brooklyn, N.Y. Founded in May 1845 as Brooklyn City Hospital, it has continued to serve its patients with top doctors and nurses to start the healing process as quickly as possible in order for them to go home to their loved ones.

Conversation with Doris J. Parris

Cambridge Who's Who: What is the most rewarding aspect of your career?
Doris J. Parris: The feedback that you get from your clients at the end of the day — to know that you have given a little bit of yourself and they have either received it or accepted what you have given to them; also, that they are able to take it and use it to improve their life.

What is your greatest professional accomplishment to date?
Everything — all the work I did in my nursing field was not for me; it was for the betterment of my patient and/or client.

What are your short-term and long-term career goals?
I am in a new job position as a nurse home visitor, so my short-term goal is to continue to learn, master and excel at what I am doing right now. It's a client-centered position (in that it is run more by the client than the nurse), so it's really learning and mastering that skill that will help me improve upon what I do for the community. My long-term goal is to strive in a supervisory position, if it's available; also, to continue learning my current position and any additional duties that come with it.

On what topic(s) do you consider yourself to be an expert?
Nursing is an ongoing and evolving profession, so I am always learning and practicing new things. I can speak on nursing.

What advice can you offer people aspiring to work in this profession?
If nursing is what you aspire to do, you must have a love and passion for the profession; you also have to be a people person to do it.

What advice can you offer fellow members who work in your industry?
If nursing is what you love, stay the course and continue to do what you do to the best of your ability.

What are you passionate about?
Being home, loving my home lifestyle, and having the opportunity to spend time with my family.

Who have been your mentors or people who have greatly influenced you?
My mom, Ruth Matthews, who has passed away, was my most valuable resource. She always said, "You can do anything you set your mind to." The sky is the limit – never stop dreaming!

What is the most difficult obstacle or challenge you have faced in pursuit of your goals?
I don't consider myself to have had any obstacles and I attribute that to my strong will. I don't look at them as obstacles, but rather as challenges.

What is the most significant issue facing your profession today?
Budget cuts have had the most impact.

How do you remain current in your profession?
Since part of this new program is run by the Department of Health, they always have ongoing training and seminars for the nurses, which will keep us updated on all the new things that affect our profession. Of course I read Nursing Spectrum; there are always online articles that you can read to keep yourself updated.

Do you have a motto or favorite quote?
"Always strive for a spirit of excellence," and "Life can become complicated and it is your challenge to keep it simple."

NURSING INFORMATICS

NANCY RAGSDALE, RN, MSN
Chief Advanced Clinical Consultant
NR Consulting Group
365 Endicott Drive
Soldotna, AK 99669 USA
nragsdale@att.net

Nancy Ragsdale is the chief advanced clinical consultant in the management department of NR Consulting Group. Her role as a specialist and advisor has taken her to numerous hospitals and clinics, where she builds relationships with facility staff and assists them in developing and implementing health care information services for electronic medical records. As a former registered nurse in the diagnostic unit of a health care center, Ms. Ragsdale has more than 35 years of relevant, hands-on experience, which includes the effective communication and transfer of knowledge to staff that will be maintaining the system.

In changing careers (after many years of bedside nursing), it took perseverance and the support of her husband Thomas to achieve success. But considering how complex it is to run a health care facility, Ms. Ragsdale — who reads the Online Journal of Nursing Informatics and Computer Informatics Nursing — maintains a keen understanding of the integration that goes on between the many areas and departments. She is flexible, compassionate and knowledgeable, all qualities that separate her from her peers. The most gratifying aspect of Ms. Ragsdale's career is seeing the spark in the people with whom she works and knowing that their newfound comprehension will benefit the patients.

Ms. Ragsdale received a Master of Science in Nursing with a minor in education from the University of California, San Francisco and a bachelor's degree in information technology from Almeda University. She is a critical care registered nurse and a cardiovascular clinical nurse specialist. Ms. Ragsdale is a member of the American Nursing Informatics Association, the American Association of Critical-Care Nurses and Sigma Theta Tau International. She is the recipient of the Award for Excellence in Critical Care Nursing from the American Association of Critical-Care Nurses.

In the near future, Ms. Ragsdale hopes to retire, at which point she will spend more time with her family, traveling, going to the beach, painting, and practicing photography.

Conversation with Nancy Ragsdale, RN, MSN

Cambridge Who's Who: What are your short term and long-term career goals?
Nancy Ragsdale: My short-term goal includes working several more years full time until I retire — I don't expect that to be any time soon. I hope to be able to do remote work a few years after that. There may be some articles or even a book in my future. Long-term goals include walking on the beach with my husband after retirement and enjoying my hobbies.

What specific steps have you taken toward achieving these goals?
The best way I have found to achieve any goal is to learn all one can and actively participate in knowledge sharing.

On what topics do you consider yourself to be an expert?
I consider myself to be knowledgeable in electronic documentation to a degree that I can assist facilities in achieving their goals.

How do you stay current in your profession?
I read articles, peruse websites, attend relevant seminars and communicate often with a wide network of colleges.

What makes you a valuable resource in your industry?
I have worked in a variety of positions within the industry. I worked at facilities that had all paper documentation, to minimal electronic functions, to being fully electronic. My years employed at the bedside, teaching and in management (prior to getting into development), give me a good sense of what the health care system should provide.

What is the most significant issue facing your profession today?
Finances, as with every other profession. Facilities have many buckets to put their budget toward; oftentimes, it is not to bring in consultants. Many facilities want to utilize the staff they have by adding new responsibilities onto their already busy days. Sometimes it works and sometimes it doesn't. Often, consultants get called in to "fix" or "redo" the process. In the long run, this may cost the facilities more than if they had brought on a consultant earlier in the project.

What advice can you offer fellow professionals in your industry?
Stay on top of federal and state regulations regarding electronic patient documentation. Many states function just fine under federal regulations, but others have very different requirements, of which the consultant must be aware. Listen to the facility with which you are working — they know what they need. Our job is to assist them to arrive at that goal.

What advice can you offer people aspiring to get into the profession?
Get an education in the field you want to approach. In my instance, if I had not been a seasoned practicing nurse, it would have been much more difficult to sell myself as knowledgeable in the field of nursing documentation.

What are you passionate about?
Getting things done and getting them functioning as desired, while looking good.

Who have been your mentors or people that have greatly influence you?
My husband, Tom, has stood by me and encouraged me through every step in my work decisions. This includes each time I pondered over advancing my education; also, joining the Navy. He has been my stay and without his support, I would not have been able to achieve all my goals.

What prompted you into this industry?
At the time I started, I just needed a change of pace or something different to do because I was getting burned out after my many years of bedside nursing. I was always interested in electronics; in fact, my first job was for an electronics assembly company, so the progression came easy. What I am doing now is not exactly in electronics. However, it is programming an electronic system to function optimally in order to assist the user and capture needed information. That makes me feel good.

Would you like us to promote any new ventures, research, affiliations, charities or awards?
At this time, I am continuing in the same direction, assisting facilities to go from paper to electronic documentation — whether it be as project manager, builder and tester, or educator.

Do you have a motto that you go by?
"Believe. Without belief, how can you expect to achieve?"

PEDIATRIC NURSING

JANE VIOLA RAPSON, RN, MSN
Assistant Professor (Retired)
University of St. Francis
500 Wilcox Street
Joliet, IL 60435 USA
trrapson@comcast.net
http://www.stfrancis.edu

As a young girl, Jane Viola Rapson spent time in a hospital unit where her aunt worked as a nurse. Observing a family member as they provided a steady level of compassionate care was incomparable to anything she had experienced. It filled her heart with such joy and gratitude that she decided to follow the same honorable path and join the nursing profession. For more than 50 years, Ms. Rapson fulfilled her calling and cared for others with strong dedication and compassion.

Ms. Rapson, who received a Master of Science from the University of Colorado, a Bachelor of Science in Nursing from De Paul University, and a diploma from Augustana Hospital School of Nursing, also taught the profession to others. She is a retired assistant professor at the University of St. Francis, where she instructed aspiring individuals looking to enter the health care industry. It became one of her favorite things to do, as she saw a little bit of herself in many of her students. Ms. Rapson was also a parish nurse for her church. She found the time she devoted to this charitable cause enjoyable as they went out, saw elderly people and checked on the safety in their homes; they also checked their blood pressure and medications. "We spent a lot of time talking to them," she remembers, "as they loved having someone come in and spend time with them."

With expertise in the spiritual and cultural aspects of nursing, Ms. Rapson handled diversity and healing well; she treated not only their bodies, but also their spirits and minds. She was adept at caring for high-risk newborns who typically need the most attention. One of the most rewarding aspects of her career was being able to interact with people and touch their lives every day. She advised them to continuously educate themselves, as new methods of care and developments constantly change the face of medicine and general health care.

In her spare time, Ms. Rapson enjoys swimming three times a week, playing baseball, basketball and reading. She also belongs to several organizations in her church.

CONVERSATION WITH JANE VIOLA RAPSON, RN, MSN

CAMBRIDGE WHO'S WHO: What prompted you to enter your profession and educate others about your profession?
JANE VIOLA RAPSON: As long as I can remember, I always wanted to be a nurse; there was no other choice for me. I feel that teaching nursing and being a nurse is the best of both worlds.

On what topics do you consider yourself to be an expert?
I am comfortable discussing nursing education, high-risk newborn nursing, pediatric and obstetric nursing, and the spiritual and cultural aspects of nursing.

What is the most significant issue facing your profession today?
The most significant issue is the [shortage of] nursing faculties due to government cutbacks on faculty member hiring; also, due to the economy, there is a shortage of support for the education of nursing students. There used to be money from the government to pay for their training. A lot of these schools could take more students into their classrooms, but they don't have enough faculty who can educate them. In nursing, they want you to have a Ph.D. now, which can be very expensive.

What is the most rewarding aspect of your career?
The most rewarding aspect of my career was teaching nursing to my students. I still have students who come up to me when I'm out shopping and remember the times they had in the nursing courses.

What is your greatest professional accomplishment to date?
My greatest accomplishment was to be on a steering committee to develop a college of nursing from scratch. This entailed building the nursing curriculum, handling hours of work and going through accreditation visits from several different agencies. It was quite a learning experience and we created a very fine curriculum.

We spent about five years because at first, we had to educate ourselves about what it would entail; then we went back to school and took some classes — it was just one thing after another. We did it professionally and got consultants in to help. When we finished and got accreditation, it was the most astounding experience. St Joseph's School of Nursing eventually became St. Joseph's College of Nursing.

What is the most difficult obstacle or challenge you have faced in pursuit of your goals?

I don't have many difficult obstacles or challenges in my life because of my faith in God.

SCHOOL NURSING

CHARLENE H. RIACH, RN, FNP, BC

School Health Care Coordinator
Wallkill Central School District
90 Robinson Street
P.O. Box 310
Wallkill, NY 12589 USA
criach@wallkillcsd.k12.ny.us

Charlene H. Riach began her nursing career in the hospital setting, where she developed a knack for treating pediatric patients. When an opportunity arose for her to become an adjunct nursing instructor and associate professor at Orange County Community College, she accepted the position as a way to improve her work schedule and apply her expertise in a new area. From there, Mrs. Riach went on to become a health care coordinator for the Wallkill Central School District, supervising nursing services for elementary, middle and high schools in upstate New York.

As the head nurse of the district, Mrs. Riach develops and implements policies regarding school safety, disease control and prevention, and regulations set by the Occupational Safety and Health Administration (OSHA). She also treats injured students at various sporting events and works with them to create anti-drug and anti-alcohol programs that focus on education, recovery and prevention. Mrs. Riach is her school's advisor for the Students Against Destructive Decisions club, and organized their first health fair, which has since become an annual event. She says, "I love interacting with students in activities outside of the clinic because it gives me an opportunity to really get to know them," which reflects her all-inclusive attitude as it relates to her work; to her, students are more than just bodies with ailments — they are colleagues from whom she learns and further develops her skills.

In addition to a master's degree from the nurse practitioner program at Pace University, Mrs. Riach also earned a Bachelor of Science in Nursing from Mount St. Mary's College and became a registered nurse at Dutchess Community College. She is a certified automated external defibrillator instructor; a certified bloodborne pathogen instructor; a certified basic first aid instructor; and a board-certified family nurse practitioner. Her professional affiliations include the New York State Association of School Nurses, the National Association of School Nurses, The Nurse Practitioner Association New York State, and the American Nurses Association.

Conversation with Charlene H. Riach, RN, FNP, BC

Cambridge Who's Who: What would you like to promote most about yourself or your business?
Charlene H. Riach: School nursing is completely different than working in a hospital because you are dealing with parents and are by yourself. You don't have other colleagues around to consult with, and you make the decisions on your own — you have sole responsibility. It is harder and there is more pressure.

What is the most rewarding aspect of your career?
The interaction with the students. I do the sports physicals and medical coverage for the football games. I'm also the school coordinator of health care and the coordinator for the wellness and health and safety committees.

What is your greatest professional accomplishment to date?
I'm an advisor for SADD and the Student Health Awareness Committee. I enjoy being the advisor to the students who are health care educators.

On what topics do you consider yourself to be an expert?
Coordinating and managing health care in the school setting.

What is the most difficult obstacle or challenge you have faced in pursuit of your goals?
The administration is my obstacle. I don't have the autonomy that I wish I had and sometimes they put up road blocks.

How do you remain current in your profession?
I attend professional nursing conferences. I do a lot of reading in nursing magazines and journals, and I go on www.webmd.com.

What makes you a valuable resource in your industry?
My ability to make decisions and interact with students, parents and the administration makes me a valuable resource.

What is the most significant issue facing your profession today?
School nurses are not valued or mandated today. Schools don't need to have

nurses in New York state. They are the lowest paid of the staff in the schools. We are wanted, but not valued.

What advice can you offer people aspiring to work in this profession?
Dealing with the parents is challenging, but very rewarding.

What are you passionate about?
When I see things that I do take hold, when I'm involved with different events that turn out well, and when I see the kids I work with do good things, it's very nice.

NEUROSURGICAL NURSING

BRENDA KAYE RITZ, RN, BSN
Registered Nurse
Humility of Mary Health Partners
3475 Darbyshire Drive
Canfield, OH 44406 USA
brenda_ritz@att.net

Brenda Kaye Ritz is a registered nurse employed in the neurosurgical intensive care unit of Humility of Mary Health Partners, an integrated health care system that delivers a full gamut of services including patient, chronic and medical intensive care and adult health assistance. Her expertise is in neurosurgical intensive care nursing, telemetry, working with ventilators, and analyzing arterial blood gas. Her daily activities include administering care for heart patients, supervising health care associates and administering medication. In addition to her duties at Humility of Mary Health Partners, Ms. Ritz is a forensic science nursing candidate and sexual assault examiner.

When Ms. Ritz had a son, he was diagnosed with attention-deficit hyperactivity disorder and behavioral problems. Since she was always visiting the doctor with him and looking up information about his condition, her curiosity was piqued. "I decided I wanted to learn more," she remembers, of the turning point leading to a career in nursing. She was 37 years old at the time. Since transitioning to a new vocation occurred later in her life than is usual, it ended up being one of the most difficult obstacles has she encountered thus far. The first step was to obtain her GED. She succeeded and immediately after went to nursing school. In 1997, she obtained a Bachelor of Science in Nursing from Youngstown State University.

While Ms. Ritz admits that nursing is a difficult and demanding profession, she points to the shortage of nursing professionals across the country as motivation to enter the field. "You should get into critical care because then you will always have a job," she asserts. She discerns that the shortage has particularly affected critical care nursing and that specialized job training is required to deal with the life-threatening problems and conditions ever-present in that setting. But the rewards are enormous and one should do it if they love it.

Ms. Ritz is a member of Sigma Theta Tau International. In fall 2010, she enrolled in the Family Nurse Practitioner program at Kent State University, where, in 2012, she anticipates earning a Master of Science in Nursing. In her spare time, she enjoys knitting, swimming and reading.

CONVERSATION WITH BRENDA KAYE RITZ, RN, BSN

CAMBRIDGE WHO'S WHO: On what topic(s) do you consider yourself to be an expert?
BRENDA KAYE RITZ: Neuroscience, psychology and forensic science.

Who have been your mentors or people who have greatly influenced you?
When I went to college, my brother, Troy Allen Cross, helped me to get through freshman registration and become acclimated with the setting; a woman named Mrs. Janoski, whom I met during my academic career also influenced me. At work, Kathy Murphy and Katarina Marjanovic have influenced me.

What are your short-term and long-term career goals?
I would like to get my master's degree. I would also like to take some time off and go on a vacation.

What is your greatest professional accomplishment to date?
I have multiple sclerosis, so the act of just getting up and doing everything I need to do every day is an accomplishment. I have been battling multiple sclerosis since 2001.

What is the most rewarding aspect of your career?
Helping the patients and their families – just being there for them. You have to try and understand what they are going through.

What advice can you offer people aspiring to work in this profession?
Don't forget where you came from when you become an older nurse — always help your fellow nurses. It seems to me like nurses are against each other. If they would just go on each other's side, it would make a big difference.

What are you passionate about?
My family; also, I love to read.

How do you remain current in your profession?
I read Nursing2010 and Critical Care Nurse.

What is the most significant issue facing your profession today?
The nursing shortage. There isn't enough staffing, so if you are working a floor, you could have six patients at one time. The pitfall is, the more you do, the more they expect from you.

What makes you a valuable resource in your industry?
I am trustworthy, honest and dependable.

Do you have a motto?
"A positive attitude may not solve all of your problems, but it will annoy enough people to make it worth the effort." — Herm Albright (1876-1944)

Nutrition and Mind-Body Medicine

George C. Sakakini, MD
Staff Physician
Marine Corps Recruit Depot
Branch Health Clinic
670 Malecon Drive
Parris Island, SC 29905 USA
gcsakakini@yahoo.com
george.sakakini@med.navy.mil

According to George C. Sakakini, CAPT, MC, USN (Ret), up to 80 percent of the illnesses we deal with today have to do with medical issues arising from people's lifestyle choices. As a staff physician for the United States Navy's Naval Health Clinic at Parris Island, S.C., he has taken on the oftentimes difficult task of steering individuals on the right track to a healthier life. With expertise in human and lifestyle nutrition, he cares for patients, emphasizing the importance of maintaining healthy behaviors. He has a firm belief that changes in a person's daily routine could prevent some of the medical issues his patients now face.

For as long as he can remember, Dr. Sakakini wanted to pursue a career as a physician. When he was 6 years old, an orthopedic doctor named Ira Canton treated his broken arm and became his first inspiration. "He impressed me so much that I decided I wanted to be just like him," he remembers. Dr. Sakakini rapidly rose up the ranks of the medical profession, working as a medical director, then in private practice, leading up to his service in the military. Dr. Sakakini has provided his medical expertise in various critical settings across the globe, including a German hospital where he treated injured soldiers from Iraq and Afghanistan, and as the senior medical officer in Kuwait and Iraq. In the near future, he intends to continue working in the health care industry and practicing lifestyle medicine.

Dr. Sakakini has earned many accolades and awards for his contributions to society and the military. From 1987 to 1989, he was awarded three consecutive Service Awards from Chincoteague High School honoring his role as their team physician. In 1981, at the Uniformed Services Academy of Family Physicians Annual Scientific Assembly in Memphis, he received an Appreciation Award for Service on the Program Committee. He holds a Commendation Medal with Gold Star from the United States Marine Corps and a Commendation Medal from the United States Army. He was the recipient of a Global War on Terrorism Expeditionary Medal, the Iraq Campaign Medal Meritorious Unit

Commendation with Bronze Star, the National Defense Service Medal with Two Bronze Stars, the Global War on Terrorism Medal, the Overseas Service Ribbon with Bronze Star, the Armed Forces Reserve Medal with Bronze "M" and Silver Hourglass, the Military Expert Pistol Award, and the Military Expert Rifle Award.

Dr. Sakakini earned an MD in 1976 from the Eastern Virginia Medical School and a Bachelor of Science in 1973 from the Hampden-Sydney College, magna cum laude. He attended the United States Military Academy from 1969 to 1971, and was the salutatorian in 1969, graduating from Fork Union Military Academy. Dr. Sakakini is a diplomate of the American Board of Family Practice and a diplomate of The National Board of Medical Examiners. He is a member of the Alpha Omega Alpha Honor Medical Society, the American Medical Association, and the American College of Lifestyle Medicine. He maintains his medical license in the states of Virginia and South Carolina.

Conversation with George C. Sakakini, MD

Cambridge Who's Who: What are your short-term and long-term career goals?
George C. Sakakini: I hope to continue consulting and helping people with lifestyle medicine issues, which deal directly with proper nutrition, exercise and basic lifestyle behaviors. Presently, I am taking care of Marine Corps recruits at Parris Island.

On what topics do you consider yourself to be an expert?
Nutrition, exercise and mind-body medicine.

How do you remain current in your profession?
I participate in online continuing medical education (CME) seminars and meetings.

What makes you a valuable resource in your industry?
My level of knowledge and passion in this field make me a valuable resource.

What advice can you offer fellow members who work in your industry?
Stay current and be involved with health care legislation that affects our profession.

What advice can you offer people aspiring to work in this profession?
After going to basic medical school and receiving specialty training, I'd recommend going to current seminars that have to do with lifestyle, functional and mind-body medicine.

What are you passionate about?
I'd say lifestyle medicine, nutrition and wellness.

What is the most significant issue facing your profession today?
Unfortunately, even with the recent passage of the massive health care bill, it is the cost and inequitable availability of health care. One of the reasons that health care is so expensive is because of the consequences of the American lifestyle. If more emphasis were placed on our life choices and prevention, health care costs would ultimately diminish.

Who have been your mentors or people who have greatly influenced you?
Recently, Dr. James Gordon has influenced me. He has made a point of promoting

mind-body medicine. He is a psychiatrist, but he has developed a mind-body institute and has been training many people. I am one of his current trainees.

Do you have a motto or principle that guides your work?
All things in moderation.

What would you like to promote most about yourself or your business?
My expertise in and passion for wellness and lifestyle medicine.

Mental Health and General Nursing

Ruthlin M. Seymour, RMN, SRN, RN
Clinical Staff Nurse
Jackson Memorial Hospital
1695 N.W. Ninth Avenue
Miami, FL 33136 USA
ruthain@comcast.net
http://www.jhsmiami.org

Being the second of eight children, Ruthlin M. Seymour learned how to care for others right in her home in Kingston, Jamaica. She always knew that she wanted to be a nurse, so she took the knowledge she gained and migrated at the age of 22 to England, where she attended nursing school. With her parents' encouragement and immense drive to be of service to others, she successfully completed training at Towers Hospital (Humberstone, Leicester) to become a registered mental nurse.

She was offered to become a staff nurse at Towers while she pursued her general training at Hackney General Hospital (London), which would have caused her to return to Towers for at least three years immediately following general training. She respectfully refused their kind offer, because she envisioned the world as her oyster, eager to see as much of it as possible while practicing. At this point, she vowed to be thoughtful and kind to the folks she met along the way. She continued her nursing education at Hackney General Hospital and graduated as a state-registered nurse. A supervisor commented, "We are training British nurses not for Britain, but for the world," which reflected her desire to provide skilled care wherever needed.

Ms. Seymour, who claims she's "never heard a cry [she] couldn't answer," knew that she would be able to function effectively as a nurse in any part of the world and decided to continue her career at a hospital in Essondale, British Columbia, Canada, where she gained further experience. Her professionalism, caring attitude and alertness carried her through to the Ontario Hospital in London, Ontario, Canada before journeying to the United States. In America, Ms. Seymour worked for the New Jersey Board of Nursing at St. Michael's Hospital, the East Orange General Hospital (NJ) and then the New York State Board of Nursing before returning to Jamaica. In 1976, she left Jamaica for Florida, where she continued serving in various capacities until her retirement in 2008.

According to Ms. Seymour, "A human being is a human being in any language," and psychiatric nursing helped her to respect individuals at their most basic levels before attempting to treat or cure their ailments. She knew that in order to effectively heal one's physical pain, she first had to understand their mind and personality. Her specialty in mental health nursing enabled her to accomplish this in all of her posts. While many joys have come to Ms. Seymour throughout her 51-year career, none have been as rewarding as the comments of her colleagues, some of whom have requested that she be their caretaker if they were hospitalized. Even in her retirement, she remains tireless in her efforts to provide comfort and kindness to all within her care.

Conversation with Ruthlin M. Seymour, RMN, SRN, RN

Cambridge Who's Who: What made you decide to become a nurse?
Ruthlin M. Seymour: I was born, grew up and lived in Jamaica. I told my mother at the age of 11 that I wanted to be a nurse, so I had to get to high school. I went to high school in Kingston and when the first university opened in Jamaica, I was accepted there for nursing. My aunt told me, "I don't want you here; I want you to go to school abroad." My father did not agree with my aunt about that subject, but I left Jamaica on November 22, 1955 and went straight to nursing school in Leicester, England. I had to keep my word because I told my dad there was no way I could fail nursing exams. I was successful and when I graduated in 1959, my tutor told me that he was arranging for me to do my general nursing at Hackney General Hospital in London. They were paying me more than the general nurses because I was a psychiatric nurse.

Who have been your mentors or people who have greatly influenced you?
My parents taught me discipline. I had a very good tutor who was like a father to me named Owen Morgan. He really protected and cared for me.

What advice can you offer people aspiring to work in this profession?
First, you have to take good care of your health. You have to love yourself to give love. If you don't have it in you, you cannot give it. You must be caring and ready to ask questions at all times to tell and be told. You have to be precise — if a mistake is made, you have to learn to speak up immediately so that something can be done about it. You cannot hide your mistakes; you are dealing with the life of somebody's loved one.

What is the most significant issue facing your profession today?
I experience time constraints with regards to taking care of myself. There have been many changes to people's perspectives on the nursing discipline. They are not embracing the responsibilities of health care as a "calling" — rather, they refer to it as a job.

What advice can you offer fellow members who work in your industry?
Having a good education, listening skills and caring will allay much anxiety.

You have to teach patients and younger people every moment that you are on the job.

What is the most rewarding aspect of your career?
I have always maintained a consistent standard of excellence.

What is the most difficult obstacle or challenge you have faced in pursuit of your goals?
I had a friend in Quebec named Pauline Patvin White, who had a whole hospital of children with special needs. She started with only one baby and expanded it into an entire hospital. She took me there one day and as conscious as I was, I had never seen a collection of so many children with Down syndrome like that. I cried for days after. I couldn't get over it and said, "What does she have that I don't have as a nurse that I am crying over it and she's happy?"

I came back to New York, left my job, and went to work for a school in Brooklyn for children with Down syndrome to challenge myself. I worked there for three years and learned a lot. You always have to look inside for what you want, not outside.

What are your short-term and long-term career goals?
I would like to go to Europe, but I had a friend in Florida who became ill so I deferred that trip until I could do better in arranging care for him — you don't walk away from your friends. My long-term goal is to be content and thank God for all of the gifts he has given me. I look back now and see my mother daydreaming about her daughter being a nurse and how happy that made her.

How do you remain current in your profession?
I own a collection of books at home. I tell everybody that the day I die, I will be learning because that will be a new experience. I am always reading publications and journals.

Do you have a favorite quote?
"To thine own self be true; and it must follow, as the night the day, thou canst not then be false to any man." — William Shakespeare

RADIOLOGY NURSING

LINDA K. STOTLER, RN, BSN
Registered Nurse
Mt. Carmel Regional Medical Center
Mount Carmel Way
Pittsburg, KS 66762 USA
lstotler@sbcglobal.net

Inspired by her mother, who was a nurse's aide, Linda K. Stotler became a registered nurse and for more than 30 years, she has worked in the radiology department of Mount Carmel Regional Medical Center. As the field of radiology continues to grow and evolve, Ms. Stotler remains at the forefront, ensuring that procedures become more efficient and accurate. As Ms. Stotler honed her skills in radiology, the branch or specialty of medicine that encompasses the use of imaging technologies such as X-rays, CT scans, and MRIs to diagnose and treat diseases, she has also sharpened her leadership skills, overseeing all diagnostic imaging and procedures for the center.

Mount Carmel Regional Medical Center has two specialty units, including an adult and/or pediatric care and intensive care. It is a short-term hospital treating such conditions as pneumonia, heart failure, sepsis, chronic obstructive pulmonary disease, heart attacks, stroke and respiratory failure. Mount Carmel holds 102 beds, of which 90 are used for adult and/or pediatric care and 12 in intensive care.

By offering health care services to people in Mexico, Ms. Stotler has found great fulfillment. A memorable moment involved witnessing a patient whom she never thought would walk or talk actually stand up and do just those things. "It made me want to work harder in helping others," she says. A member of the Kansas State Nurses Association, The American Nurses Association, Inc., and the American Radiological Nurses Association, she attributes her success to her faith in God, and her knowledge and desire to learn.

Ms. Stotler earned a Bachelor of Science in Nursing from Pittsburg State University in 1967 and hopes to obtain certification in radiology nursing in the future. She volunteers her time as a campus minister for the United Methodist Campus Ministry and is a public speaker on health-related topics, particularly conditions such as hypertension and diabetes.

Conversation with Linda K. Stotler, RN, BSN

Cambridge Who's Who: On what topics do you consider yourself to be an expert?
Linda K. Stotler: Critical care.

What characteristics help to separate you from your competitors?
My faith. When handling critical situations, I stay calm and do not panic.

What motivates you?
My faith and my job motivate me. There are so many people who don't have the same opportunity as I to do what I do.

What lessons have you learned as a professional in your field for the past 37 years?
I've learned to take one thing at a time and do it as well as you can. Concentrate on what you are doing and don't juggle too many things and.

What short-term and long-term career goals are you currently pursuing?
My short-term goal is to retire.

What is the most difficult obstacle or challenge you have faced in pursuit of your goals?
There is not a lot of flexibility in my area — although there are different patients, it's the same thing day in and day out. Things are not as challenging as they could be and tend to be monotonous.

Did you ever consider pursuing a different career path or another profession? If yes, how did you end up working in your current field?
Yes — I did lay ministry work in my church. I became a nurse because during my time, it was what the women did.

What do you find to be most rewarding about your profession?
The satisfaction of seeing people get well.

What is your favorite or least favorite work-related task to do and why?
My least favorite aspect of work is not being able to help someone get well.

Who have been your mentors or people who have greatly influenced you?
My mother, Frances Mae Stotler, inspired me.

What changes have you observed in your industry/field since you started?
The electronics; everything used to be paperwork and now they use computers.

How do you see these changes affecting the future of your industry?
I think that it has improved care and things have become more efficient.

If you could be an advocate or spokesperson for any major health issue, what would it be and why?
I would want fair and equal health care for all.

CLINICAL GYNECOLOGY

JOHN E. TURRENTINE, MD, D.MIN.
President, Chief Executive Officer, Medical Doctor
JET Investments, LP
P.O. Box 24414
St. Simon's Island, GA 31522 USA
jet@optilink.us
http://www.turrentinemivh.com

Dr. John E. Turrentine was in private practice for more than 25 years, during which time he focused primarily on all aspects of female health care, from general conditions such as the common cold to screening for more serious ailments, cancers and even surgeries. Known for providing individualized care with compassion backed by knowledge and experience, he developed a minimally invasive vaginal hysterectomy, which is an innovative method that allows for faster recovery time and lessened pain for patients. Dr. Turrentine currently teaches this procedure along with alternative care, epidural anesthesia, female urinary incontinence, and pelvic reconstruction to medical students in various stages of their education. Having completed training throughout the United States and in Ireland, he is highly conversant with topics concerning maternal and child health, and has delivered more than 10,000 babies during his career.

Dr. Turrentine has written five medical textbooks, including three editions of "Clinical Protocols in Obstetrics and Gynecology" and two editions of "Surgical Transcription in Obstetrics and Gynecology." He is board-certified by the American College of Obstetricians and Gynecologists and completed postgraduate studies in general surgery, pediatrics, radiology, and CPR at Memorial Medical Center, Gracewood Hospital, the Medical College of Georgia, and Georgia Baptist Medical Center and Women's Hospital (now Atlanta Medical Center). In order to offer comprehensive care that encompasses physical and spiritual healing, he acquired a Doctor of Ministry degree from Trinity Theological Seminary and currently provides marital, premarital and family counseling.

While his career has been dedicated to treating patients, Dr. Turrentine also maintains interests in the great outdoors as an avid diver and traveler. He received postgraduate training in travel medicine, aviation medicine and human underwater biology, which have been great assets as he has traversed remote areas of the world completing medical missions for 30 years. A pilot, scuba diver and public speaker on new aspects of technical diving, Dr. Turrentine hopes that by raising awareness of decreasing marine life and ocean pollution, he will be able to continue pursuing his passion for many more years to come.

CONVERSATION WITH JOHN E. TURRENTINE, MD, D.MIN.

CAMBRIDGE WHO'S WHO: What is the most rewarding aspect of your career?
JOHN E. TURRENTINE: I have kids come up to me and tell me I delivered them, and I have former patients who tell me stories that are satisfying. I love to teach and that's what I'm mostly doing now. I teach MIVH robotic surgery using the robotic- and computer-assisted da Vinci Surgical System, obstetric epidural anesthesia, and board review for physicians taking the certifying exams.

What is your greatest professional accomplishment to date?
I developed and was the first to perform minimally invasive vaginal hysterectomy (MIVH). I still teach that procedure in different operating rooms and at Johnson & Johnson Ethicon Endo-Surgery in Cincinnati.

What are your short-term and long-term career goals?
My short-term goal is to teach history at a university full time. I will also eventually need to get a Ph.D. in archeological history or biblical history to teach at a university. I still want to continue doing my medical mission work and legal consulting. I would like to dive in Antarctica and get some shark dives in southern Australia. There's a lot of traveling that I would like to do. There are the giant squid down in Los Cabos. I would also like to spend more time with family; this has been difficult due to my work schedule.

What is the most difficult obstacle or challenge you have faced in pursuit of your goals?
One of my obstacles many years ago was getting to and through medical school – it was very competitive back in those days. I had a fire that burned my entire practice down in 1991. That was a challenge to rebuild and I was underinsured, which didn't help.

How do you remain current in your profession?
I receive articles from Johns Hopkins and take continuing medical education courses with Oakstone Medical Publishing company; they send out DVDs and offer a test. I also do postgraduate studies through Johns Hopkins and receive the OB/GYN Clinical Alert (a journal). The state requires you to have 50 CME hours every three years, but I usually have about 300. I also write my books and teach physicians and medical students while on mission trips.

What makes you a valuable resource in your industry?
In terms of medicine, I have to keep up so that I can consult on medical aspects of legal cases that are referred to me. The attorneys refer me for cases. I review the cases to tell them if anyone has performed any malpractice.

On what topics do you consider yourself to be an expert?
MIVH, female urinary incontinence and sling procedures, obstetrical anesthesia, technical scuba diving and marine medicine, and mission medicine and surgery.

What is the most significant issue facing your profession today?
With health care reform, the biggest issue is that if the Senate passes anything, I think Americans ought to demand that all members of the House and Senate be a part of it. If they don't all accept the same things, then we shouldn't pass it.

What advice can you offer fellow members who work in your industry?
If you take care of patients, think of them first, always spend time with them, and do a good job, then you will be fine. You're always going to make a living if you're a good doctor. If you just think of it as just running a business, you will not enjoy it as much.

What advice can you offer people aspiring to work in this profession?
With all the upheavals going on, you have to love it to be able to do it. I don't know what's going to happen to the health industry with this socialization of medicine.

What are you passionate about?
I'm passionate about family, individual freedoms, and letting people live their own lives.

Who have been your mentors or people who have greatly influenced you?
I grew up with a lot of World War II veterans, including my father, Paul Turrentine, who was a big influence. Another man named Fred Norman was also a World War II veteran. I was influenced by the great generation. I feel like they did a whole lot for us. Christ is, of course, the greatest of mentors. If we could all live as close to the way he lived, the world would be so much better.

Do you have a motto or favorite quote?
"Sacrifice your life rather than your word." — Stonewall Jackson

What would you like to promote most about yourself or your business?
If you give your credit to the Lord, everything else takes care of itself. I am a clinical professor at the Medical College of Georgia, having taught third- and fourth-year medical students during their core rotations.

I now teach medical and nursing students mission medicine. I would like to let physicians know that if they are not board-certified, I can help them with my tutorials to pass the boards. I still teach MIVH through Johnson & Johnson. I am also available to attorneys to review their cases, as I am an expert witness in OB/GYN.

Reiki Healing

James S. Bolton
Researcher
Independent Contractor
2623 W. Philadelphia Avenue
Oley, PA 19547 USA
boltz2z@gmail.com

James S. Bolton is a researcher and independent contractor with expertise in environmental engineering. He has more than 12 years of experience in the field and his daily activities included recording smokestack emission data and studying the impact of several environmental factors on plants. In the past seven years, Mr. Bolton experienced a major spiritual awakening, which stirred him to explore, study and research as much of the spiritual world as possible. He began to study the concept of universal vibrational energy, whereby humans, plants and animals each manifest their own energy frequencies. As he further explored the mechanisms and functions of vibrational energy further, he conducted his own garden experiments and learned how to manifest healing energy towards plants. He has progressively increased the amount of energy work he does through Reiki to help other people heal themselves.

To Mr. Bolton, healing is a very humbling and rewarding experience. "We are just creating a balance within the human body," he describes, "which allows the human body to heal itself." The highlight of his career was being told by a master Reiki practitioner of 12 years that the healing energy he gave off was stronger and more loving than the master had ever felt before in his life. Mr. Bolton, who attributes his success to his perseverance, curiosity, devotion and efficiency, continues to experiment and develop new healing practices and hopes to open a healing center in the future.

Mr. Bolton received a Bachelor of Science in Environmental Engineering in 1996 from Rensselaer Polytechnic Institute. He holds level I and level II certification in Reiki. A charitable individual concerned with the welfare of his fellow man, woman and animals, Mr. Bolton donates regularly to local hunger relief organizations, Habitat for Humanity International and The Humane Society of the United States.

In his spare time, Mr. Bolton enjoys hiking, mountain bicycling, spending time outdoors, practicing yoga and Reiki, meditating, performing consciousness calibrations, gardening, energizing water and developing new technologies.

CONVERSATION WITH JAMES S. BOLTON

CAMBRIDGE WHO'S WHO: What is your greatest professional accomplishment to date?
JAMES S. BOLTON: I've been able to review what I was doing and I'm at the point where I can begin to share the information with other people who understand healing energy. I have had very powerful experiences recently where I use the mind-body-soul techniques; people can feel it, so they look at me and say, "Wow, thank you!" I have a small group of people with whom I practice and we are all really in-tune with the healing energy.

What are your short-term and long-term career goals?
My short-term goals are to experience personal growth, learn to relax, and heal myself more deeply. My long-term goal is to invent things. Right before I graduated, I promised myself I would invent something. I do want to have a company, a group of people developing technology and using it to augment what we know about the mind, body and soul.

On what topic(s) do you consider yourself to be an expert?
I consider myself an expert on energy healing, defining consciousness, elementary particles, technology, consciousness calibration, health, the environment, and understanding how intention travels through the universe.

What is the most difficult obstacle or challenge you have faced in pursuit of your goals?
My view is that if an obstacle comes my way, it is there to help me grow. Some people might look at it as an obstacle, but I see it as a learning experience. One of the difficult obstacles I faced involved public speaking. Everyone knew that I was the most nervous getting in front of the class.

Do you have a motto?
"Every obstacle is there for us to grow and learn." "Everything is always perfectly perfect."

What is the most rewarding aspect of your career?
Helping and observing other people grow is the most rewarding aspect.

What advice can you offer people aspiring to work in this profession?
I always tell people to follow their hearts. Be very specific with what you want and it will come. One must take initiative to show the universe your intention and then comes patience in following the signs to your goal.

How do you remain current in your profession?
I stay current by using my intuition and techniques, and meeting new people. I typically encounter new people through seminars, holistic expos and meetings, etc. We all have valuable information to share that can raise everyone's consciousness.

What would you like to promote most about yourself or your business?
I would like to promote learning to love everything around oneself, unconditionally.

What prompted you into this industry?
I wanted to have an understanding of the entire universe, which lead to my looking into vibrational energy and the highest and most pure form of unconditional love.

And what specific steps have you taken toward achieving these goals?
I have been learning how to increase unconditional love through intuition, meditation and visualization. I study the works of experts in the field, such as the consciousness calibrations defined by Dr. David R. Hawkins, to gain more insight.

What makes you a valuable resource in your industry?
I am a valuable resource because I combine intuition with experience and augment my "knowingness" further through consciousness calibrations.

What is the most significant issue facing your profession today?
The most significant issue facing my profession has to do with toxic frequencies; also, having to remind people of the fact that we have all created this together and what we have created is absolutely perfect.

What advice can you offer fellow members who work in your industry?
Everything is always perfect. It goes beyond an understanding; it is a feeling, a sense of being. Stay tuned to your body and how it feels, witness every thought and begin to transfigure your thoughts to peace and perfection. Never fear the amazing changes that begin to take place. Changes always feel different, but the simple act of knowing this makes the process more and more effortless.

What are you passionate about?
I am passionate about absolutely every single aspect of this whole entire connected universe.

Who have been your mentors or people who have greatly influenced you?
I have had many mentors who have influenced me in profound ways, but the top ones are Criss Angel, the "Mind Freak" master magician; David R. Hawkins a master of enlightenment; and Gerald O'Donnell, a master of remote viewing and influencing. I feel I connect with their works in a very unique, spiritual way that I am still exploring. The most powerful author I've ever read is David R. Hawkins. I've read most of his books. He has written the book, "Truth vs. Falsehood," which has had a profound impact on me.

EMPLOYMENT LITIGATION

CHARLES R. BAILEY
Attorney
Bailey & Wyant, P.L.L.C.
500 Virginia Street E.
Suite 600
Charleston, WV 25301 USA
cbailey@baileywyant.com
http://www.baileywyant.com

In any career, a favorable reputation is a testament to one's work ethic, ability and commitment to achieving satisfactory results. Whereas many in the legal profession have unfortunately been deemed as untrustworthy or duplicitous, Charles R. Bailey is regarded by clients and colleagues as an outstanding litigator who takes on challenging cases and remains on the cusp of new technologies that affect legal proceedings. Although much of his practice is focused on employment and labor law, Mr. Bailey is also highly adept at handling regulatory matters, mediation and alternate dispute resolution, professional liability, insurance coverage, constitutional law, and civil rights cases. With an influx of cases that involve injuries sustained due to automotive accidents, he has adjusted his repertoire to include trucking litigation and representation for all affected parties.

In 1982, he penned the article "Toward a More Complete Notice of Proposed Rulemaking: A Judicial Overview and Suggestions for Change" in the West Virginia Law Review, Volume 84. Additionally, he has lectured on federal court rules and procedures in West Virginia, current issues in municipal law, the Civil Rights Act of 1991, education law, and public contracts and procurement. As a lecturer on legal matters for the National Business Institute and Lorman Education Services, Mr. Bailey provides exceptional continuing education for lawyers in all stages of their careers. His fascination with medicine and functions of the human body prompted him to learn more about medical negligence litigation and how ever-present changes regarding this field can be tempered to suit individual needs. He says, "While the law doesn't change, breakthrough and new medical technologies are always challenging," which he manages through constant self-erudition and publications from legal associations.

Mr. Bailey received a Bachelor of Science from West Virginia University's School of Journalism in 1976 and a JD from the West Virginia University College of Law five years later. He is a member of the West Virginia Bar

Association, the American Bar Association, the Defense Trial Counsel of West Virginia, the Eastern Mineral Law Foundation, and three United States district courts. He also serves on the Employment Committee of the West Virginia State Bar and maintains involvement with the Defense Research Institute, an international organization of defense attorneys in civil litigation.

Conversation with Charles R. Bailey

Cambridge Who's Who: What would you like to promote most about yourself or your business?
Charles R. Bailey: We are the go-to firm for the West Virginia Office of the Governor. When they need help with litigation, they come to us.

Who have been your mentors or people who have greatly influenced you?
I was inspired by my grandfather, who was a magistrate. He enjoyed politics and law, although he was not a lawyer, and he always thought it would be neat if I went to law school. I think he was a frustrated lawyer at heart.

What advice can you offer people aspiring to work in this profession?
If you're interested in being a lawyer, then you should be curious. A lot of lawyers say they don't like science because they aren't good at it, but when you become a lawyer, you have to know [scientific] principles. Talk to people who are professionals in the field and listen to them very carefully. If you ask the right questions, you will get good answers. You need to find an expert who is going to teach you.

What is the most difficult obstacle or challenge you have faced in pursuit of your goals?
If you do not come from a family of attorneys or have not had close relatives who are attorneys, to some extent, you have to fight your way upstream. Many of your classmates' parents or close relatives may be attorneys, so therefore their name is already known in the legal community and among clients. If you are a first-generation lawyer in your family, there is a certain hurdle to overcome because you have to distinguish yourself. I think...that is more of an issue...in smaller states such as West Virginia.

How do you remain current in your profession?
I go to national seminars and the National CLEs (Continuing Law Education conferences), whether they are on employment, labor or medical issues. I read American Bar Association journals, the Defense Research Institute magazine, and in the evenings, I try to read as much as I can about the profession — especially in trial litigation. I try to keep up with what's new regarding technology and presenting at trials because juries now expect to see films and animation. Technology in the courtroom is important. Some litigators use it sparingly, but powerfully — what they use, they have carefully crafted and designed. I also try to stay abreast of the psychology of voir dire,

which is [an oath regarding] questions you can ask the jury, and how jurors react to information. I think lawyers need to read a lot about that.

What advice can you offer fellow members who work in your industry?
Don't take anything at face value. Always try to dig very deep into any situation to find answers. If you are very curious, your curiosity will lead you toward uncovering a fact or principle that other people may have overlooked.

Do you have a favorite motto or slogan?
"Curiosity does not kill the cat, curiosity wins the case!"

Criminal Intelligence

Lt. Pierre R. G. Clemens
1) Commanding Officer 2) Commanding Officer
1) South Pacific Islands Criminal Intelligence Network 2) International
Criminal Police Organization
Pago, Pago, American Samoa
milodada@blueskynet.as
http://spicin.com

Lieutenant Pierre R.G. Clemens is a commanding officer of the South Pacific Islands Criminal Intelligence Network and the International Criminal Police Organization. Each agency works hand-in-hand as a joint effort criminal intelligence agency and law enforcement organization. His expertise is in drug enforcement, police corruption, white-collar crime, and human trafficking — evils he learned to combat while attending the Federal Bureau of Investigation's National Academy, from which he graduated second in his class. Additionally, Lt. Clemens specializes in handling escalating forces and conducting traffic crash and DUI investigations.

Before his successful career in criminal investigations and drug enforcement, Lt. Clemens was unsure what he wanted to do with his life. He had tried accounting, but admits that he "quickly became bored with it." One of his friends suggested that he sit in on a criminal justice class with him; that was all it took. He honed in on his investigative skills and cultivated a knack for interacting with all walks of life within the community, for the purposes of intelligence gathering and surveillance. Lt. Clemens admits that one motivating force that emerged early in his career is his passion for protecting people. "I want to do justice for them because there is so much injustice happening," he explains. In the 20 years that he has been in his profession, he has seen a lot that would send anyone to early retirement, but his persistence to facilitate order in the communities in which he works remains. "You have to keep moving, keep driving and remember that people come first," he remarks.

Lt. Clemens holds certification from the Institute of Police Technology and Management, U.S. Customs and Border Protection, the Federal Bureau of Investigation, the United States Secret Service, the United States Coast Guard, the Drug Enforcement Administration, the Asia Pacific Center for Security Studies, and the Bureau of Justice Assistance. He is also certified in pressure point control tactics through PPCT Management Systems. In addition to his contributions as a commanding officer for the U.S. Department of Homeland Security, he has also worked for SDA Investigations, LLC.

Conversation with Lt. Pierre R. G. Clemens

Cambridge Who's Who: On what topics do you consider yourself to be an expert?
Pierre R. G. Clemens: Corruption and human trafficking. Corruption is the root of all evil — that's why we have so many problems.

What characteristics help to separate you from your competitors?
I am intensely driven; I truly wanted to be a cop. Twenty years later, I still believe that you never stop learning and you try to do better than you did the year before. Some people put on the badge because it [signifies] power, but it is more than that.

What motivates you?
When someone comes to me and tells me that they have been victimized, I do everything I can to help them.

What is the most significant issue facing your profession today?
Injustice due to the rapid corruption in government.

What advice can you offer fellow members or others aspiring to become involved in your profession?
Get an education. You really have to want it; don't just go into it because you have nothing else to do. If you are looking to be rich one day, don't become a cop, because it's not going to happen.

What is your favorite or least favorite work-related task to do and why?
I enjoy the public and we work with the community. There is no us against them — we work together.

Who have been your mentors or people who have greatly influenced you?
My father.

Labor and Employment Law

Dorothy Fleming Green, JD
Partner
Latham, Shuker, Eden & Beaudine, LLP
390 N. Orange Avenue
Suite 600
Orlando, FL 32801 USA
dgreen@lseblaw.com
http://www.lseblaw.com

Dorothy Fleming Green, a partner at Latham, Shuker, Eden & Beaudine, LLP, is board-certified as a specialist in labor and employment law by The Florida Bar. She is AV-rated by Martindale-Hubbell and has 27 years of experience representing clients. Ms. Green is well-versed in defending individuals brought before the National Labor Relations Board, the State of Florida Public Employees Relations Commission and the Department of Labor's Wage and Hour Division. She also provides defense to employers in federal and state courts. This includes civil rights litigation involving race, sex, national origin discrimination, sexual harassment, disability and age discrimination. As an expert advisor to employers, she is adept at clarifying the Equal Pay Act, Family Medical Leave Act, COBRA and Fair Labor Standards Act, and federal and state statutes.

Ms. Green lectures and speaks publicly on issues related to labor and employment law. Additionally, she is a graduate of Leadership Orlando and Leadership Winter Park and participates in local civic activities in the Orlando area. She is valued by the community as a resource.

Ms. Green received a JD from American University Washington College of Law in 1983, a master's degree in library science from the University of Kentucky in 1972 and a bachelor's degree in history from Baylor University in 1970. She is a member of the Winter Park Chamber of Commerce, the Society for Human Resource Management, the Central Florida Association for Women Lawyers, The Virginia Bar Association and the Federal Bar Association. In 2004, 2005 and 2006, Ms. Green was featured in the Orlando Business Journal's "Best of Bar." Since 2005 she has been recognized as a Top Lawyer by Orlando Magazine, and in 2004, 2005 and 2006, she was listed as one of Florida Trend's Legal Elite.

Conversation with Dorothy Fleming Green, JD

Cambridge Who's Who: What would you like to promote most about yourself or your business?
Dorothy Fleming Green: My expertise is in labor and employment law for employers.

What do you find to be the most rewarding aspect of your career?
Advising clients, offering guidance and keeping them out of trouble.

What are your short-term and long-term career goals?
My goal is to continue to provide timely and excellent service for my clients.

And what specific steps have you taken toward achieving these goals?
I keep up with my field and am board-certified in labor and employment law by The Florida Bar.

On what topics do you consider yourself to be an expert?
Labor and employment law for management.

How do you remain current in your profession?
We are required to do continuing education. I also read professional journals and publications.

What makes you a valuable resource in your industry?
My experience.

What is the most significant issue facing your profession today?
The public's perception of lawyers.

What advice can you offer people aspiring to work in this profession?
Train yourself to be the best that you can be. Absorb everything you can that is relevant to labor and employment law.

What are you passionate about?
My family, reading, the choir, traveling, and my dogs.

Who have been your mentors or people who have greatly influenced you?
James G. Brown, who is the person that I worked with for the longest period of time. He is an experienced labor and employment lawyer whom I worked with for about 20 years. He is a colleague and mentor of mine.

Hair Artistry

John E. Kelley
Instructor (Retired)
Los Angeles Unified School District
West Valley Occupational Center
6200 Winnetka Avenue
Woodland Hills, CA 91367 USA
jekelley@dishmail.net

John E. Kelley considers himself to be an artist in many rights, mostly as a talented hairdresser for more than 20 years. He stumbled upon this career by chance, having survived a terrible motorcycle accident that left him critically injured in a hospital for three weeks. Though the ordeal was trying and he eventually received government assistance, Mr. Kelley was determined not to lose hope for a more promising and fulfilling future. After taking an aptitude test that measured his IQ, manual dexterity and interests, he found that he had the potential to excel in seven professions, all of which would challenge his intellect and specific skill set.

Mr. Kelley chose to pursue cosmetology because it allowed him to get back on his feet quickly and offered him a welcome career change from his previous occupation as a truck driver. He had served the Army National Guard for 13 years and retired from the Air Force Reserve with five honorable discharges, so embarking on a new journey was certainly enticing. In Studio City, Los Angeles, he styled ordinary citizens and high-profile celebrities before opening La Parisienne Hair Salon in North Hollywood. Accented by a distinct attention to detail, his obvious talent for tailoring styles, colors and cuts to his clients' personal tastes helped him to develop personal relationships that extended further than the station and swiveling chair.

The salon operated for a decade before Mr. Kelley became an instructor in the Los Angeles Unified School District. Owning a business prepared him for the challenges he would face in the classroom, including how to function on a schedule, manage others, and interact with various personality types. He advises young people to undergo testing before graduating high school in order to determine their strongest areas and pursue careers that will satisfy their interests and future goals. A lifetime member of the California Rifle & Pistol Association and the National Rifle Association, he also belongs to the California Teachers Association and AARP.

CONVERSATION WITH JOHN E. KELLEY

CAMBRIDGE WHO'S WHO: What would you like to promote most about yourself or your business?
JOHN E. KELLEY: I had a business for 10 years, which facilitated my ability to go into teaching. I'd like people to know the story of how I became a hairdresser. I like to play "What's My Line?" with people I meet and they never come close to guessing what occupation I had. [Many] of them are homophobic and have a preconceived idea about hairdressers, which I deal with all the time. That is the first thing many of my customers wanted to know, if I was straight or not.

What is the most rewarding aspect of your career?
Being able to make people look good and help them with their little problems is the most rewarding aspect. Hairdressers are like psychologists; when customers come to a hairdresser, they expect him to keep his mouth shut and only put in his two cents worth.

On what topics do you consider yourself to be an expert?
I consider myself to be an expert in the field of art. I did a show in 1965 and won the Hollywood Coiffure Guild Award. I also put a model airplane in the Smithsonian Institute. It took me two years to build and was an exact replica of a crop duster that flew in Bakersfield. I took pictures of crop dusters, went home and built everything one part at a time. When I finally finished it, it hung for eight months in a model shop and the woman who owned the shop said to me, "They are building a new Air and Space Museum in Washington, D.C. You ought to send a letter to them and see if they are interested." We did that together: wrote a letter and took pictures. After my plane went into the museum, I didn't do much more modeling; I had done it for seven years. I found different ways to apply my art and I think that's the crux of the whole thing.

What are your short-term and long-term career goals?
My short-term goal is to get through this life and my long-term goal is to meet my maker and hope he's grading on a curve.

What is the most significant issue facing your profession today?
In the hairdressing field, I think that the state and the government are not regulating it as they should. There was one time that I went to a salon and asked for a haircut. A woman came up to me and introduced me to her daughter-in-law, who was an apprentice. She was going to do my hair, but she had no formal training and was being trained by this woman in the salon. What kind of protection is that for the public? When I went to beauty school, there was a two-day session and we had to answer everything in the book, and be able to do all the operations too. The business is slowly deteriorating because of the state's attitude and I think money has something to do with it as well.

What is the most difficult obstacle or challenge you have faced in pursuit of your goals?
It's sad — people are at risk because of untrained people. The training and expectations of a hairdresser today are far less than what they were when I went to school.

What advice can you offer fellow members who work in your industry?
Be as astute and aggressive as you can possibly be. Go to all the beauty shows and read the magazines or journals. American Hairdresser and a couple of others are journals just for hairdressers. They [feature] almost everything that's going on in the world.

What are you passionate about?
I am passionate about God and doing things for other people.

Do you have a motto?
Always try to do more for your clients and treat them as you would like to be treated! Do unto others as you would have them do unto you.

What is your greatest professional accomplishment to date?
Giving thousands of students the skills that are needed to succeed in their chosen profession.

What makes you a valuable resource in your industry?
Staying abreast of my field, and passing on my skills to better my profession.

WASTEWATER TREATMENT AND DISPOSAL

LEN L. REDMON-BENNETT
President
Lenco Industrial Services, Inc.
P.O. Box 111
Gardendale, TX 79758 USA
len.red@sbcglobal.net
http://www.lencoindustrialservices.com

Wastewater management is a dirty job, but Len L. Redmon-Bennett has chosen to do it. In a male-dominated field, she has fearlessly stepped up to the plate, which happens to be filled with grimy water. She prides herself in providing tools and resources for safety to her customers, and maintains a strict code of green practices to protect the environment. Her company, which manufactures, sells and rents industrial-grade, portable wastewater treatment systems (as well as oil infusion tanks for the oil industry), has grown at a rate of 300 percent annually for the past six years.

Mrs. Redmon-Bennett has eight years of experience in wastewater treatment systems and eight years as president of her company. Establishing and operating her own business that would focus on green practices was something she always desired. "I have always strived to provide the best, environmentally safe products while delivering accurate customer service," she says. She believes that friendly customer relations should also be a top priority for any company to succeed. Additionally, she feels the most efficient way to ensure continued growth is to constantly research green products and continue to further advance all technology used in her current business.

Mrs. Redmon-Bennett is a member of the Odessa Chamber of Commerce and the National Small Business Association. In turn, her professional affiliates are helping her company to formulate greener products. She received certification in electrical engineering from Siemens Energy & Automation, Inc. and certification in advanced overcurrent protection from Cooper Bussman, Inc.

Mrs. Redmon-Bennett is thankful to her parents, her faith in God, her honesty, and the support she receives from her family and friends for making her the successful businesswoman she is today. In the future, she hopes to travel with her husband, update herself with the ongoing changes in her profession, and serve her community. When she's not trying to make the world a more sanitary place, Mrs. Redmon-Bennett enjoys golfing, deep sea fishing, gardening, caring for her new colt, and spending time with her husband, children, grandchildren, great-granddaughter and friends.

Conversation with Len L. Redmon-Bennett

Cambridge Who's Who: What would you like to promote most about yourself or your business?
Len L. Redmon-Bennett: I would like to promote my portable wastewater treatment systems. We design, manufacture and rent aerobic, portable wastewater treatment systems as well as several other products, including trash trailers, individual lift systems and odor-controlled charcoal filter systems. I also have a new, totally green oilfield chemical.

What prompted you into this industry?
My friend and mentor, Ted Lawson, prompted me into the industry, but I was also ready to go into business for myself. I felt that I was not meeting my fullest potential while I was working for someone else.

What are you passionate about?
I have a great passion for life. God gave us a beautiful land on which to live and the only way to keep it beautiful is for people to be open and honest with themselves and others. We need to keep a safe, clean and green environment for us and for our future generations. We must work daily to improve our lives and living conditions on this great land.

What are your short-term and long-term career goals?
My short-term goals are to continue providing my customers with well-maintained rental equipment and a friendly, well-trained service staff to meet their needs. I will always continue my research to develop and/or acquire products that will help us to meet our goals of maintaining a green environment, while always watching the bottom line for our customers.

My long-term goal is to continue to improve my existing products. I am always ready to try new materials and once the testing and research is complete, the product will be introduced to the market place. To meet our goals of a green environment, product testing takes many twists and turns. I want every product to be completely safe for our environment and customers.

And what specific steps have you taken toward achieving these goals?
There are a number of organizations that are helping to achieve these goals such as the Odessa Chamber of Commerce, the National Small Business Association, the Water Environmental Federation and many others. By being a part of these organizations, we are able to network with many individuals that have the same goals and desire for the environment as we do. We have the opportunity to learn about new products and innovations that will soon be introduced to the market, and sometimes I actually hear about some of the new research and development that is taking place in different parts of the country. I enjoy research and development and I am extremely lucky to have several companies that are willing to try out some of my new ways or products before we release them to the public. I am not afraid to try new products while we are in the research process, as long as I know that they will not harm our environment or our customers.

On what topic(s) do you consider yourself to be an expert?
Portable wastewater treatment systems, gas plants, waste water treatment plants, environmental safety products, and green chemicals.

How do you remain current in your profession?
I have very skilled and professional people who work for me who are constantly reading, attending trainings and networking with others in our field. We spend many hours brainstorming together. I attend training seminars and am a very avid reader. I perform all types of research and development projects to keep up with the new happenings in the industry.

What makes you a valuable resource in your industry?
I feel that I am a conscientious and prudent business owner. I am not only here to make money and provide jobs; I have a personal responsibility to the land owner to do the best job that I possibly can to ensure that the products that my company use are EPA-rated, and will not harm the land or the animals. I am always looking to better our living conditions and the environment while keeping it affordable.

What is the most significant issue facing your profession today?
Maintaining the quality of service and trained staff; also, keeping the same equipment when the industry is down. What I am presently facing is costs that have to do with insurance, equipment training, research and development, taxes, office space and daily expenses. These have not changed, even though the market and oil companies have.

What advice can you offer fellow members who work in your industry?
Make sure that you regulate yourself and take care of our environment to ensure safety for many generations to come.

What advice can you offer people aspiring to work in this profession?
One must really enjoy this profession. It is dirty, the work never ends and it's a 24/7 job if you are a business owner. You'd better be ready to study all the time as things will change daily in this industry. You must be very committed or you will not be able to cut the mustard, as we would say; also, you have to be motivated.

Who have been your mentors or people who have greatly influenced you?
There have been several people who have influenced me. My father, who is a Marine of World War II and a survivor of Bataan and Corregidor, was captured by the Japanese and remained a POW for three and a half years. He is my hero. He adopted me and taught me all of the same positive things that the Marines stand for, such as value, strength, good work ethic, leadership, bravery, trust, kindness, and — most of all — unconditional love.

My mother made me a lady in spite of myself. Both of my parents always told me that there was nothing in this world I couldn't do if I set my mind to it. My friend, Ted Lawson, who talked me into this business, was a mentor; I wish he was still here for me so I could confer with him. My best friend and general manager, Charlie Kirkpatrick, stood by me 24-7 as I struggled to get my business started. From day one, he proudly stood by my side and I am able to bounce ideas off of him.

Do you have a motto?
I have always followed my parents' mottos: "Do an honest day's work for an honest day's pay!" and "You should always give more than you receive."

Aerial Acrobatic Performance

Ekaterina Arnaoutova
Performer
kat_aclysme@hotmail.com

Ekaterina Arnaoutova is the third generation of the Arnaoutova circus family from Russia. Throughout her 23-year career, she has performed for major entertainment companies around the world (including the Moscow Circus) and for charities such as the Children's Starlight Foundation. Her performances are unrivaled, as she brings enormous talent, a captivating stage presence and an admirable level of devotion to each show.

It doesn't get much better for an aerial acrobatic performer as it did for Ms. Arnaoutova, who has been an intrinsic part of Cirque du Soleil for several years. She is currently a performer in "The Beatles LOVE" by Cirque du Soleil, which is a tribute to the legendary band that can be experienced at The Mirage in Las Vegas. It is considered one of the most successful shows in the world. Additionally, she has been featured in the "Nouvelle Expérience" (Cirque du Soleil's fourth touring circus-styled show) and "Fascination" (another Cirque du Soleil production that was staged in Japan). Her daily routine is one that may seem overwhelming to someone not used to the rigors of circus performance and includes the upkeep of strength and flexibility exercises, rehearsing for different parts of the show, applying makeup and hairstyling, selecting costumes and performing on stage.

For Ms. Arnaoutova, the process remains a true test of her will and strength, as she continually overcomes obstacles, remains relevant and takes adequate steps toward the upkeep of her health. Through it all she has her parents to look to for support and inspiration, as at any given time they can be found on some kind of stage around the world. "My parents are touring with Cirque du Soleil in Japan," she asserts. "My father, Dmitrii, is now a trainer and my mother Irina, who is a former performer, now works in the wardrobe department." In the near future, Ms. Arnaoutova intends to be a part of productions that continue to amaze, touch and mesmerize audiences. She also hopes to continue evolving, creating, transforming and improving herself as an aerial acrobat.

CONVERSATION WITH EKATERINA ARNAOUTOVA

CAMBRIDGE WHO'S WHO: What would you like to promote most about yourself or your business?
EKATERINA ARNAOUTOVA: I am a versatile and creative artist with lots of experience and priceless knowledge. I took part in the creative process on many different productions throughout my career. My skills and imagination have contributed to my unique and original circus acts.

What is the most rewarding aspect of your career?
The best part of my job is having the ability to touch people in the audiences and see them smile after a performance.

What is your greatest professional accomplishment to date?
My greatest accomplishment to date is always being at the top of my game, where I give my best in every performance that I give to the audience. Generally, it has been about my perseverance and ability to overcome many obstacles along the way. Right now, of course, it's about being a part of one of the best shows in the world, which is "The Beatles LOVE" Cirque du Soleil show.

What are your short-term and long-term career goals?
Short term, I would like to remain creative, innovative and always achieve a higher level of performance. Long term, I intend to continue working in the performing arts; I hope to stay in the business for as long as I can. I am committed to taking care of my body. Eventually, I would maybe like to work behind the scenes at entertainment venues. I will also try and always be a positive influence for others.

What specific steps have you taken toward achieving these goals?
Practice makes perfect, so I'm always working out and surrounding myself with very talented people who are creative and positive. In terms of the long term, I would continue collaborating with the best in the industry.

What is the most difficult obstacle or challenge you have faced in pursuit of your goals?
Sometimes it's easy to lose motivation or creativity; other times, an injury

can be in the way. It's not always easy to find ways to reinvent yourself. There's obviously always a lot of competition in the field; you always need to prove yourself and stay on top.

On what topic(s) do you consider yourself to be an expert?
In show business, I specialize in circus art, more especially in the aerial acrobatics.

How do you remain current in your profession?
I work with many people who share the same interests; we stay open to all kinds of different, new art and continue to always go to different shows around the world. This includes music, dance, variety shows and film.

What makes you a valuable resource in your industry?
I have so many years of experience; I'm an adaptable and creative artist who is not afraid of challenges.

What is the most difficult obstacle or challenge you have faced in pursuit of your goals?
The economy: it's hard to get people to come see a show when they want to save money, pay their rent and buy their food. Another challenge has to do with keeping the industry going, because people don't always want to invest in this business — other parts of their lives seem to be more affected by the economy. Right now, it's a lot harder to get people interested to attract bigger audiences.

What advice can you offer fellow members who work in your industry?
Never give up. Always find new ways to be creative. Find inspiration around you and don't be afraid to take risks.

What advice can you offer people aspiring to work in this profession?
Have a lot of perseverance. Realize that sometimes, it takes time — you've got to start somewhere and you always have to start small. Before you get to where you want, you're going to have to go through a lot. Always aim higher and try to go further. In my business, try and perform as much as you can to gain recognition and experience. Practice a lot and treat your body like a temple.

What are you passionate about?
My biggest passion is being onstage, in the spotlight, flying high, seeing people's faces after the performance and knowing I've mesmerized somebody or touched someone. As much as I enjoy being onstage, I am also passionate about seeing other people onstage. Watching movies or other shows always brings food for a greater thought.

Who have been your mentors or people who have greatly influenced you?
Being third generation in a circus family, I would have to say my family, particularly my father Dmitrii, who has been a performer all his life. He's the one that got me into this and always pushed me to go further. He's my greatest hero. His passion for his work has always inspired me. To this day, he is still involved in the business.

Do you have a motto or principle that guides your work?
Dream big and nothing is impossible.

CINEMATOGRAPHY

DOUG J. MILSOME
Director of Photography
Individual Production Services
Wootton Farm
Eardisley, Hereford HR3 6LS UK
dougmilsome123@btinternet.com

While he was working under the legendary film director Stanley Kubrick, Doug J. Milsome learned a valuable lesson. The motion picture maker told him, "Photography is not just artistic interpretation; it's unquantifiable. It's the authorship of the original work rather than the simple recording of a physical event." The message stuck and has permeated every single project in which Mr. Milsome has been involved. A director of photography with more than 55 years of experience in the film production industry, he has provided cinematography for a wide range of projects, including major motion pictures. Mr. Milsome has received a handful of nominations and awards, including an Emmy Award nomination for "Lonesome Dove" in 1989, an Oscar nomination for "Full Metal Jacket" in 1985, and a Camera Operations Award for his contributions to "Highlander" in 1982 — in the ultra-competitive film industry, no small feat.

As early as the age of 16, Mr. Milsome excelled in the arts, learning the ropes as a camera assistant. He began his career in 1957 with the J. Arthur Rank Organization at Pinewood Studios, serving as an apprentice for five years and learning about special visual effect photography, stop frame model animation and rostrum camera work. He was trained in the Rank Film Laboratory processing division and in the camera department as a staff assistant cameraman for feature film productions. He then worked as a freelance first assistant cameraman, participating in the production of many major motion pictures, which include "Modesty Blaise," "Magnificent Showman," "Woman of Straw," "Sands of the Kalahari," "Casino Royale," "Houston/Bob Parish," "Blow-Up," "Sinful Davey," "Where's Jack?" "A Clockwork Orange," "The Horseman," "Barry Lyndon," "Ryan's Daughter," "The Spy Who Loved Me," "Pink Panther Strikes Again," "Ragtime," "The Shining," "Kind David," and "Plenty."

He then contributed to the photography of two Australian movies, a six-month shooting after which he returned to England at the invitation of Stanley Kubrick to photograph "Full Metal Jacket." He was also involved with the productions of "The Shepherd," "Until Death," "The Hard Corps," "Second in Command," "The Legend of Simon Conjurer," "Dracula III: Legacy," "Dracula

II: Ascension," "Standing in the Shadows of Motown," "Ritual," "Highlander: Endgame," "Dungeons & Dragons," "Legionnaire," "Breakdown," "The Sunchaser," "Rumpelstiltskin," "Body of Evidence," "Sunset Grill," "The Last of the Mohicans," "Robin Hood: Prince of Thieves," "If Looks Could Kill/Teen Agent," "Desperate Hours," "The Beast," "Hawks," and "Wild Horses."

Mr. Milsome attributes his success to his dedication and passion for the film industry. His work as a cameraman is a reflection of his personal authorship, a perspective that only he can bring, that becomes open to interpretation. Mr. Milsome is a member of The British Society of Cinematographers, the Guild of British Camera Technicians, the Directors Guild of America, the Motion Picture Association of America, Inc., the The American Society of Cinematographers and Local 600, the International Alliance of Theatrical Stage Employees.

CONVERSATION WITH DOUG J. MILSOME

CAMBRIDGE WHO'S WHO: On what topics do you consider yourself to be an expert?
DOUG J. MILSOME: Cinematography.

What characteristics help to separate you from your competitors?
The public makes up their own minds as to what is exceptional in terms of the cinematic eye. It is all a question of choice and what the personal view of people in this area is.

What motivates you?
If you think you have not attained the great level you wish to get to, keep going. It's like the Olympics — you strive to conquer your own goal and go out as an achiever in your field. That's the drive that keeps you there and as long as you have your sanity and health, the age doesn't really [matter]. There are a lot of cameramen who are my age.

What lessons have you learned as a professional in your field for the past 56 years?
Lessons are not always a good thing because every time you are associated with a project, it [involves] a different psychology. Each director is different. You have to go along with knowing all areas of the script, how to make them feel comfortable with you and heading a big team. Short of the director, you are the other important person on the team. You have many people under you and likability is an important aspect; they all need to get along with you in a professional manner. Do the best job you can with the time you are allotted. I have learned to let go in areas where I don't think it counts.

What short-term and long-term career goals are you currently pursuing?
I have been working with John Paul Van Dam for the past few years as a co-director mainly on TV shows and I will be helping him with a project about his life in the near future. We are also working on a movie called "Cross Meglan," about the IRA and the British Army in the 1970s. We are hoping to start on that very soon. I am working on two projects, "The Tower" and "The Weapon." I am always getting scripts — it's about deciding for which scripts I am prepared to go away for a long time.

288

What is the most difficult obstacle or challenge you have faced in pursuit of your goals?

Every one of them has been a challenge; I don't think there has been an easy [task]. In each of these cases, you have to visualize a style and approach, which always depends on the director. Approving the crew is always a challenge. It's also a challenge to make the footage look good and make sure that the mood and tone of the light is effective, all with minimum reset time between setups. People want to move quickly these days. The problem here is that you try to produce a magnificent, gold medal movie on bare money with hardly any time. It's hard to get good scripts. Sometimes, you will get a script that has a beginning and no end, which means you really don't have a beginning.

What is the most significant issue facing your profession today?

There are a handful of really great directors, and I don't know who is coming up in their tracks, but they are my age and still working.

What are some questions that an individual interested in your services can ask to ensure a more productive relationship?

They have to understand what you have shot before. Sometimes, I won't even meet directors, but you have to somehow create a good first impression for them. The general questions directors ask have to do with the way I shot another film and whether or not I could bring the same look to their project.

Did you ever consider pursuing a different career path or another profession? If yes, how did you end up working in your current field?

I don't think I would be good at anything else. I enjoy this business and there is no way you can get the variety of work and meet the people you do in any other profession. I am trying to preserve the image of film and will continue to use film for all its brilliance. I have a trained eye for what is shot on film and what isn't, and I can still tell the difference. I think that is the perceptive eye that cameramen who are in the business as long as I have been possess.

What do you find to be the most rewarding about your profession?

I think the best part was when I gave a talk about Stanley Kubrick's movie "Full Metal Jacket" last year in a warzone. Some did not understand the movie, but others [related to] that confusion and a sense of hopelessness. I had the privilege of working on three of his films as an assistant cameraman and two as a director of photography. I have worked on more than 100 movies, but the ones I am most proud of are "The Shining," "Full Metal Jacket" and "Barry Lyndon," which won an Oscar. Stanley Kubrick's films have content, mystery and beauty. They are often greeted with reservations by critics and only after a period of time did the status of his work emerge as something special. That's how I'd like my work to be: the status will hopefully re-emerge, people will see them later on and see something truly special.

What is your favorite or least favorite work-related task to do and why?
What I enjoy most is being part of a successful project. The job is demanding; it's six days a week, 12 to 16 hours a day. You just keep going and don't stop for a period of time, which may be two to three months — and then it's a dead stop.

Who have been your mentors or people who have greatly influenced you?
Stanley Kubrick. I treasured working with him and I consider him to be a true artist.

Have you contributed to any publications or research in your field?
I created a CGI (computer-generated imagery) practical guide for American Cinematographer magazine.

What changes have you observed in your industry/field since you started?
When I first started, everything was done organically through film, with the expertise of the cinematographer and his crew; there was no trickery or electronics. Now it is all digital and things can be done post-film.

CIVIL AIR PATROL ADMINISTRATION

MARGOT LEVEQUE
Wing Adminstrator
Civil Air Patrol
13186 Tonopah Street
Arleta, CA 91331 USA
levequeyes@aol.com

Marguerite "Margot" Leveque remembers when she was a child and her father introduced her to the telescope. Peering up at the stars and the sky through its lens, somehow she realized all those years ago that she would become involved in the aviation industry. While her calling came as a "second career," her passion remains as strong as it did those many years ago.

The Civil Air Patrol is a nonprofit organization that provides cadet and aerospace programs and conducts search and rescue operations for the U.S. Air Force. As a wing administrator for the Civil Air Patrol, Ms. Leveque is responsible for managing the administrative duties of the California wing. She attributes her success to her knowledge and strong communication skills, which help her share information with many different departments that work together.

Prior to her role at the Civil Air Patrol, Ms. Leveque was a teacher for 35 years and taught kindergarten. "I love the little ones," she remarks. She retired from teaching and then dedicated 23 years as a volunteer for the Civil Air Patrol (she started in 1986). Recently, she became a member of their staff and, for the past two and a half years, she has helped her peers conduct searches for missing aircraft. Since the Air Force pays for the fuel required for the mission, it is her duty to help finish up the mission paperwork and get people paid. In 1994, Ms. Leveque took her love for aviation to the next level. She became a pilot — a process of training and instruction that she recalls taking up to 18 months to complete. Additionally, with her newly accrued skills, she went on to provide flight instruction for the Civil Air Patrol.

Ms. Leveque holds a Bachelor of Arts in English and a Bachelor of Arts in History from Immaculate Heart College (which closed in 1981). In her spare time, she enjoys flying and spending time with her 89-year-old mother.

Conversation with Margot Leveque

Cambridge Who's Who: What motivates you?
Margot Leveque: The opportunity to help people motivates me. This job gives me an opportunity to get to know a lot of our members who are very special people. They are devoting their time and energy toward doing a very important job.

What lessons have you learned as a professional in your field for the past 23 years?
It's all related to being a part of the Civil Air Patrol, whose members come from every part of life. We have street repairmen, teachers, firemen and policemen, and aerospace engineers — people from all walks of life. To see that these people can come together in a united and respectful way, working as a team together to complete their mission [is great]. Also, to be a part of that has been probably the best thing that I have gotten out of my association with Civil Air Patrol. [I love seeing the] respect from all the people from all levels of life. Everybody does their own job and it is a united front.

What short-term and long-term career goals are you currently pursuing?
My short-term goal is to continue learning more about my job and do a better job every day. Things are always changing and [you need to] stay current with the different aspects of the program.

How do you plan to achieve goals?
I want to gain more proficiency in each of the areas that come along because there are always new programs in Civil Air Patrol that I need to keep abreast of and understand. I am hoping to be able to [continue to] participate in the administrative end of it, as well as being involved in actual searches.

What is the most difficult obstacle or challenge you have faced in pursuit of your goals?
Making the time to become proficient in it all.

What is the most significant issue facing your profession today?
Staying abreast of the technology that is available for us.

Did you ever consider pursuing a different career path or another profession? If yes, how did you end up working in your current field?
I had retired from teaching and became a volunteer. I had the opportunity to

work here with people I love and respect, and it was a new challenge for me because there would be new things to learn. It was completely different from what I had been doing so I knew I would have more energy for it. The people with whom I would be working were those who I knew well and respected; also, they respect me.

What is your favorite or least favorite work-related task to do and why?
Working alone is my least favorite, because I am at my best when I am working with others.

Who have been your mentors or people who have greatly influenced you? Why?
My flight instructor, Tim Quinn, influenced me through his confidence boosting. He was also a part of the Civil Air Patrol. He gave me an opportunity to be able to participate in missing aircraft missions and instructed me on being more proficient.

My direct supervisor, Jim Crum, has influenced me with his patience in dealing with others and his attention to detail. He has a way of being able to kindly tell people that they have made a serious mistake and need to fix it. My mother, June Leveque, has been an inspiration to me my whole life for her deep faith in God and dedication to her family.

What changes have you observed in your industry/field since you first started?
In just the couple of years that I have been working here [Civil Air Patrol], we are turning more and more to the Internet and electronics.

How do you see these changes affecting the future of your industry?
We all have better capability with the new technology; it is making us more efficient. I get the paperwork e-mailed from the incident commander of a mission, which makes receiving them a lot faster. There are some instances where I am getting the paperwork, when before I might not have.

What do you find to be the most rewarding about your profession?
The most rewarding aspect for me is the contact with the members, because they are volunteers and give their time. For me to be able to make their lives a little bit easier by giving them information or by helping them with something is also the most rewarding.

What advice can you offer fellow members or others aspiring to work in your industry?
[You should] have an attitude of looking forward to what's next rather than

being afraid of change. Accept things that are coming as challenges rather than things to be concerned or worried about.

Do you have a motto or philosophy that guides your work?
Look for the possibilities. This means that when a possibility appears on my horizon, I see it as an opportunity to grow.

What characteristics help to separate you from your peers?
I have a great enthusiasm for life and all that it can bring. Life is an adventure and I always strive to learn what the next adventure has in store for me, as well as what new skills it will require.

RECORDS MANAGEMENT

FRANCES McGINNIS
Clerk
Bethel Baptist Church
P.O. Box 276
Corryton, TN 37721 USA
kest491@yahoo.com
http://www.bethel-corryton.org

Frances McGinnis is a clerk at Bethel Baptist Church, where she applies her strong desire to help people to the benevolent cause of prayer, reflection and spiritual development. With expertise in record management and program coordination, she is responsible for managing church activities, maintaining church baptism records, obtaining letters from new members of the church, recording minutes for meetings, sending cards to shut-ins, and organizing Sunday school education. Having a functional church that can properly serve its parishioners is one of those things that takes dedication and hard work, two qualities that Ms. McGinnis has acquired through her years employed by the church.

Ms. McGinnis has worked as a Sunday school teacher for 53 years at Bethel Baptist Church. She became involved in her profession after she was recruited by a pastor to perform clerical work. That was 38 years ago and she hasn't turned back since. In 1997, Ms. McGinnis was recognized by Bethel Baptist Church with an award for 25 years of dedicated service.

The church clerk is one of the organization's most important contributors, in that they are charged with numerous vital responsibilities. Ms. McGinnis not only can be found maintaining the church's list of registered parishioners; she is also the go-to person for individuals who have transferred in from other churches. Additionally, she can be found at crucial business meetings, acting as Bethel Baptist Church's secretary. "I have been able to stay well enough to be present for each business meeting," she remarks. While she has recently turned 73, Ms. McGinnis hopes to continue working in her current position in the near future, although she remarks, "Retirement is right around the corner."

In her spare time, Ms. McGinnis enjoys solving puzzles, including word searches and crosswords. Additionally, she volunteers her time at a local hospice center.

CONVERSATION WITH FRANCES McGINNIS

CAMBRIDGE WHO'S WHO: What would you like to promote most about yourself or your business?
FRANCES McGINNIS: Our church is thriving and growing every day. We have nearly 350 members and our pastor's name is Tim Inklebarger.

What is the most rewarding aspect of your career?
Being around people who are loving and friendly. Our business always goes smoothly and we don't have any big problems; everything goes as it is supposed to. Everyone is in one accord and it makes all the difference.

What are your short-term and long-term career goals?
I am 73 years old, so retirement is my next goal.

What is the most difficult obstacle or challenge you have faced in pursuit of your goals?
I haven't had any obstacles; everything goes so smoothly.

On what topic(s) do you consider yourself to be an expert?
Teaching Sunday school, which I have done since I was 20 years old.

How do you remain current in your profession?
I depend on the Lord to give me what I need.

What makes you a valuable resource in your industry?
People will come to me for my knowledge and if they need anything, they know they can come and ask me.

What advice can you offer people aspiring to work in this profession?
Pray and ask God to lead you and guide you.

What are you passionate about?
My church, loving the people that come here, and seeing the lost come to the Lord. We had seven people saved recently and will have a baptism for each of them.

Who have been your mentors or people who have greatly influenced you?
Stella Arwine, who has passed away, was in one of my Sunday school classes and she really influenced me over the years.

Is there a saying that you live by?
"Do the best you can do and let God lead you."

FINANCIAL MANAGEMENT CONSULTING

BRIAN P. VICKERS
Chief Executive Officer
Vickers Consulting Services, Inc.
brianv@vickersconsultingservices.com
http://www.vickersconsultingservices.com

Brian P. Vickers, CEO of Vickers Consulting Services, Inc., has worked for over 16 years as a volunteer firefighter. While the experience has been rewarding, he noticed that his department never received any grants to support the cause. With a newfound determination to make an even bigger difference, Mr. Vickers then decided to pursue a career in grant consulting. Today, he consults on grants for the public safety sector, contacting clients and assessing their needs, creating funding plans and utilizing those plans to assist nonprofit organizations. This includes the replacement of equipment, and the provision of much-needed commodities.

Determination, a desire to be successful, and the drive to help communities have propelled Mr. Vickers to the forefront of this specialized form of financial management consulting. Since 2001, his operation has provided aid for more than 2,000 fire departments, and rescue and EMS squads, with competitive grants and private and local non-competitive funding totaling more than $250 million.

With the slogan, "Preparing Today's Responders for Tomorrow," Mr. Vickers' cause is just as important to his clients as it is for the communities which they serve. Aside from consulting, Vickers Consulting Services, Inc. offers one-and two-day workshops where attendees gain a more in-depth understanding of the grant-writing process. Most recently, the firm has expanded to help nonprofits with organizational development to ensure that they are able to operate for years to come through any type of economic conditions and still provide full assistance to those in need. They have also begun advising clients on their strategies for needs and risk assessment, strategic financial planning, and marketing services. Since he is an expert in financial management consulting, Mr. Vickers believes it is important to get the word out on grant availability for public service organizations. He has published numerous articles, authored a chapter in Brady Publishing's "Principles of Firefighter Safety and Survival" (2010), recorded numerous podcasts, and spoken publicly on the subject across the country.

Mr. Vickers, who was a computer software programmer before entering the field of financial management consulting, is presently pursuing a Master of Business Administration from the University of Phoenix, Inc. In 1998, he received a bachelor's degree in computer information systems and management from Delaware Valley College.

Conversation with Brian P. Vickers

Cambridge Who's Who: On what topics do you consider yourself to be an expert?
Brian P. Vickers: Financial planning, consulting, and public safety.

What characteristics help to separate you from your competitors?

In-depth analysis and unique approaches to problem solving are the two main components in our success. Both require a lot of time to perform properly and too many other companies don't want to take that time to do things the right way. We do, and it shows in our success rate.

What motivates you?

The desire to make things better no matter how great they are right now. No process or situation is perfect and since the world changes around us, we have to constantly re-evaluate everything in order to just maintain status quo, let alone make improvements. It's our responsibility to make all possible improvements so future generations don't have to deal with too many major issues.

What short-term and long-term career goals are you currently pursuing?

My short-term goal is to expand to other nonprofit genres since we are still mainly known for our public safety efforts. The principles that apply there are just as valid for any nonprofit, so while slower in growth, the potential is still great for us in that genre. Also, like any progressive company, we need to continue to increase our staffing and infrastructure to meet the demands that our customers have for us so that we can continue to meet their future needs and expectations.

How do you plan to achieve these goals?

Networking and relationship-building are at the core of any growth, whether personal or corporate. We continue to make contact with new potential clients every day and always leave them with a sense that we can help them now or later if we can't do anything for them at that time. That has helped us to build relationships quickly through referrals. Also, continuing to educate myself and our employees is something that has to happen in order to succeed. In a changing world, yesterday's knowledge is only the foundation for what we will learn tomorrow to continue to be successful.

What is the most difficult obstacle or challenge you have faced in pursuit of your goals?

Time and information management are the greatest challenges we have because there is constant, ongoing change all around us, and with the Internet so accessible, it takes a good investment of time to separate information and misinformation from various sources to ensure we're still doing the right thing.

What is the most significant issue facing your profession today?
Like any business, the economy always comes into play, not so much for our survival, but more for our clients. All nonprofits always need funding from other sources to survive, whether the economy is good or bad. As times get tough, our business increases as donations to organizations go down since they rely on us to help them find the funding they need. What makes it hard is that when the economy is down, many grant makers also reduce their funding levels so we don't have as many opportunities to help clients as we do during the good times.

What are some questions that an individual interested in your services can ask to ensure a more productive relationship?
Actually it's the questions that we ask that help make the most productive relationship. The information we need from clients to make the most of any venture with our company includes their organization's long-term vision, planned projects and needs, current ventures, and any shortfalls they may have in providing their services right now. The world of grants is very large, but there isn't always something for nonprofit organizations or projects, so we do the legwork to ensure that we're not wasting anyone's time or money chasing something that won't have a high chance of success in the long run.

Did you ever consider pursuing a different career path or another profession? If yes, how did you end up working in your current field?
Yes, I was actually in the software industry before I went into consulting, which fit into my passion for solving difficult problems. The move to grants and the consulting work that we do was a small step going from solving computer-related business problems to solving financial ones for nonprofits. Both require a lot of work and planning in order to be done right the first time and still allow for long-term flexibility in any solution.

What do you find to be the most rewarding about your profession?
Seeing the improvements in clients and their abilities to serve their communities better is huge success metric for us. Nonprofit organizations, whether they are a public safety agency, a church, a school, or a single cause-focused group like a cancer research organization, all exist to learn from the past and improve the future in handling the issues they face in their communities.

What is your favorite or least favorite work-related task to do and why?
My least favorite work-related task is the paperwork; my favorite part is the

challenge of having the grants funded and the networking. I enjoy being able to talk to so many different people and organizations and see tangible results of our efforts through the improved services that our clients can provide to those that they serve.

What advice can you offer fellow members or others aspiring to work in your industry?
Treat everyone with respect and be honest when dealing with clients. Sometimes, we have people come in who would like a grant, but it's just not possible and we have to be honest with them and tell them that it just doesn't exist, rather than take their money, make them wait for weeks, and then come up empty-handed. They appreciate the fact that we will check things over to ensure that there is something we can do for them first.

Who have been your mentors or people who have greatly influenced you?
My parents, Steven and Dorothy Vickers, were the biggest ones. They instilled in me the value of working hard and treating everyone with respect, no matter how they treat me. That's the basis for relationship-building, let alone the fact that it's the proper moral way to live.

What changes have you observed in your industry/field since you started?
There's more funding out there for different programs and more grant money available at the federal, state and private foundation level than there was 10 to 15 years ago. That has attracted more organizations to seek funding, because they realize they are eligible and there are things they can do with the assistance of a grant where their local fundraising efforts have fallen short. Unfortunately, this has also increased the occurrence of fraud, both in the writing of applications and in the use of the awarded funding. As money gets tighter, more applicants are willing to stretch the facts or outright lie to beat out everyone else to get the funding. Sometimes even legitimate applicants do the wrong thing once they get the money in hand just because the temptation is there. Luckily everyone gets caught eventually and it hasn't affected the willingness of the grant makers to continue their programs.

How do you see these changes affecting the future of your industry?
There are more regulations put in place to minimize the potential for wide-scale fraud issues, so we have to stay on top of those. But otherwise, not a whole lot has changed within the grant programs themselves.

Have you contributed to any publications or research in your field?
Yes, Firehouse Magazine, Firehouse.com and a textbook called "Principles of Firefighters and Survivors Safety and Survival."

Do you do any public speaking?

Yes, I have done appearances at conventions. Firehouse Magazine hosts three conventions every year around the country, which I have spoken at on various occasions. We also have our own brand of workshops that teach organizations about pursuing grants, from planning to research, to effective writing skills.

SGT. MAJ. HUBERT D. WALKER
Commander (Retired)
Disabled American Veterans
320 Sand Bar Road
Chuckey, TN 37641 USA
hjwalker@embarqmail.com

Sgt. Maj. Hubert D. Walker served for 38 years in the United States Army Special Forces Green Berets. A six-time recipient of the Bronze Star Medal, Sgt. Maj. Walker engaged in numerous tours of active duty to Korea, Vietnam and Japan. As a man whose leadership and courage abilities have been tested to the highest extreme, he is very familiar with the struggles of his fellow comrades. Now retired, Sgt. Maj. Walker is presently affiliated with Disabled American Veterans, an organization that is dedicated to providing assistance and improving the lives of Americans wounded during their tour of duty, and their families.

A unique opportunity to serve in the National Guard prompted Sgt. Major Walker to enlist in the United States Army. He ended his military career as a sergeant major, one of the highest ranks attainable by enlisted servicemen and women. He has dedicated the last 17 years of his life to Disabled American Veterans, providing various forms of financial assistance, transportation to and from medical appointments, and support in completing everyday tasks. Additionally, he visits veterans who are unable to return to their families due to ongoing medical conditions that may require continuous hospitalization. As he gets on in age, Sgt. Maj. Walker has enlisted the help of three service officers who visit the veterans and take care of them. "If they need to join their organization, they sign them up right there," he explains. In 2009 alone, he and his three service officers signed up approximately 15 new members, which also includes younger soldiers who have returned from Afghanistan and Iraq.

Sgt. Maj. Walker, who attributes his success to his interpersonal skills and the solid training he received while serving in the United States Army Green Berets, is a member of Greene County Veterans Services, The American Legion and Veterans of Foreign Wars of the United States. When he's not working with and assisting 272 Disabled American Veterans, he enjoys fishing, vegetable gardening and spending time with his six living children, 18 grandchildren and 23 great-grandchildren.

Conversation with Sgt. Maj. Hubert D. Walker

Cambridge Who's Who: What would you like to promote most about yourself or your business?
Hubert D. Walker: I would like to promote the business itself, and the services that we provide to disabled veterans and their families. We help them pay their bills during the wintertime and sometimes, we help them with food, around Thanksgiving and Christmas; we also help them with clothing. There are a lot of needy families and we all get together and fill up boxes of clothes to give out. We provide transportation if they need to go to the hospital. We are working with about 270 individuals so we continue to grow and help others.

What is the most rewarding aspect of your career?
The most rewarding aspect of my career is seeing the faces of those people who are in really bad shape, when we help them out, giving them a little something extra and watching theirs and the kids' faces, especially around Christmas. They just open up to you.

What is your greatest professional accomplishment to date?
I'm still alive! I am grateful for all the things I have, such as my wife, family, house and 17-acre farm.

What are your short-term and long-term career goals?
Right now our goal is to get more veterans and try to sign more people up. As soon as we sign them up, I give them a job right away. If you give them something to do, then they keep themselves interested and will keep on working.

What is the most difficult obstacle or challenge you have faced in pursuit of your goals?
I find out that most of them, about 75 of our members, are like me — they are getting old. There are a lot of World War II, Korean War and Vietnam War veterans, and like with me, it's hard to get them to come if the weather is bad; they don't want to get out in this rain or snow. Fortunately, the young members want to do something and are taking charge.

On what topics do you consider yourself to be an expert?

Leadership — without it, you don't have anything; also, project management.

How do you remain current in your profession?
I read journals and publications. We have two conferences a year where a lot of studying and presentations occur.

What is the most significant issue facing your profession today?
Bringing the new and younger people in and keeping them trained. Getting that new blood in really helps.

What advice can you offer fellow members who work in your industry?
You put God first, family second, and then your country. If you keep your life in that sequence, I think you'll be doing all right.

What advice can you offer people aspiring to work in this profession?
Keep yourself out of trouble, get back in school, and once you get through school, get a job where you know what you are doing and stick with it. Keep training and you will be all right.

What are you passionate about?
All my life it's been my position and my family.

Who have been your mentors or people who have greatly influenced you?
A man named Mac Arthur had a pretty good pull on me. My father and mother, Raymond Nelson and Bonnie Mae Walker, along with my church, Tuscan Baptist Church, kept me out of trouble all the time.

Do you have a motto or principle that guides your work?
Never put off for tomorrow what you can do today.

Mortgage Planning and Preparation

Maria De Lourdes Greenberg
Senior Mortgage Planner
Golden Empire Mortgage, Inc.
361 N. Bender Avenue
Covina, CA 91724 USA
mgreenberg@gemcorp.com

Maria De Lourdes Greenberg is a senior mortgage planner at Golden Empire Mortgage, Inc., a mortgage banking company that provides mortgages and federal housing administration loans. She utilizes her expertise in mortgage preparation to interview clients and, while working with a team that includes a product manager and branch manager, lock in the most favorable real estate deal. Her exceptional talents and abilities have certainly helped her to gain recognition and in 2006, she was the recipient of the Golden Empire Mortgage, Inc. Award for Excellence.

Golden Empire Mortgage, Inc. is a company started by a husband and wife team several years ago. To this day, the business remains family operated. Additionally, the same personnel can be found working with Ms. Greenberg and company. "It's not very common in this industry, so that means something to us," she states. Ms. Greenberg, who is bilingual, became involved in her profession after her husband asked her to help him in translating the conversations he was having with various Spanish-speaking communities. It was from this experience that she learned about the field of real estate and recognized her strong passion for the work.

With branches all throughout California, Golden Empire Mortgage, Inc. offers a complete line of real estate loan programs without the inclusion of a middleman. The setup enables clients to close on a property with lower interest rates and lower closing costs. Ms. Greenberg, who attributes her success to the support she receives from the team with whom she works, hopes to utilize her skills as a senior mortgage planner to continue developing the business.

In her spare time, Ms. Greenberg enjoys spending time with her family, skating, and bicycling. Additionally, she enjoys donating her time as a volunteer at a local school, and to an animal protection organization and environmental protection agency.

CONVERSATION WITH MARIA DE LOURDES GREENBERG

CAMBRIDGE WHO'S WHO: What would you like to promote most about yourself or your business?
MARIA DE LOURDES GREENBERG: We are a mortgage banking company dealing with direct lenders.

What is the most rewarding aspect of your career?
The most rewarding aspect is seeing a family obtain their house — and keep it. It is also rewarding to know clients who refer us to their family members and co-workers. It shows that we did a good thing for them because they are confident enough to refer us to someone else.

What is your greatest professional accomplishment to date?
Still being in business and keeping very busy is an accomplishment.

What are your short-term and long-term career goals?
My short-term goal is to move forward and balance my career and family life.

And what specific steps have you taken toward achieving these goals?
We always try to keep up with all the changes in the market and adapt to them. By understanding all the changes, it becomes less of a challenge to close a deal, which is the main point.

What is the most difficult obstacle or challenge you have faced in pursuit of your goals?
The changes in the field are the most challenging things because not everyone understands them. The bottom line is that we have to document everything; otherwise, we may not get an offer. This can be challenging for us because we have to change the mentality and show them. That's not what I want, but what the field requires.

On what topics do you consider yourself to be an expert?
We do a lot of things, including FHA programs and dealing with single-family residences.

How do you remain current in your profession?
Our corporate office sends us all the materials concerning changes; they guide us very well. I read magazines related to my industry also.

What is the most significant issue facing your profession today?
The regulations are constantly changing and a lot of it doesn't always make sense, so it is hard for some people to follow them. The regulations are insane.

What advice can you offer people aspiring to work in this profession?
Be flexible and learn to adapt to the changes — that is key.

What are you passionate about?
My family is my passion and my life.

Who have been your mentors or people who have greatly influenced you?
My husband, Hank Greenberg, has greatly influenced me.

Antique Sales and Restoration

Carolyn Anne Bergam
Owner
Antiques & More
1030 Oakwood Drive
Yuba City, CA 95991 USA

Ever since her birth in the Historical Stonewall Jackson House in Virginia (where the library served as the delivery room) Carolyn Harwood Bergam has been immersed in the rich history and culture of our country. She takes pride in her firsthand knowledge of chronological facts — a tremendous asset when it comes to her job combing the world for valuable items as the owner of Antiques & More. She uses her expertise to discern firsthand the relevance of artifacts, which she sells and sometimes restores. These antiques come from all over the world, including China, Australia, England and Europe. Ms. Bergam also collects and resells tea bricks, didgeridoos, brass rubbings and camel saddles. Additionally, she teaches brass rubbing to students in the United Kingdom and Australia.

Both sides of Ms. Bergam's family come from England, where they lived not far from Harwood Avenue (which happens to share her maiden name). They arrived through Jamestown in the early 1700s. First moving to Philadelphia, Pa., they eventually decided to move to Old Salem, N.C., where her father's family purchased property. It was here where a major battle was fought during the American Revolutionary War between General Green and General Cornwallis. During this battle, they opened up their home to help injured soldiers. When the battle was over, her forefathers gave the property to the state of North Carolina and it is now called "The Guilford Battleground." The movie, "The Patriot," was filmed on that very estate. "A lot of people can read out of books," she points out, "but it's another thing to actually see firsthand how people lived during that period of time."

With 31 years of experience in her profession, Ms. Bergam has dealt with antiques from China, Australia, England, and Europe. Her family life, like the keepsakes in which she deals, reflects a certain worldliness that has impacted her to this very day. From the time she was born to the age of 22, she traveled all over the world with her father, who was a cryptologist with the United States Coast Guard, visiting the seven continents; he was also a senior officer at the USCG Academy at Fort Trumbull in New London, Conn. He taught as a communication officer and broke the Japanese code, the Enigma code and the Soviet code. Ms. Bergam met her future husband as a cadet at the USCG Academy. One of her great-great grandfathers, Ellis Hoskins, was one of the founders of The Old Salem Quaker College. Her second great-great grandfather, Col. Thomas Holcomb, was a colonel in the Confederate States Army from 1862-1865. Ms. Bergam still has his sword and saber in her home, alongside other artifacts that he used during the Civil War.

In 1966, Ms. Bergam received her Associate of Arts from New London Business College. In 1987, she received her travel agent training certification and SABRE computer reservation system training, and in 1989, she earned her national tour operator certification from Yuba College. She is a board member and docent of The Mary Aaron Memorial Museum, and is a Queen of the Red Hat Society. She is also a member of Veterans of Foreign Wars of the United States.

Conversation with Carolyn Anne Bergam

Cambridge Who's Who: What would you like to promote most about yourself or your business?

Carolyn Anne Bergam: I have the history, knowledge and context behind my restoration work. Unlike a lot of people who talk about the United States of America, I can say firsthand that I was raised around its history. My knowledge is directly from my family. We had five generations alive until I was 16 years old. My great-great grandmother lived until she was 105 years old and was very keen until the last week of her life. My artifacts from my family are furniture, china, silver pieces, wedding dresses and Quaker lace items.

What is the most rewarding aspect of your career?

Living with my family antiques during my lifetime makes others very interested in my life. Traveling all over the world with my family heirlooms with me lets me share my family's rich history. The useful factor was that antiques were used for different periods of time, which makes it interesting to others. This is the most rewarding aspect of my career.

What is your greatest professional accomplishment to date?

My extensive travel: I lived in Guantanamo Bay, Cuba, during the time of the Cuba Missile Crisis, for instance. It's not only about my travels; it's being in the places where things actually happened. For example, I lived in Alaska when it became a state. It's not something I just read out of a book; it's about knowing the people and the places. Being from the South, we are very keen about keeping the history alive. My southern heritage on both sides of my family has been an asset to me. The knowledge of living in many parts of the world had educated me on acquiring a lot of history.

What are your short-term and long-term career goals?

My goal is to stay in the United States so I can share more of our true history with our fellow countrymen. Since I am an international travel agent, I can relate to what others may like to see and do, and why. My long-term goal would be to write or speak to others on what the effects of knowing history in our country and in other parts of the world [has done for me] and how it has enriched my life. This combines my history and knowledge.

What is the most difficult obstacle or challenge you have faced in pursuit of your goals?

I would have liked to have been able to do this sooner than I did. Due to my father and husband being in the military, it was harder to do while living overseas. I had other obligations and I had to wait until later in my life. However, it actually worked out for the best. I've found that the time has really been a saving grace because all the things that I have are that much more appreciated. So much of our American history seems to be disintegrating. The joy I have in being in history and telling others all the unique things I have done seems to make others more excited. I would love for other people to see that there is always a challenge in getting to reach your goals. Many people are fascinated about the things I have inherited and acquired through living in other parts of the world.

How do you remain current in your profession?

I read quite a lot about the new things that are happening. I read the Preservation Magazine and history books, published by the National Trust for Historic Preservation. I receive many monthly and yearly journals on my antiques, and I am active in the museum I work with. I get about eight magazines and history books. I receive books from Mt. Vernon, Civil War Preservation, Confederate History, Williamsburg Magazine, and Living with Antiques, Kovals, and Antique Roadshow.

What advice can you offer fellow members who work in your industry?

I think when people work in antiques, they should not just to do it because of the financial part; it should be more about the uniqueness of the items. Some of the items are so distinctive and served their own purpose.

What are you passionate about?

I've done a lot of public speaking. I love teaching others about antiques. If you have an antique and you really know the history behind it and connect with it, it makes it so much more meaningful than just having an item that is worth a certain amount of money. It's the history behind it, not the monetary value. I also love gardening. When an event or a special time of the year approaches, I love dressing in period dresses and outfits with a parasol, gloves, the ornate fans and purses, and my Quaker lace. So many people comment on how unique it looks and it shows the social graces of an era begone. My gardening helps to display items because I dry some of my flowers. I love to have formal teas to share social graces and my love of cooking.

Who have been your mentors or people who have greatly influenced you?

My father, Clarke Russell Harwood, was my biggest mentor because he carried along the legacy, which he did fantastically. I really do love the historical fact of my family and I try hard to keep that intact because someday, that could be gone. All the research he did on the family was fascinating. My dad was such an inspiration to myself and to all the family. In the Quaker belief, they honor the living as well as past generations. This way, dates and historical events stay current.

Do you have a motto?
"Semper Paratus," which means "Always Ready." This truly applies to me because it comes directly from my father who served 31 years with the U.S. Coast Guard. He is buried in Arlington Cemetery with high honors. At his burial, the entire Coast Guard Band and Honor Guard came from New London, Conn. to play and march to his grave site!!

On what topic(s) do you consider yourself to be an expert?
I can say the topics that I consider myself to be an expert on are two sources: my extensive travel and antiques. In the 63 years of my life, I had the opportunity to live an expanded life. I moved 52 times to different states or other countries. Once we were there, we traveled from within the state or the country. With my dad, it was 22 years and with my husband, 24 years. Once I got to a location I knew in one and a half to two years, I would be moving and setting off to get organized in a new location. Since I grew up with antiques, I had many different generations around me that talked about the love they shared with them and the period of times that they acquired them. Life for me has been one big adventure. I love it and the only regret I have is that there are some places that I cannot go to see old friends, but I love to write them.

What makes you a valuable resource in your industry?
I feel I am a valuable resource in both of my industries because I can speak firsthand the knowledge of historical places I have lived and shared. The antiques I have are from my families and ones that I have purchased in many different states in the U.S, to the countries I have also lived in. I have carried the traditions forth for many generations. I can reflect back with my photos and items that I have around me. This instantly puts me back in that period of time. Times are changing and so many things are getting lost in the process. Many people want an item for its value, but the meaning that it was passed along with or the person who gave it to me, means a lot more to me. Some people may think of it as far too messy, but when I look around I see my loved ones that are here or have gone before me. Many people thank me for sharing these two assets. For that feeling, I feel rewarded.

Agricultural Operations

JARVIS D. GARETSON
Partner
Garetson Brothers
2394 120th Road
Copeland, KS 67837 USA
garetsonbrothers@yahoo.com

Jarvis D. Garetson is a partner at Garetson Brothers, a farm that raises corn, wheat, cotton and milo. He, alongside his father, is responsible for the farm's daily operations and operational planning, which includes overseeing irrigation and nutrition management, applying pesticides, scheduling crops, harvesting, and maintaining the crucial relationships that help to sustain and grow the business. The farm, over which he has presided for more than 20 years, has been in his family since 1902. "Our blood is in the land," he says, referring the passion and gusto he puts into his homestead. Mr. Garetson, who reads High Plains Journal and Farm Journal to remain abreast of new developments, finds that the most gratifying aspect of his career is the fact that he is able to work alongside his mother, father and brother.

Innovation and defining the curve, rather than heading the curve, have placed the Garetson Brothers farm on the map. Over the past recent years, irrigation issues have threatened the yielding of one of Garetson Brothers' primary crops, irrigated corn. In order to make up for the shortage, and to grow a crop that didn't require so much water, around 2004 the family decided to plant one of the first 50-acre plots of cotton in the area. Within a short time, other farmers in Kansas — who perceived the threat of being wiped out due to water shortages — joined in and by 2003, Kansas had tens of thousands of acres of cotton to help sustain its economy.

Mr. Garetson received a Bachelor of Science in 1995 from Kansas State University. He is a member of the Kansas Farm Bureau, the Southwest Kansas Irrigation Association and the Kansas Milo Growers Association. In 2004, the Garetson Brothers farm was selected as a runner-up for the Top Producers distinction by Agweb.com powered by Farm Journal. In his spare time, Mr. Garetson enjoys the outdoors, including waterskiing. He also takes great pleasure in football.

Conversation with Jarvis D. Garetson

Cambridge Who's Who: What advice can you offer people aspiring to work in this profession?
Jarvis D. Garetson: Have your whole heart in the profession and don't get sidetracked. You need to make smart choices every day; there is a tight margin for error in the farming profession. You have to be comfortable taking risks due to Mother Nature having an effect on your crops. Farming is a very capital-intense profession.

What would you like to promote most about yourself or your business?
I have a passion for farming because my family has been a part of the industry for generations.

What is the most rewarding aspect of your career?
The most rewarding aspect is working with my family and having the opportunity to raise my five sons on the farm.

What is your motto?
My motto is the same belief that my grandfather held, which is, "Do the best that you can each and every time."

What is the most significant issue facing your profession today?
Significant issues facing my profession today are global warming and carbon credits.

What is your greatest professional accomplishment to date?
Helping to start a commercial grain storage facility to help fill the need of grain storage in the area. Using technology, GPS guidance, and automated section shutoff on our sprayers and planter helps to maximize efficiency of inputs.

What are your short-term and long-term career goals?
My short-term goal is to survive until next year by making the best-informed decisions every day. My long-term goal is to grow the farm so that any of my sons or nephews have the opportunity to get into the farming profession if they choose to.

And what specific steps have you taken toward achieving these goals?
Our farm utilizes crop consultants, crop insurance, market management, tax planning and a host of other available resources.

On what topic(s) do you consider yourself to be an expert?
Equipment operation and seed selection for the conditions that exist. It's hard to think of myself as an expert when I learn something new every day.

How do you remain current in your profession?
To remain current, I attend workshops annually, attend crop plot tours, visit with equipment personnel, and read different agriculture periodicals.

What are you passionate about?
I am passionate about my wife, five sons, extended family and, most importantly, my personal relationship with my Lord and Savior, Jesus Christ.

Weapon Manufacturing

Kelly J. Milne
General Manager
Atlantic Research Marketing Systems, Inc.
230 W. Center Street
West Bridgewater, MA 02379 USA
kelly@armsmounts.com
http://www.armsmounts.com

Kelly J. Milne goes to work every day with a mission to make her loved ones proud. As the general manager of Atlantic Research Marketing Systems, Inc., she has helped usher the family-run business into its 30th year of successful operation. The company, which designs and manufactures specialized system mounts for weapons used during the day and night, has provided products and services for military and civilian use since the early 1980s. In addition to system mounts, A.R.M.S.® offers scope rings, spacers, specialized apparel, self-cooling handguards for safety and comfort during firing, and the custom patent-pending Selective Integrated Rail® System. The S.I.R. system, which has been used in Iraq by soldiers in the United States Marine Corps, is specifically designed to allow for efficiency, and easy cleaning and repair. In 2006, the company's president and chief executive officer, Richard Swan, received The George M. Chinn Award from the National Defense Industrial Association for his contributions to the field of small arms and infantry weapons systems.

Ms. Milne, who is best known for her managerial skills, is also quite the marketing genius when it comes to showcasing her company's products in front of potential clients. She attends trade shows throughout the nation to inform enthusiasts about the latest development of weapons or accessories, and maintains contact with a number of private and military clients interested in small arms weaponry. Additionally, Ms. Milne is integral in research and development endeavors, many of which have led to the acquisition of more than 40 patents and 13 trademarks. Through collaborative business efforts across a worldwide network of distributors, she has helped A.R.M.S., Inc. to become a recognizable asset to the defense of the United States.

The recipient of a Bachelor of Arts in Psychology from Eastern Nazarene College in 1997, Ms. Milne is currently pursuing a master's degree to increase her knowledge of business practices. When not working or attending shows, she enjoys spending time with her children Emily and Matthew, and volunteering for a local conservation commission.

Conversation with Kelly J. Milne

Cambridge Who's Who: What would you like to promote most about yourself or your business?
Kelly J. Milne: I have excellent customer service, communication and management skills, which are very important in my profession and make me an incredibly valuable asset.

What is the most rewarding aspect of your career?
Not only do I work with my family, but I enjoy it.

What is your greatest professional accomplishment to date?
Working with the company for 10 years.

What are your short-term and long-term career goals?
I would like to finish my master's degree and move into a higher managerial position.

And what specific steps have you taken toward achieving these goals?
I work consistently and continue to educate myself, which I enjoy.

What is the most difficult obstacle or challenge you have faced in pursuit of your goals?
Living up to my family's expectations, although I have proven myself many times over. The fact that I work with my family does not detract from my abilities.

On what topics do you consider yourself to be an expert?
Coordinating trade shows, scheduling and management.

What is the most significant issue facing your profession today?
Being able to stay current with management policies.

Restaurant Management

Keita Sato
President
Hatsuhana of USA, Inc.
17 E. 48th Street
New York, NY 10017 USA
brooceli@aol.com
http://www.hatsuhana.com

With two locations in the heart of New York City's bustling Midtown and one in Honolulu, Hawaii, Hatsuhana Sushi Restaurant is continuously surpassing expectations for traditional Japanese cuisine in America. A well-respected favorite among sushi and sashimi lovers, the eatery is known for its excellent customer service, delectable fresh fish, and selection of high-quality warm dishes for those whose palates may not favor raw seafood. Hatsuhana's owner is Keita Sato, who prides himself on a customer base that trusts in the quality of the food and its ability to consistently satisfy.

According to Mr. Sato, many chefs and owners are concerned with monetary gain rather than creating a product that will keep patrons returning to fill dining room seats. He frequently gathers their input to implement changes to the menu and specials while retaining the familiar, lively and energetic atmosphere. In addition to ensuring customer satisfaction and managing daily operations, he supervises dining services, which include an efficient delivery option for late-night customers or workers on their lunch breaks. Although he has only officially been a proprietor for nine years, he has spent nearly his entire life in the business, since his father began in the restaurant as a chef and eventually assumed ownership. Mr. Sato himself went through rigorous culinary training, and can often be seen serving customers at the sushi bar when not at the captain's desk.

Reviews in New York Magazine, Saveur and Gourmet laud Hatsuhana as "a treat," "my favorite sushi place in the city ever," and "a very authentic sushi spot." This uncompromising attitude has only benefited Hatsuhana, which has since earned favorable reviews from The New York Times, New York Magazine, Saveur and Gourmet, not to mention an enviable reputation for authenticity. It is Mr. Sato's hope that with affordable prices and an atmosphere that provides a venerable escape to Japan in the center of a great metropolis, the restaurant will be able to sustain itself for many years to come.

CONVERSATION WITH KEITA SATO

CAMBRIDGE WHO'S WHO: What advice can you offer people aspiring to work in this profession?
KEITA SATO: You have to love it, first of all. Only do it if you love it and feel that you have something to share. If you feel you have great food and great service, you want to share it with people; you want people to experience this. I think that's the philosophy of a successful restaurant — you can't go for the big bucks right away.

How do you remain current in your profession?
I go by what I feel and I get customers' feedback all the time. People stop by and say, "Why don't you try doing this?" If it seems like a great idea, I'll do it. I don't want to absorb things that I get from outside. I want to try to set my own trends and standards for what we should be doing, not what other people are doing. I want to do things that make magazines write about us, instead of doing what magazines tell us we should do.

What is the most significant issue facing your profession today?
There's too much mixing going on, too much fusion of cuisine. Ideally, what I want other restaurants to do is concentrate on a specific type of cuisine and keep it very traditional and classic. I don't like these new types of restaurants that are one-stop shops. If you are going to a convenience store, you want everything under the same roof, but if you go to a restaurant, look at the menu and see many types of food, you won't be able to figure out what kind of restaurant it is. I want people to stay away from that. I don't like going to a restaurant where I'm looking at the menu and trying to figure out what they sell. That's why I consider a good sushi restaurant to be equivalent to a steakhouse in America.

What are your short-term and long-term career goals?
We've been here quite a long time; the restaurant is going to be 34 years old this year [2010]. We set the standards for the sushi industry quite a long time ago and we are looking forward to a glorious future. The company's business philosophy is to prioritize authenticity, tradition and extremely high quality.

CUSTOMER SERVICE MANAGEMENT

JOYCE E. WEISS

Customer Service Representative
Wal-Mart Stores, Inc.
7256 61st Avenue N.
Saint Petersburg, FL 33709 USA
wolves48.1@juno.com

In the beautiful waterfront area town of St. Petersburg, Fla., Joyce E. Weiss is a source of joy and radiance to everyone she encounters as a customer service manager in Walmart, one of the nation's largest and most popular retailers. The chain, which offers online and in-store purchasing options, has stores located throughout the entire country and is known for affordable prices and an assortment of products. Early in her childhood, Ms. Weiss was affiliated with the Girl Scouts organization, a membership she maintained through four of the six designated age levels. As she progressed through the ranks, she took with her many valuable tools, including leadership skills and the ability to work cooperatively with others on a team. Moreover, she learned how to listen to others' viewpoints with a fair and discerning ear. Ms. Weiss was also a member of her local 4-H club, inspired by her older sister, Lucy Lambert, to join the organization and enrich her immediate community.

After spending much of her young adulthood developing into a strong leader with outstanding interpersonal skills, she entered the workforce and obtained a position in accounting with the Sears Corporation. Upon learning the inner workings of the business and training for the appropriate amount of time, she then became an office manager and grew in her profession even further. Currently as Wal-Mart's customer service manager Ms. Weiss encounters a number of situations, many of which are genial and resolved easily. Others involve angry patrons and frustrated employees who may both require her assistance at some point in the transaction. Through it all, she remains calm and in control, channeling her 35 years of experience and pleasant demeanor to quell even the most volatile situations.

Since assuming her position in late 2009, Ms. Weiss has consistently delivered effective solutions and improved relations between employees and customers. Although she looks forward to retirement in the near future, she is determined to continue enjoying life and making it easier for others. In her free time, she enjoys reading mysteries, collecting unicorn paraphernalia, and creating liquid stained glass projects.

CONVERSATION WITH JOYCE E. WEISS

CAMBRIDGE WHO'S WHO: How did you become involved in the retail and merchandising industry?
JOYCE E. WEISS: It was one of the easiest to get into because of the benefits offered, especially by Sears at the time [at which I applied] in 1970.

Would you like us to promote any new endeavors for you?
I have been promoted to the position of customer service management as of October 2009. I have more front-end control with associates at the cash register. I do scheduling and management.

What is the most rewarding aspect of your career?
Customers who come back to say they love to shop at our store and that we have friendly people who are helpful to them. I'm from Pennsylvania and when we came down to South Florida in 1990, there were no Walmart stores.

What is your greatest professional accomplishment to date?
Growing with the company — moving up from doing accounting and being an office manager to becoming a customer service manager.

What are your short-term and long-term career goals?
My long-term goal is to retire, although I'm sure I'll be looking for something else [to work on]. I may not stay in retail, but I'll be helping people, possibly in the accounting area.

Who have been your mentors or people who have greatly influenced you?
There was Mrs. Whitehead, who influenced me when I went through 4-H, and Onegene Hahn.

What is the most difficult obstacle you have faced in pursuit of your goals?
When I first went looking for a job, being a woman [I heard] "You're only going to spend a certain amount of time [here]. You'll get pregnant, have kids and quit." Even when I went to Walmart, for women, moving up depended on the store manager. He wanted more men in managerial positions. Back in 1990 it was still that way, but now it's changed a little bit.

What advice can you offer to someone aspiring to work in this profession?
If a customer is very aggressive, it turns the person they're talking to off; they don't even want to help them. Customers need to understand that if they come off as aggressive, they won't receive good customer service. When I first started speaking on the phone with people, I really didn't think I wanted to do it, but I didn't have a choice. I found out that it wasn't as bad as I thought it was. When speaking with a customer, you have to take the time and try not to interrupt them — I still find myself doing this — because you're in a hurry and want to get [work] done. You have to be patient and just listen to them. Take a deep breath and count to 10. You may not always like what they say, but give them attention and eye-to-eye contact.

Biblical History and Archeology

James Fleming, Ed.D.
Chief Executive Officer
The Explorations in Antiquity Center
P.O. Box 3900
LaGrange, GA 30241 USA
biblicalresources@earthlink.net
http://www.explorationsinantiquity.net

As the chief executive officer of The Explorations in Antiquity Center, Dr. James Fleming documents the visual side of history, creating interactive experiences for the general public to explore and enjoy. His strategy is to take the dry and technical — in this case, faith documents throughout history — and form tangible exhibits where laypersons may experience them in a lively and more interesting way. In addition to overseeing the museum operations, conducting programs and conferences and raising money to fund the museum, Dr. Fleming organizes archaeological tours in Israel and the United States. He personally trains prospective tour guides of Jewish, Christian and Muslim descent who are bound for Israel, which is no easy feat in dealing with a region that is rife with sociopolitical and religious conflict. "Interfaith work...is so difficult, but it is important in that part of the world," he states. Dr. Fleming posits that there is a lot more in common between these people then they realize, and that most of them want three things: respect for the past, service for the present and responsibility for the future.

A profound interest in ancient history, archeology of the Roman period and biblical studies of the New Testament prompted Dr. Fleming to pursue a career in museum operations. Since 1973, he has worked and lived in Israel, where he has helped to organize eight excavations. He currently spends two to three months a year in Israel, travels to four to six U.S. cities a month, and visits England and Australia once a year to speak at conferences. He is a scholarly lecturer in archeology at the Hebrew University in Jerusalem, and professor of geography and archeology at the Tantur Ecumenical Institute for Advanced Theological Studies.

Dr. Fleming received a Doctor of Education in Philosophy of Education in 1973 from Southwestern Baptist Theological Seminary, and completed coursework in biblical archeology and theology the same year at The Hebrew University of Jerusalem and the New York Theological Seminary. He is an advisory board member of the Biblical Archeology Review Board and a member of The Galilean Resort & Campus.

Conversation with James Fleming, Ed.D.

Cambridge Who's Who: What would you like to promote most about yourself or your business?

James Fleming: We're building new phases to our Museum of Daily Life in Ancient Times. We hope to buy more property to expand The Explorations in Antiquity Center with additional displays and annexes.

What is the most rewarding aspect of your career?

We do museum tours. Every year, we are always adding some new kind of tour to Middle Eastern and Mediterranean countries. It's very rewarding to see a new tour catch on with travel participants. People who go on those tours have great interest and appreciation for what they've learned. The other rewarding aspect is implementing new programs at the physical museum in LaGrange, Ga., which elicits a good response from visitors. For example, we are just now building a new Roman theater, which will offer some very rewarding programs.

What is your greatest professional accomplishment to date?

Even though it no longer exists, we built and maintained a museum and learning center in Jerusalem, Israel. It was very hard to construct and sustain a company in an area of conflict and tension. But because we had programs that were open to Jews, Christians and Muslims — in a country where there is so much intolerance in terms of different faith traditions — it was meaningful to see the progress of people wanting to learn about traditions different from their own. We had to close it down eventually.

What is your motto?

Can you understand your faith documented, in light of its original cultural meanings? History and archeology can help interpret what these artifacts might have meant in their original context (when they were written) and then people can get excited about that.

What are your short-term career goals?

Short term, the main thing I have now is I'm trying to get the museum going with a firm foundation of new programs, new replicas, and with that, endowment so we can endure during the rough times. It's been a rough year for museums, generally. Educational and nonprofit organizations have been suffering more than churches, synagogues or schools. We're a little more esoteric in people's minds. Our attendance is up, but our donations are down. I suppose if we had to choose, it is better than having our donations up and our attendance down.

What is the most difficult obstacle or challenge you have faced in pursuit of your goals?

In difficult times, the challenge is to help people buy less, but give more. This translates to them valuing what is important, not just thinking about materialistic stuff. We ask people to fund things that are educational, important and of value; you can feel good about that. A related challenge is helping people to value the significance of giving to something important, which is good for your heart. Generally, when people saw their nest egg shrink, to invest in an experience became a good investment.

On what topic(s) do you consider yourself to be an expert?

The ancient history, geography and archeology behind religious documents.

How do you remain current in your profession?

I do lots of reading about new archeological digs. In our field, there are the American School of Oriental Research (ASOR), the American Academy of Religion and the Biblical Archeological Society (BAS), which I often reference. Additionally, I attend meetings and conferences where there are new reports with new information.

I'm at the stage now where I'm trying to do more writing and publish a book each year, which also helps me to remain current. Two years ago, I wrote "The Life of the Shepherd Farmer and Village in Biblical Times." Last year, I authored "Jesus' Last Night with His Disciples," which was 250 pages with 500 color illustrations. Now I'm working on a title called "The Good Shepherd: The Life of the Ancient Shepherds." It will also have 500 photographs; I hope to have it completed by the end of 2010.

How do you compile all the photographs?

I have an archive of approximately 350,000 photographs. Obviously, I focus on new archeological sites and have made several trips to expand the archive. The photographs are important as are the words; also, most people are visual people.

What advice can you offer fellow members who work in your industry?

Be interactive — museums and academic institutions that are purely lectures and books are not doing well. Do something to help people feel that they are better experiencing, say, the ancient world, or faith tradition; take the subject, relate it to an object and have visitors interact with that object. Our museum is all-interactive. This is why we have full-scale replicas, not just stuff behind the glass, which is not interesting for most people. This is a continuous process where we see how these things work and our creative docent relates these exhibits to the past to convey their relevance.

We try to move from the area of knowledge to understanding. One reason we want this Roman theater replica is so we can do more outdoor activities and drama, and not just look at the architecture of a theater. In the four Gospels about the life of Jesus, a lot of his ministries were around the Sea of Galilee. In our next phase, we would like to purchase some land next door and make a football field-sized pond the shape of the Sea of Galilee, put some ancient harbors, have a fishing boat (replicating one that was found 12 years ago), and use the shoreline as the setting to talk about some of the teachings. It would be an interactive walk covering what was said where and the conditions of certain parts of the sea.

What are you passionate about?
The broad answer is being a teacher and seeing the sparkle come to people's eyes when they understand something. I'm also passionate about designing activities, programs and physical settings of exhibits to help that sparkle come to people's eyes. In the scientific age, in one sense, the truth is largely yet to be discovered and ahead of us. But there's also a lot of interesting truth from the past to be uncovered. It's nice to have people excited about both directions; to me, it's more about getting people excited about the past. When you stop to think about it, one definition of a cultured person is that they can appreciate the value of something old. I say this without intending to sound judgmental against someone who doesn't yet have that appreciation. How can you get them excited about the past as well as the future?

Who have been your mentors or people who have greatly influenced you?
George Earnest Wright and his writings — he was an archeologist from Harvard University and a biblical theologian. You usually don't find a theologian who is into dirty fingernail work like archeology. He was interested in taking the dry, technical and scientific [aspects] and applying it to a faith document.

Randolph Crump Miller, a philosopher of education, was also someone who greatly influenced me. He really stressed experiential learning activities such as involving the subject with the object. This influenced me in the direction I took of wanting to guide tours and build replicas you can see, touch and experience.

LABORATORY SCIENCE AND MEDICAL TECHNOLOGY

ANN L. MALTBY, MS, MT, SH (ASCP)
Medical Technologist (Retired)
Laboratory Alliance of Central New York, LLC
P.O. Box 399
Liverpool, NY 13088 USA
amaltby@twcny.rr.com
http://www.laboratoryalliance.com

Ann L. Maltby is a retired medical technologist, formerly employed by the Laboratory Alliance of Central New York, LLC. Her expertise in laboratory analysis and medical technology education comes from a career spanning more than 40 years. She has overseen a hematology laboratory, analyzed tests, reported results to hospitals and doctors' offices, and tested for disease. Ms. Maltby, who reads Laboratory Medicine to remain abreast of new developments in her field, also has extensive experience teaching medical lab technician students.

To this day, she considers honesty to be one of the most important characteristics that set her apart from others. Her ability to engage learners while maintaining a cheerful yet professional etiquette enabled her to get into the minds of her students and make sure they absorbed the necessary information. One solid hint of advice comes from the bottom of Ms. Maltby's heart: "Always follow your dreams. Go as far as you can with education and never give up."

The Laboratory Alliance of Central New York, LLC is a for-profit medical reference laboratory that provides upstate New York with extensive, high-quality laboratory testing to more than 500,000 patients each year. In keeping up with the newest medical and information system technology, the company is able to offer more than 1,400 tests and test combinations. With a number of operating sites throughout western New York, the Laboratory Alliance of Central New York, LLC employs more than 400 individuals. In one year, the company performs more than 8,500,000 tests and generates revenues in the approximate amount of $46 million.

In 1985, Ms. Maltby received a master's degree in medical technology from the Upstate Medical University. She is a licensed medical technologist in the state of New York and certified in hematology by the American Society for Clinical Pathology. In her spare time, Ms. Maltby enjoys traveling, creating jewelry and crafts, and admiring artwork, watercolors and acrylic painting.

Conversation with Ann L. Maltby, MS, MT, SH (ASCP)

Cambridge Who's Who: What would you like to promote most about yourself or your business?
Ann L. Maltby: When I was upstate, I taught hematology to undergraduate medical students. For several years, I taught residents while working in the hematology lab for several years. I also taught medical technician students.

Do you have a motto?
Honesty is the best policy.

What is the most rewarding aspect of your career?
The most rewarding aspect was teaching the residents and medical students; also, when I worked in a special hematology lab.

What is your greatest professional accomplishment to date?
My master's degree is my greatest professional accomplishment.

How did you get involved with health care?
When I was young, I wanted to be a nurse. Yet, I was discouraged from being a nurse because I had a disability. They thought that standing on my feet all the time wouldn't be good for me, but I wanted to work in the medical field. I looked into physical or occupational therapy, or medical technology and I chose to be a medical technician.

What is the most difficult obstacle or challenge you have faced in pursuit of your goals?
The undergraduate courses were heavy in science, which I found to be very difficult.

How do you remain current in your profession?
The main thing I do to remain current in my profession is partake in continuing education through work.

What advice can you offer people aspiring to work in this profession?
You need hard work and perseverance.

On what topic(s) do you consider yourself to be an expert?
Hematology and medical technology education.

What are you passionate about?
I am passionate about traveling, health care and art.

Computer Hardware and Software Technology

David William Scott
Systems Administrator, Government Contractor
National Oceanic and Atmospheric Administration
308 16th Street S.E.
Washington, DC 20003 USA
david.w.scott@noaa.gov

David William Scott is a systems administrator and government contractor for the National Oceanic and Atmospheric Administration (NOAA) Department of Commerce. With expertise in computer hardware and software technology, he is responsible for delivering technical support, managing desktop applications, hardware and software, working on the Uniplexed Information and Computing System (UNIX), and maintaining records. The NOAA is a federal agency that assesses and evaluates conditions of the oceans and atmosphere. They provide an assortment of services, including the prediction of severe weather conditions, coastal restoration, and information and infrastructure to help support economies around the world (including one-third of America's gross domestic product). From the first computer repair course he took in 1993, Mr. Scott was hooked on software and hardware. That day, he went home and took apart his then-brand-new Intel i386SX computer and put it all back together. "When it was done, I pressed the power button hoping it would come on and it did," he remarks. That moment, he realized that he had the zeal and the courage to learn and apply his knowledge to innovation and highly technical functions.

To this day, after 21 years in the profession, Mr. Scott admits that a lot of what he does now is self-taught, based on knowledge he has gained over the years through talking, listening and studying. Working for a company that is known for cutting-edge research and high-tech instrumentation, he attributes his success to his tenacity, learning skills and willingness to do whatever it takes to get the job done. In the near future, he would like to explore opportunities in computer forensics, the branch of forensic science that deals with evidence that is stored digitally and/or on computers.

Mr. Scott received a bachelor's degree in computer science from The University of Maryland. He is a member of IEEE and the Alpha Sigma Lambda National Honor Society. In his spare time, Mr. Scott partakes in photography, studying the history of the Civil War, tutoring, reading about genealogy, and working on computers.

Conversation with David William Scott

Cambridge Who's Who: What has been the key to your success?
David William Scott: I do a lot of research and take proactive steps to continue learning. My passion for learning keeps me going and if I have any free time, I will begin to look up things I don't know or that I may want to know more about. I just love to learn, so I never stop learning.

Who have been your mentors or people who have greatly influenced you?
There have been several, from professors to friends and family.

Do you have a motto or principle that guides your work?
Put the Lord first and let everything fall into place.

What is your greatest professional accomplishment to date?
Becoming a member of Who's Who Among Students.

Audio-Visual Forensics

Larry Howell Williams
Deputy Administrator, Commander
Houston Police Department
11810 Terrero Court
Tomball, TX 77377 USA
lhwilliams8@yahoo.com
http://www.houstontx.gov/police

"It's CSI on TV versus the real thing," says Larry Howell Williams, when asked to describe his position as deputy administrator and commander for the Houston Police Department. In 2000, a new show called "CSI: Crime Scene Investigation" surfaced, where forensic criminologists use DNA along with other crime scene evidence to capture the bad guy. His biggest problem with the program was that it gave him and his colleagues a new job responsibility — that of "explaining the reality of fact versus fiction." According to Mr. Williams, the techniques, technology and events that occur on the boob tube just aren't feasible. Also, the unknowing public doesn't know the difference between those two, so it is up to him to make sure the rumors and misinformation are dispelled.

Mr. Williams has 36 years of experience working with the Houston Police Department, where he oversees 12 employees and manages the operations of three laboratories, which includes acquisition, budgeting and grant funding. His expertise includes the supervision of forensic laboratories for homeland security, audio, video, and photographic forensics, and photography and grant management. The most gratifying aspect of his career is being successful in his investigations and prosecutions. By all means possible, Mr. Williams promotes integrity within his profession. "You must understand that your integrity is more important than any other outside influence of any type," he says.

Mr. Williams is a man of many great accomplishments. He created the first forensic laboratory in Texas; he has been featured in the Texas Journal of Forensic Analysts; and, in 1991, he even led the Houston Gunners, the football team of the Emergency Services League, to their first national championship. Mr. Williams has also participated in the photography competition conducted by the International Association for Photography Art Dealers. In the near future, he would like to have made a meaningful impact on current technology.

A certified forensic-audio analyst, Mr. Williams completed coursework in forensic audio and media through the University of Houston and the

University of Michigan. He also received training in forensics from the FBI and the Michigan State Police. He is a member of the Intelligence Group of the Texas Gulf Coast Region, the Law Enforcement Emergency Services Video Association, the Joint Terrorism Task Force, the International Association for Identification, and a Fellow of the American College of Forensic Examiners.

Conversation with Larry Howell Williams

Cambridge Who's Who: What is the most rewarding aspect of your career?
Larry Howell Williams: The most rewarding aspect of my career is being able to exonerate innocent people and convict those who are truly guilty.

What is your greatest professional accomplishment to date?
My greatest professional accomplishment is being able to successfully assist agencies.

What are your short-term and long-term career goals?
I would like to retire soon and I want to go back into professional photography. If people can find me, I am always willing to assist them.

And what specific steps have you taken toward achieving these goals?
My short-term goal is to move forward and balance my career and family life.

What is the most difficult obstacle or challenge you have faced in pursuit of your goals?
The most difficult obstacle I have faced is having to explain the reality of fact versus the fiction that gets presented in so many instances. There are things that can be done, but the processes, software and hardware are actually classified, so people are never going to see them on a TV show. It's just never going to happen.

On what topics do you consider yourself to be an expert?
I consider myself to be an expert on audio and video forensics and digital photography.

How do you remain current in your profession?
I provide my staff with every opportunity for training that they can acquire. I think it's very important for the newer and younger members getting into in the field to receive as much proper and adequate training that they can possibly achieve.

What makes you a valuable resource in your industry?
I am a valuable resource in your industry because of my experience and management methods.

What is the most significant issue facing your profession today?
The most significant issue is the fact that audio and visual forensics is very expensive. There are changes and modifications to programming software and hardware that take place annually. It becomes very costly to keep up with the technology, which is everyone's problem — it's an ongoing, number one issue. Ultimately, it's [about] how much justice you can afford. That's where the credibility and integrity come in because you have to have people who won't go too far, and people who won't be slackers and not go far enough.

What advice can you offer fellow members who work in your industry?
You have to be immune to political pressure. You must understand that your integrity is more important than any other outside influence of any type for your entire career. You have to have an impeccable history because you can't have anything in your background that someone could use against you. You have to resist everything and with experience and practice, you can.

What advice can you offer people aspiring to work in this profession?
You will find it absolutely fascinating because you will be privileged to things that very few other people ever will.

What are you passionate about?
I am passionate about getting it right and doing it right the first time. Never rush anything so that you have to come back and do it again. Accuracy and integrity are everything.

Who have been your mentors or people who have greatly influenced you?
Stephen Hawking, Albert Einstein and P.T. Barnum have greatly influenced me. What [a person is able to do] is only as limited as any individual's capability and perseverance. If they just quit, they gave up too soon. You have to do this on such a consistent basis so that you know what to do and what not to do, inherently based on your own experience. Training is one thing, but you have to get in there and actually do it.

Do you have a motto or principle that guides your work?
It's more important to be correct independently, than to just be one of the guys.

336

BEHAVIORAL HEALTH COUNSELING

HILDA F. BOOTH
Clinical Intake Coordinator
Palmetto Health Alliance
3134 Prentice Avenue
Columbia, SC 29205 USA
hbooth@sc.rr.com
http://www.chilel.com

Humans may need counseling for a variety of reasons and it takes a strong-willed person to assume the position of a counselor and help people, no matter what they are going through on a daily basis. Caring for individuals with mental health problems has been Hilda F. Booth's strong suit for over 20 years and she enjoys helping them recover and turn their lives around. With more than 15 years of experience as a clinical intake coordinator for the Palmetto Health Alliance, Ms. Booth uses her expertise in counseling to help with emergency room crisis intervention. She uses her persistence every day when speaking to individuals and feels that it has made her successful.

Ms. Booth became involved in her profession due to the inspiration from her husband, whom she lost to a motorcycle accident in 1990. Less than a month after the incident, she was forced to do grief therapy with a young woman whose husband had also been killed. That was when she decided she needed to leave the agency where she was working and take a break. She knew she had to stop outpatient therapy because she wouldn't be able to resolve her crisis while working with someone in a similar position to hers. In order to justly serve patients, Ms. Booth needed to identify their issues and devise methods with which to treat them.

The profession of behavioral counseling has more to do with the mind than with medicine. According to Ms. Booth, simply prescribing pills for someone with a mental disability is not sufficient; therapy helps an individual to heal and lead a better life. To complement her formal training, she has been studying the art of the Dragon's Way of Qi Gong, which is a Chinese meditative practice used to help stress management and health. When employing this method, she uses her intuition and instincts to develop her level of understanding even further.

Ms. Booth received a Master of Science in Clinical Psychology from Valdosta State University and is a certified Qi Gong instructor and national certified counselor. The highlight of her career was receiving the Employee of the Year award while working for Coastal Empire Community Mental Health Center.

CONVERSATION WITH HILDA F. BOOTH

CAMBRIDGE WHO'S WHO: What would you like to promote most about yourself or your business?
HILDA F. BOOTH: I've been to China four times and studied Qi Gong with different masters. I am studying the movement and spiritual aspects of it and teaching one class. I am being certified in the Dragon's Way of Qi Gong, which is used for weight loss. It's a combination of diet, stress management, lifestyle change and exercises, which take 20 to 25 minutes a day. You have to do it in a relaxed state or it will not work properly. I am also a certified teacher supervisor in Chi-Lel Qi Gong.

On what topics do you consider yourself to be an expert?
I'm truly an expert in counseling, with a specialty in emergency room crisis intervention.

What is the most rewarding aspect of your career?
Seeing people change their lives. It's seeing someone who was absolutely hopeless and helpless turn things around so that they are productive again.

What is your greatest professional accomplishment to date?
In 1990, I was Employee of the Year for the agency in which I was working. Now I am privileged to be able to contribute to the training of the psychiatry residents in Richland Memorial Hospital.

What are your short-term and long-term career goals?
My main goal is to teach the new way for weight loss through the Dragon's Way of Qi Gong when I retire. I would also like to continue with the hospital for the next three or four years.

How do you remain current in your profession?
I do continuing education every year and go to a week-long conference called "The Psychology of Health Immunity and Disease." I get caught up with that and then I do some readings and trainings as we go along. It's sponsored by the National Institute for the Clinical Application of Behavioral Medicine.

What makes you a valuable resource in your industry?
My tenacity — I don't give up and I don't back down. I've listened to my instincts and intuition.

What is the most significant issue facing your profession today?
We have [very little] resources because of budget cuts and hospital closures. There's nowhere to put anyone and they can't get the therapy they need in order to get better. People don't get into the situations they are in overnight and they are not going to get out of them overnight. Insurance companies give them three sessions and that's about it, but it depends on the situation. When I started out, it was nothing to keep somebody in therapy for a year, but now we give them a pill and send them off. The pills are great, but the therapy is more necessary in my opinion. The community mental health systems are reduced to doing nothing for the chronically mentally ill people unless they are so sick that they are going to be dangerous to themselves. They're only given enough treatment until they're not dangerous anymore; then they go back on the street. It's a revolving door, and I think that is the biggest challenge.

What advice can you offer people aspiring to work in this profession?
Find yourself a stress management technique that works for you and practice it. Any energy exercise is better for stress management than any of those aerobic activities. Find yourself an outlet that's practical and that you can keep up with because if you can't do it every day, it's not going to work.

INDEPENDENT TECHNICAL CONSULTING

ELEANOR BROWN
Owner, Independent Contractor
E.S. Brown and Associates
949 Aberdeen Avenue N.E.
Apartment D313
Renton, WA 98056 USA
eaglegazer1@gmail.com

For most people, death is considered an end — a definitive closing to a life that may or may not have fulfilled its purpose. Eleanor Brown, however, was presumed dead for an astounding 26 minutes, during which she claims to have seen a bright light and been visited by her deceased father. After speaking with him, Ms. Brown realized that she had not yet chosen a career path, and awoke from a coma 10 days later with the determination to rebuild her life. To do so, she obtained reports from the local fire department about the events leading up to her experience before conducting independent research. Learning to drive again was one of her more secondary tasks, while regaining her teaching abilities was of the utmost importance.

Prior to establishing her consulting company, E. S. Brown and Associates, Ms. Brown assisted in the development and building of Washington state's Everett Public Market and tested data systems for the Lunar Orbiter program missions by the Boeing engineering company. Using the knowledge gained from these experiences and others, she presently offers a variety of services to her clients, including strategic business advisement, organizational assistance, consulting on structural systems, and basic computer instruction. She also provides sound marketing schemes to increase revenue, encourage business relationships and garner new clientele.

Ms. Brown holds a master's degree in psychology with minors in whole systems design and arbitration from Antioch University West (now Antioch University Los Angeles), and a bachelor's degree in sociology with minors in architecture and mathematical statistics from the University of Washington. Her latest venture, a book entitled "Piercing the Fog," recounts her near-death experience and encourages others who have undergone similar situations to chronicle their post-recovery life progression. A member of Mensa International Limited, she was nominated for and featured in the Who's Who Among America's Teachers prestigious publication.

CONVERSATION WITH ELEANOR BROWN

CAMBRIDGE WHO'S WHO: What are you passionate about?
ELEANOR BROWN: I really have a passion for learning, so I look for new ideas and new experiences. I love to meet new people.

Do you have a motto or principle that guides your work?
"There is an opportunity to grow every day."

What is the most rewarding aspect of your career?
The most rewarding thing over the years – whether it's teaching or creating systems or organizations – is watching other people. I love to open doors and share this passion with others, so that they too can grow.

What is your greatest professional accomplishment to date?
There was an old historic building that the owners wanted to keep, but they had to find a use for it — it's more than 100 hundred years old. I did research on its history and surveyed what type of businesses might work in the downtown area. I did a lot of interviewing of business owners and finally decided to turn it into a public market. I surveyed what they did in other public markets that would help it maintain itself. I was told by many people that it was in a dying town, but [the market] has been around for 30 years now and became a model for other communities. You can create public markets anywhere; it's like a collection of little shops. I had a place on the main floor where entertainers could come in during the day and it became a high-activity area.

On what topics do you consider yourself to be an expert?
I'm an expert in systems, whether human brain or computer systems. My degrees were in sociology and psychology.

What are your short-term and long-term career goals?
I love the educational community. I have been applying for jobs at a local community college and begun to write stories and a book about the process I used to create a public market. My main goal is to get the cash flow back.

What makes you a valuable resource in your industry?
Understanding how the brain works, how people learn and taking neuro-linguistic

programming (NLP), I learned that there are what you call learning modalities. Females are auditory-visual, so I would see my female students listening and writing notes — that's how they learn. Males are visual-kinesthetic and I taught more toward the male style. If you can hook your students into learning through their five senses, they will have a better chance of remembering what they learned.

How do you remain current in your profession?
I have a lot of magazines and watch a lot of discovery, history and science programs. I have given talks to different groups and before my incident, as a professional counselor I used to do teaching sessions as a corporate trainer.

What is the most significant issue facing your profession today?
The main thing is the slow economy. Even really good businesses are letting people go because there just aren't any jobs.

What advice can you offer people aspiring to work in this profession?
I will give the same advice that my father gave, which was "Follow your passion; what's your life without passion?" That was his favorite saying. Both of my parents followed through with what they wanted to do. My mother worked until she was 86.

I had a student in one of my classes who was not doing any of the work, so I asked him why he was taking this class. He told me that his parents had decided that he should major in computers. I told him what my father had told me and said, "If you can go home, get the courage to stand up to your parents and tell them that this is not what you want to do, I will give you at least a D."

BRAILLE TRANSCRIPTION AND INSTRUCTION

MIRIAM ELIZABETH DIXON, M.ED., BA
Braille Teacher
North Carolina Division of Services for the Blind
305 Ashe Avenue
Raleigh, NC 27606 USA
miriam1@mindspring.com
http://www.dhhs.state.nc.us/dsb

A man named Louis Braille was only 15 when he developed the system that would change the way blind people live and interact with others. In 1812, he was playing in his father's shop when he had a terrible accident that left him blind. By 1824, he had created what we know today as Braille, which consists of a six-dot cell and is based upon character sets of various languages. Miriam Elizabeth Dixon, a Braille teacher for the North Carolina Division of Services for the Blind, entered into the field of teaching the blind and visually impaired because of her own visual impairment and interest in reading. She credits the inspiration of her parents and the family's interest in literacy for the success she has today. It is estimated that as many as 80 percent of all blind people are unemployed and through her current profession, she hopes to affect change that lessens this figure.

As a person who enjoys reading and is very passionate about it, Ms. Dixon believes that every visually impaired or blind person should have the opportunity to learn how to read. She focuses on adults who have recently lost their vision and teaches them to read using Braille, while remaining careful not to show pity or treat them as if they are handicapped. She feels that Braille literacy is too important to stop teaching it, and hopes that she never has to retire after 32 years of doing what she loves.

In 1984, Ms. Dixon received a Master of Education in Special Education, with a concentration in visual impairment from North Carolina State University. She also received a Bachelor of Arts in Psychology from The University of North Carolina, Chapel Hill in 1977 and a certification in literary Braille transcription from the National Library Service for the Blind and Physically Handicapped in 1978. She is a current member of the Association for Education and Rehabilitation of the Blind and Visually Impaired, and the National Braille Association.

Conversation with Miriam Elizabeth Dixon, M.Ed., BA

Cambridge Who's Who: What would you like to promote most about yourself or your business?
Miriam Elizabeth Dixon: My biggest accomplishment is following the ongoing progress of one of my former student's research and development. He has a patent on a new Braille cell for the Braille displays for computers. The new Braille displays, instead of one line of text, will be a full page Braille display. This will enable the Braille reader to obtain information more quickly and read the Internet web pages more efficiently. The price of the future Braille technology will be less expensive than it is today.

How did you become involved in this industry?
I was interested in working with the blind and visually impaired since I was 8 years old and I am interested in Braille literacy. I enjoy reading, and I did not like thinking about a newly blind or visually impaired person not being able to read.

What are your short-term and long-term career goals?
I have worked for more than 30 years as a Braille teacher for adults who have recently lost their vision. My goal is to work as long as I can and I do not plan to retire anytime soon; Braille literacy is too important. When I do retire, I will continue to work on some aspect of Braille literacy, either through contract teaching or transcribing.

And what specific steps have you taken toward achieving these goals?
I co-founded the North Carolina Braille Literacy Council and I plan on continuing to be active on this Council. I will also continue to work on my skills in the area of Braille transcription.

On what topic(s) do you consider yourself to be an expert?
Braille teaching and adjustment to blindness for adults who have recently lost their vision.

How do you remain current in your profession?
I am a member of the National Braille Association. I visit websites, network, read many journals and attend conferences about Braille.

What makes you a valuable resource in your industry?

I have been in this field for over 30 years. My personal experience, enthusiasm and interest in Braille literacy make me a valuable resource.

What is the most significant issue facing your profession today?

The main obstacles are the 80 percent unemployment rate for the blind and visually impaired, the exorbitant price of Braille technology, and the threat that Braille will become obsolete in the future. There is no other alternative written medium for the blind.

What advice can you offer fellow members who work in your industry?

I would like my fellow professionals to have compassion and belief in the blind and visually impaired, but not to pity them.

What advice can you offer people aspiring to work in this profession?

It is important not to think of this as a 9-to-5 job, but to work hard for the newly blind individuals. It is important to have the special skills and knowledge to rehabilitate them.

Who have been your mentors or people who have greatly influenced you?

My eighth-grade European history teacher and headmaster in Florence, Italy, and my first supervisor, who hired me to be a Braille teacher.

What is your favorite quote?

"Give a man a fish and you feed him for a day. Teach a man to fish and you feed him for a lifetime." — Chinese proverb

Children's and Family Services

Rosanna L. Michela
Child Protective Case Worker
Albany County Department for Children, Youth and Families
New York, USA
spiltjoe@aol.com

Rosanna L. Michela always knew that she wanted to work with children in some way. Her initial plan to become a teacher didn't quite come to pass as she had expected, so she earned an Associate of Applied Science from Hudson Valley Community College and entered the field of social work. Since joining this often selfless class of professionals, Ms. Michela has been a champion for children's rights and a voice for youngsters whose lives need guidance. In Albany County, N.Y., she conducts in-home visits to ensure the health and safety of children and monitors their progress as the Department for Children, Youth and Families responds to various claims about their welfare. Ms. Michela also attends family court with her clients, collaborates with other agencies to reduce the number of youth entering the system, and schedules necessary services to protect their interests. Focused on empowering families to become more involved in their children's welfare, she works with parents to help them face challenges and seek support, information and advocacy.

Although her main goal is to strengthen and reunite families, Ms. Michela must unfortunately sometimes facilitate a child's removal from their home if abuse, abandonment or neglect is suspected. Reducing the number of placements in foster care is equally important to her, but above all, she is concerned with securing an environment in which children are allowed to thrive, flourish and live up to their greatest potential. One of her career highlights was helping a little girl in foster care to enroll in school; she later found out that the girl graduated from high school and college, and knew that her dedication had paid off. While being recognized as a two-time recipient of an Employee of the Month award has certainly been gratifying, nothing warms Ms. Michela's heart more than to know that a child or children have benefitted from her tireless efforts.

Just as she has served as an inspiration to many of the youth she encounters, Ms. Michela credits her supportive friends, colleagues and late parents, Elissa and Joseph Camuglia, with the encouragement she needed to pursue her dreams. Though she receives much satisfaction from interacting with children on a daily basis, she also enjoys attending her son Joseph's sporting events, traveling, entertaining guests, cooking and baking.

CONVERSATION WITH ROSANNA L. MICHELA

CAMBRIDGE WHO'S WHO: What has been the most difficult obstacle or challenge you have faced in pursuit of your goals?
ROSANNA L. MICHELA: Family court is a big obstacle. We have to remove children from their homes, follow up with petitions, and take them to family court. Sometimes they just don't understand; they can't see the whole picture. They see what's on paper, but we're [social workers] the ones who are out there every day in these homes trying to make a difference with these families. When we can't, the judges are the ones who send the kids right back and it's very frustrating. When you have to continue working with the family, a lot of times you end up having to remove the children again because the family hasn't changed.

What prompted you to become involved in this profession?
I really wanted to be a teacher, but couldn't work in that capacity, so I figured doing something like this would allow me to work with children.

What are your short-term or long-term goals?
By next year, I'll be retired.

Have you ever become really attached to a particular child?
It's hard not to. I take [my work] home with me, but I don't talk about it when I go home — it's in the back of my mind. I had three siblings in my care who went home with their mother after three years. This little boy was a year and a half when he went in and now he's 5 years old. I went there one day and he was getting out of a van. I said hello to him but he didn't [recognize] who I was. He got out of the car and said, "Oh Rosanna, I've missed you." I would spend my whole day with them, transporting them back and forth, and I developed an attachment to them. Some of the kids I've worked with have been adopted and it feels good.

On what topics do you consider yourself to be an expert?
Every time we have new [social workers], I always take them out and teach them the job because it's a lot to learn. I'm different from some of my co-workers — some of them are very hands-on with their clients. My interest

is in the children; adults can do what they want. I don't take it personally if they yell and scream at me.

How do you remain current in your profession?
I attend trainings every time a new law comes out.

CLINICAL SOCIAL WORK

JOHN T. SLOMA, LCSW, LP
Licensed Clinical Social Worker
Associated Counseling
24 E. 12th Street, Room 4E
New York, NY 10003 USA
jtsloma@optonline.net
http://www.associatedcounseling.org

For more than 35 years, John T. Sloma has been helping others focus on and improve their well-being by following the example of his late father, John Anthony Sloma, a concert violinist who always worked hard and maintained a "can-do" attitude. Mr. Sloma recalls his father as the type of person who could "take lemons and make lemonade all the time." A licensed clinical social worker for Associated Counseling, an insurance-based private practice located in Middletown, N.Y., Mr. Sloma also maintains an office in New York City. He offers services such as individual and group therapy, and family and couples counseling. Associated Counseling is an affiliation of therapists that shoulders the responsibility of giving the best care it can to every patient it receives.

Though he had been encouraged by his father to consider a career in engineering, Mr. Sloma developed an interest in psychotherapy at a fairly young age. He reminisces about reading works like Salinger's "The Catcher in the Rye," and Camus' "The Stranger," and learning of Sigmund Freud and existentialism. Now an established professional, he brings his expertise in psychotherapy and marriage counseling to the treatment of three to 13 patients on a daily basis. Within the realm of psychotherapy, professionals focus mainly on building relationships with their patients, which can be difficult at times. While working with each patient, they must maintain belief in themselves and in their intrinsic value of basic human caring in order to build trust with their patients. It is only once this trust is formed that the counseling can move forward and the patient is able to achieve personal growth.

Even though he is faced with obstacles and frustration at times, Mr. Sloma finds great pleasure in helping each of his patients experience emotional growth and self-understanding. "It is very rewarding and fulfilling when the patient finds self-love and self-acceptance based on the work that I have been doing," explains Mr. Sloma. He believes that it takes more than sitting on a couch and hearing his patients' words. It requires intent listening and the desire to help each individual through whatever trial he or she is facing.

A member of the American Society of Group Psychotherapy &

Psychodrama, Mr. Sloma received a Master of Social Work from the Graduate School of Social Service at Fordham University in 1980, followed by a fellowship in research at the New York State Psychiatric Institute. He became a licensed psychoanalyst by the state of New York in 2006. In 2009, Mr. Sloma was recognized as a Professional of the Year in Clinical Social Work by Cambridge Who's Who. In spring of 2008, he appeared in an MTV documentary called "True Life: I Need Anger Management."

Conversation with John T. Sloma, LCSW, LP

Cambridge Who's Who: What lessons have you learned as a professional in your field for the past 40 years?
John T. Sloma: The key words that come to mind are perseverance, devotion and commitment. These values are the bedrock of my competence, self-confidence and effectiveness with my patients.

On what topics do you consider yourself to be an expert?
Psychoanalysis, group psychotherapy and role playing.

What characteristics help to separate you from your competitors?
My dogged perseverance. I exemplify that old phrase, "Success is 10 percent inspiration and 90 percent perspiration," because I work and just go. I have a forward momentum and a powerful goal-setting, can-do ethic. If I picked a goal, I will attain it sooner or later. There is a certain article of faith that operates in that too: faith in myself.

What motivates you?
Learning how to have faith in yourself, and believe in yourself and your own strength, capacity and abilities. These are the characteristics that I learned from my father; he was very strong and believed in himself. He used to say, "The 'difficult' we do today; the 'impossible' takes a bit longer!"

What short-term and long-term career goals are you currently pursuing?
My short- and long-term goal is to continue to provide a wide range of effective mental health services to my local Orange County community in New York, as well as my New York City population.

What is the most difficult obstacle or challenge you have faced in pursuit of your goals?
On a very personal level, years ago when I was in my 20s, I had a defiant attitude of "Why do I need a license to help people?" That attitude proved to be a stumbling block for seven years until I decided that I would go get the license so that I could help others. I had a lot of other training, which allowed me to be effective, but it was outside the mainstream of mental health for licensing.

I was able to eventually alter my attitude and I began to realize that it was the public who needed to feel safe because they don't understand the training that is involved. It was a personal growth process for me.

What is the most significant issue facing your profession today?
The biggest issue for me is that they keep calling it "mental health" and "mental illness," which is a misnomer, and distorted. It creates a stigma that keeps people away from getting help. The real issue is that it is about emotional health. "Mental" health connotes a loss of cognitive capacity to think clearly. We lose our cognitive capacity to think clearly due to anxiety states that impair cognition and judgment. It's emotional health that facilitates clear thinking and affects functioning using intelligence, judgment and so forth. We should be teaching emotional education as a basic part of our American curriculum.

What are some questions that an individual interested in your services can ask to ensure a more productive relationship?
They are free to ask any questions that they may need to; questions from the patients are never discouraged. When people come for help, counseling and treatment, they usually come with what is called a presenting problem. They will come and tell us how they have been feeling and ask how we can help them. My responsibility is to provide the best treatment that I can. The patient's responsibility is to commit to a process of growth and change. The real test is having the patient commit to 10-15 weekly sessions to gain trust between them and the counselor, and once that trust has been built, then the counselor can begin to work on the real issues.

Did you ever consider pursuing a different career path or another profession? If yes, how did you end up working in your current field?
When I was in junior high school, I had an inkling toward engineering, but that was more my father's agenda for me. I first became interested in the field I am in now while I was in high school, but it did not all come together until I was in my 20s.

What do you find to be the most rewarding about your profession?
What is most rewarding is when it is clear that the patient is beginning to develop self-understanding that has some depth, insight and substantial self-awareness so that I feel like all the efforts I had been making are bearing fruit. It's much more than just sitting, listening and collecting money.

What is your favorite or least-favorite work-related task to do and why?
My favorite task is being able to offer a completely accurate and useful piece of interpretive feedback to the patient at the time when it is really going to

register. It is very satisfying when that all comes together and the patient is ready to hear the interpretation.

What advice can you offer fellow members or others aspiring to work in your industry?
Trust your own devotion and commitment, and use the strengths and the belief in yourself.

Who have been your mentors or people who have greatly influenced you?
My father, John Anthony Sloma, was a very powerful, "can-do" man who never took "No" for an answer. Also, there were my early teachers, notably James Sacks, Ph.D.; Hannah Weiner, MA; Zerka Moreno; Martin Sulkow, Ph.D.; Murray Kagel, JD; Charlotte Schwartz, LCSW; and my current clinical supervisor, Joan Klein, LCSW. Each of these wonderful mentors has provided encouragement, support, common sense, expertise and clinical acumen, which have honed my own skills to their ever-improving level of proficiency.

What changes have you witnessed in your industry/field since you first started?
In the realm of psychoanalysis, things have changed to become much more relational; that is to say that there is much more recognition to the kind of co-equality of patient and therapist as two individuals working together in a co-equal sort of way to understand what is being experienced in the session. This is in contrast to the old model where the therapist knew everything and the patient knew nothing. It used to be that the authority of the analyst was incontrovertible and the patient was often overwhelmed and intimidated just by that power and inequality. It has gone full circle to where it is much more the two individuals having a co-therapeutic effort to understand what is being experienced.

Have you contributed to any publications or research in your field?
Yes, there is a group called the International Forum for Psychoanalytic Education, and in Boston at a conference in 2008, I was invited to present a paper, which was entitled "Love and Fear in the Analytic Encounter." I will be presenting another paper at their conference in Nashville in 2010, entitled "The rhythms of psychoanalysis and the 'counterpoints' of therapeutic spontaneity."

Air and Missile Defense Operations

Michel T. Closson
Senior Principal Systems Engineer
Raytheon Company
1330 Inverness Drive, Suite 250
Colorado Springs, CO 80910 USA
mikeclosson0067@msn.com

U.S. military-trained Michel T. Closson has taken the high level of integrity he earned as a soldier and become an upstanding civilian whose paramount concern is for the safety of his country and the world at large. Presently the senior principal systems engineer in the Network Centric Systems division of the Raytheon Company, he is responsible for managing three missile defense task orders for exercises and war games, and distributing training worth more 31 million dollars annually. Additionally, he oversees analytical data and mission systems integration, leads an organization responsible for the deployment of integrated exercise and training environments, addresses concerns involving the engineering of system-of-systems architecture and mission systems integration. He also works as a member of several integrated-product teams comprised of members from numerous functional disciplines, which include: modeling and simulation, systems analysis, enterprise integration and infrastructure. Throughout his career, he has led more than 50 contractors of various disciplines through proposal development, contract negotiation, technical planning, program management, design, and the execution and analysis of missile defense exercises and training events.

Mr. Closson enlisted in the Army at the rank of E1 and retired as a chief warrant officer 3. With 20 years of experience in the military, he has developed a mission-focused approach with considerable expertise in completing operations, air and missile defense, program management, system engineering, and problem identification and resolution. He demonstrated his capability to assemble and organize teams for success and possesses the ability to develop complex strategies, and communicate concepts and technical summaries. In 2007, Mr. Closson was presented by the Raytheon Company with Technical Honors.

Mr. Closson completed a leadership course in 2007 through his employer, Raytheon. In 2004, he obtained Six Sigma certification and received a Master of Science in Space Systems Engineering Management from Webster University. In 2001, he earned a Bachelor of Science in General Sciences with a concentration in electronics and psychology from Excelsior College. He is a member of the Military Officers Association of America.

Conversation with Michel T. Closson

Cambridge Who's Who: What would you like to promote most about yourself or your business?
Michel T. Closson: For myself, it's about the integrity and productivity I put into this business. In my field, the continual technology advancements force me to remain abreast.

What is the most rewarding aspect of your career?
The most rewarding aspect of my career is having the opportunity to train and mentor others, work with people and watch them advance and grow.

What is your greatest professional accomplishment to date?
Completing my military career and doing everything that I set out to do while in the military. I left on my terms, after I had accomplished all of my goals.

What are your short-term and long-term career goals?
My short- and long-term goals are the same: to remain productive and continue enjoying the challenges.

And what specific steps have you taken toward achieving these goals?
Complete the educational goals, continue to work with people and maintain a trained workforce. I challenge myself every day, in that I make sure that I am in a position that I enjoy and that I remain responsible for the things that I enjoy.

What is the most difficult obstacle or challenge you have faced in pursuit of your goals?
We live in an ever-changing environment so the most difficult obstacle is staying current with regards to threat perspectives, technology and capabilities.

On what topic(s) do you consider yourself to be an expert?
Project management, and air and missile defense.

How do you remain current in your profession?
I take advantage of training opportunities. Most of the work I do is in the classified realm, so there aren't many publications that I can subscribe to in

order to keep technically current. Missile defense has documents and publications that come out and I try to stay current by reading up on them. I also participate in many Integrated Product Teams (IPT) that involve communications with subject matter experts who work together for integrated solutions.

What makes you a valuable resource in your industry?
My communication skills and overall knowledge.

What is the most significant issue facing your profession today?
It has to do with the technologic advancement of our adversaries. There is a growing global threat concerning missile defense and ballistic missiles, which continues to grow and change.

What advice can you offer fellow members who work in your industry?
As an individual, you have to maintain your integrity. Never let anybody question the information you are providing or the manner in which you behave. You also need to think outside of normal logical processes. You have to be able to expand outside of the box into the entire realm of possibilities.

What advice can you offer people aspiring to work in this profession?
Become an expert in a specific discipline, but keep your eyes open and understand the bigger picture of how your discipline fits into the larger goals.

What are you passionate about?
I am a mission- and goal-oriented type of individual. I am passionate about accomplishing whatever the mission is and being effective in whatever my responsibilities are.

Who have been your mentors or people who have greatly influenced you?
My mother, Myrna Hancock. Watching her struggle and handle challenges while I was growing up had a big influence on me. Other than that, I had many role models, both positive and negative. In my career, I had one mentor: Chief Warrant Officer 5, Ed Byrd.

Do you have a motto?
My personal motto: "I am what I am, this is who I am."
My professional motto: "Clear, concise communication."

Aerospace Administration

Gary Colgren

Chairman, Chief Executive Officer
Viking Aerospace, LLC
824 S.W. 128th Street
Seattle, WA 98146 USA
garycolgren@hotmail.com
http://www.vikingaero.com

Gary Colgren is the chairman and CEO of Viking Aerospace, LLC. He is responsible for the long-range plans and focus of the company, as they remain dedicated to excellence in the design, production and support of unmanned aerial vehicles and their systems, including flight test services. "Our experience and research on intelligent aerospace vehicles and systems, especially in the development of cutting-edge embedded control technologies, allows the realization of autonomous vehicles capable of conducting safe operations even in conjunction with other unmanned vehicles," he describes. "This is required to achieve a high level of mission effectiveness in varied and complicated system operations."

Mr. Colgren became involved in his profession through the example and influence of his oldest brother, Arthur Lew Colgren, who was an electrical engineer with McDonald Douglas. Throughout his 40 years in his vocation, Mr. Colgren has contributed his knowledge to other members of the profession. His first four years at Boeing were spent as part of the instrumentation staff. He transferred to the Minuteman Project Ground Test Group, which designed and built the test stations for assembly testing in Seattle and the final assembly test stations at Vandenberg Air Force Base and Hill Air Force Base. This was an opportunity to participate in the circuit and packaging design, manufacturing process, and to write and conduct the test procedures for individual units and the test station. After 16 years on the Minuteman program, he move to the IUS program, where he worked as a design engineer and lead engineer to the acting supervisor on packaging the ground test stations. After a retirement period, he joined the Viking Aerospace as chief executive officer and was added as chairman of the board in 2009.

Mr. Colgren received a Bachelor of Science in Electrical Engineering from Washington State University. He holds a professional engineer's license in the state of Washington.

CONVERSATION WITH GARY COLGREN

CAMBRIDGE WHO'S WHO: On what topic(s) do you consider yourself to be an expert?
GARY COLGREN: Personal relations. I am able to keep the whole system in view, while concentrating on the main goal. I have experience in instrumentation circuit design, packaging, and testing and due to my participation with design reviews with the Air Force, I also have experience with presentations and the critique of designs.

What characteristics help to separate your company, Viking Aerospace, LLC, from your competitors?
Viking Aerospace, LLC is fortunate to have top-of-the-line employees in the engineering industry. Additionally, we have great business relationships with other companies and universities. For example, Viking Aerospace, LLC, which has advanced technical equipment, interfaces with a Swiss autopilot company and other aviation organizations.

What motivates you?
My children's enthusiasm and encouragement help motivate me to succeed.

What lessons have you learned as a professional in your field for the past 37 years?
I feel that you need to take risks in your profession. People should not be afraid to do anything they normally would not. I have seen so many engineers who have more experience than I do, but they are unsure about themselves and the decisions they make.

What are your personal aspirations you wish to accomplish over the years?
I aspire for my company to rapidly grow with this exciting and expanding field of unmanned aerial vehicles. I am hoping my company will have the opportunity to expand into a new facility base that would be closer to where my children live.

What are your short-term and long-term career goals?
My long-term career goal is to ensure the success of Viking Aerospace, LLC. The field of unmanned aerial vehicles can revolutionize many areas, including those found in the legal, insurance, police and military professions. This

includes building upon the revolution in battery design. In addition, there are so many opportunities for use of UAVs, building upon the tremendous advancements in autopilot controls; also the capabilities of these developments have opened up.

How do you plan to achieve these goals?
Collaborating with universities and building relationships with other companies is giving my company an opportunity for great exposure. We must be ready to respond to the wide variety of possible UAV applications, and to set the standard of excellence in the UAV community.

What is the most difficult obstacle or challenge you have faced in pursuit of your goals?
Seeing a lot of our competitors downsizing due to the economy shows the challenge we face. We must make sure that our product's quality is better than theirs and our service is first-rate. A real challenge we face is how to make different industries aware of the opportunities they could have with the use of UAVs.

What are some questions that an individual interested in your services can ask to ensure a more productive relationship?
An individual should ask, "How can Viking Aerospace, LLC help my company grow in a more efficient way by using UAV technology?"

Did you ever consider pursuing a different career path or another profession? If yes, how did you end up working in your current field?
In high school, I wanted to pursue forestry because I loved being outside in the environment. I ended up in the engineering field, because of the influence from my father and brother. They both had engineering minds, where they were good with numbers and at building things.

Electronic Design and Engineering

Harry J. McIntyre
Engineering Staff Consultant
Xerox Corporation
800 Phillips Road
Webster, NY 14580 USA
hmcintyre1@rochester.rr.com
http://www.xerox.com

When one thinks of Xerox, the first thing that may come to mind is a copy machine, which is one of the many products made by the Xerox Corporation, where Harry J. McIntyre has worked as an engineer for the past 29 years. The Xerox Corporation is a document production and management company that provides office products and equipment, electronics design, and document, outsourcing and consulting services.

Out of his many years of experience in engineering, Mr. McIntyre has dedicated them all to one company as a loyal engineering staff consultant. His areas of expertise include problem analytics and electronics design, both of which require some thinking outside of the box. He states that his imagination is something that makes him valuable in his profession, and it is this creativity that is just one piece of the puzzle needed when performing his job in electronics design. When facing various difficulties that may arise in design engineering, he relies on his technical prowess and problem-solving skills to guide him toward cost-effective solutions that will benefit the company and its clients to a level of complete satisfaction.

Retrieving correct information is a large part of Mr. McIntyre's job description and unfortunately, at times can be somewhat of an obstacle. The advice he gives to others aspiring to work in his profession is that one must look at the company they are working for as a customer, and always try to meet their needs as best as possible.

Mr. McIntyre has received a total in excess of 50 awards and honors for professional excellence during his tenure at Xerox. He earned a Bachelor of Science in Engineering from the University of California, Los Angeles in 1982 and is a member of IEEE, the Institute of Electrical and Electronics Engineers.

In his spare time, he enjoys golfing, tennis, and photography, and reading Design News and EE Times.

Conversation with Harry J. McIntyre

Cambridge Who's Who: What is the most rewarding aspect of your career?
Harry J. McIntyre: It would be my patents, of which I have quite a few.

What is your greatest professional accomplishment to date?
My greatest professional accomplishment is the accumulation of design work.

On what topics do you consider yourself to be an expert?
I consider myself to be an expert on analog integrated circuit (IC) designs, sense and control circuits, and electrical optical-driving circuits.

What is the most difficult obstacle or challenge you have faced in pursuit of your goals?
Acquiring information is the most difficult obstacle I have faced.

How do you remain current in your profession?
I am a member of IEEE and have been an officer for the past two to three years.

What is the most significant issue facing your profession today?
The most significant issue facing my profession is the paradigm change in the work environment, which is a change from [showing] company loyalty as an employee to simply being your own business person.

What advice can you offer fellow members who work in your industry?
Plan your career early — 40 years in advance. [It cannot] just be an idea in your head.

What advice can you offer people aspiring to work in this profession?
Because engineers are more like entrepreneurs now, you have to know your customer, which is the company you're working for and think of them as such.

Umbilical Systems Engineering

Einar Mjelstad
President, Chief Executive Officer
Ultra Deep, LLC
11757 Katy Freeway
Suite 1300
Houston, TX 77079 USA
einar.mjelstad@ultradeep.com

In umbilical systems engineering, one needs to anticipate upcoming changes of the future in order to stay in business — whether in regards to business models or technology. Einar Mjelstad, president and chief executive officer of Ultra Deep, LLC, does so by keeping his finger on the pulse of the industry, intricately learning how trends are changing, he says. Ultra Deep is an independent consulting company working with the subsea oil and gas industry. The company develops software, designs cables, consults with clients, and handles research and development. It also offers several different services to oil and engineering companies, and umbilical and steel tube manufacturers including umbilical system engineering, cross-section component and umbilical cross-section design, umbilical mechanical properties and capacities assessment, and dynamic analysis.

Mr. Mjelstad has worked in engineering for 25 years, with the four most recent spent as president and chief executive officer of Ultra Deep. For 10 years, he worked alongside Knut I. Ekeberg, vice president and chief technology officer, in building up the umbilical department to one of the major manufacturers in the industry. During this process Mr. Mjelstad was the head of department while Mr. Ekeberg served as the head of umbilical systems design.

Earning a Master of Science in Electrical Engineering in Norway was just the beginning for Mr. Mjelstad. After serving numerous clients through his company, he acknowledges that it is important to clarify what each customer needs and to break the complex information down in simple terms for them to understand. Uncovering the service they require while ensuring their happiness with the product takes top priority.

In addition to a Master of Science, in 1990 Mr. Mjelstad also earned a Master of Business Administration in Strategic Management from the BI Norwegian School of Management, the largest business school in Norway and the second largest in all of Europe. In 2003, he was awarded global recognition for sales and performance. When he is not answering his clients' many questions, he enjoys listening to jazz music, walking and biking.

Conversation with Einar Mjelstad

Cambridge Who's Who: On what topics do you consider yourself to be an expert?
Einar Mjelstad: I have been testing people in order to define their brain code. Everyone has a different brain code.

What characteristics help to separate you from your competitors?
I have a philosophy for management and an ambition to do things efficiently. I also put together a team dedicated to complete any task given.

What motivates you?
I am very passionate about what I do and I also have the curiosity to learn and understand the things in my field. Our curiosity can be used to predict the future. In order to stay in business, you need to know what is going to happen in your industry.

What lessons have you learned as a professional in your field for the past 30 years?
I have learned that businesses today need to sell more, but at the same time need to cut costs — that should be number one on the agenda. Number two is technology and product development. Intelligent simplicity is important. I can solve a complicated mathematical problem and explain it in simple terms because a client needs an answer they can use.

What short-term and long-term career goals are you currently pursuing?
In my position, I do not wish to [manage] more than 50 people. I would like to keep 25 specialists.

What is the most difficult obstacle or challenge you have faced in pursuit of your goals?
Building the client base and managing each of the clients.

What is the most significant issue facing your profession today?
Offshore drilling.

What are some questions that an individual interested in your services can ask to ensure a more productive relationship?
We work best when the clients know exactly what they need and are able to depict that to us. Needs analysis is very important.

Computer Operations Management

Kimberly B. Santilli
Computer Analyst
The Hartford Financial Services Group, Inc.
Asylum Avenue
Hartford, CT 06105 USA
john_santilli@comcast.net

Computer analysts are always in demand. Our nation has quickly become computer based, which makes Kimberly B. Santilli, a computer analyst for The Hartford Financial Services Group, Inc., a vital resource. Hartford is a financial company that provides investment and insurance services including annuities, mutual funds, college savings plans, life, business, automobile and homeowners' insurance, and group and employee benefits. Ms. Santilli has 29 years of experience in her field, in which her area of expertise is computer operations management. With the Hartford Financial Services Group, Inc., she coordinates the help desk team for the entire company and supports 30,000 employees while working on Blackberry networking systems. She says, "We try to assist [with] any application that Hartford has." By communicating through the Internet, she oversees spam issues and e-mail support services, and reviews e-mail encryption software.

Change is a big factor when it comes to computers and technology. Ms. Santilli offers, "You have to really be able to deal with change," since many advancements take place over the years and affect the way a company operates. As the "first line of support for all Hartford employees," she considers herself to have a great relationship with the customers, which is important in any business to communicate with clients and satisfy their needs.

Besides adding to her professional resume, Ms. Santilli's experience at Hartford Financial Services Group, Inc. provided her with something a little more personal: a romance. She met her husband, John, while working at the company. They have been married for 22 years and she has a stepson named Jim.

Ms. Santilli, who attributes her success to her hard work, and technical and learning skills, received the Hartford Hero Award in 2001. In five years, she hopes to expand her knowledge of e-mail support systems and experience professional growth. When she is not working with computers, she enjoys car racing and gardening.

Conversation with Kimberly B. Santilli

Cambridge Who's Who: What advice can you offer people aspiring to work in this profession?
Kimberly B. Santilli: Change is on an hourly basis. You have to be a quick learner and keep up with the fast-paced industry.

How did you become involved in your profession?
I went to a job fair while I was working down the street at another company. I started at the bottom and wasn't doing any computer work at the beginning. I learned hands on. I've been working for The Hartford Financial Services Group, Inc. for 27 years.

What would you like to promote most about yourself or your business?
I am very customer-focused and have strong communication and organizational skills. I also keep a good relationship with the customers.

What is the most rewarding aspect of your career?
We were involved in Sept. 11. I received an award for that in 2001, called the Hartford Hero Award.

What are your short-term and long-term career goals?
I'm looking to retire in the next two to three years and then I want to do something else. I would also like to do some volunteer work for a good cause after I retire.

What is the most significant issue facing your profession today?
We need to stop all the outsourcing. It's making things a lot harder on a lot of companies. It's tough to work and get things done in a timely manner.

How do you remain current in your profession?
I did a lot of work with e-mail and Blackberry networking systems, so I used to keep up with everything. I still read technical things here and there and keep up with what's going on.

Do you have any hobbies?
I enjoy flower and fruit gardening.

CARGO AND FREIGHT SHIPPING SERVICES

LEYDA E. COLÓN
President
Dependable Carriers Corp.
52 Lefferts Road
Yonkers, NY 10705 USA
dtrans13@verizon.net

Few people would dare turn back and revisit such traumatizing events in their lives as becoming homeless. Leyda E. Colón is the exception. She, alongside her oldest daughter, lived in a shelter for five months while Ms. Colón went to school in an earnest attempt to get out of the oftentimes difficult system and go out on her own. Now, as she regards those experiences as distant memories, she continues to donate her time and resources to individuals who are less fortunate than she, including needy children and the homeless.

As president of the Dependable Carriers Corp., Ms. Colón is charged with the oversight of business operations. The company provides cargo and freight shipping services to, among others, big companies such as Costco, Sam's Club, and BJ's. But they also donate and transport furniture to formerly homeless individuals who, like herself, are able to move out of shelters and into their first homes. Additionally, on Thanksgivings, Ms. Colón and her family cook food — not only for themselves, but also to place in trays that are distributed to areas in Manhattan with high concentrations of homeless people. She takes her four children with her in order for them see what blessings they have received in their lives, for which they should be thankful.

Since her childhood, Ms. Colón, who reads Worth and Time magazine, experienced the trucking business firsthand, because her father was in the industry. She was trained by her father in the business and in 1989 began her career as a truck driver. Ms. Colón has more than 20 years of experience on the road, seven of which she has spent operating Dependable Carriers. The brunt of her daily activities includes managing sales, marketing the company to prospective clients, negotiating contracts and subcontracting.

In the near future, Ms. Colón hopes to expand her trucking business while experiencing professional growth. Additionally, she aspires to help solve the problem of funding for elementary through high schools. She would like to be remembered as someone who fought her way toward her goals, because she is one of a few women in an industry dominated by men; also, because she overcame great odds to achieve success.

Conversation with Leyda E. Colón

Cambridge Who's Who: What would you like to promote most about yourself or your business?

Leyda E. Colón: I would like to promote the activities of my business. When we do subcontracting with other companies, especially with furniture, we take items that have been donated and help to furnish the first apartment of someone who is moving out of a shelter. We also transport cargo and freight. We have a small truck that moves the furniture. We have a larger truck that is contracted by big companies such as Costco, Sam's Club, and BJ's. We do the same thing with Toys "R" Us when they have toys for charities. We collect the toys and take them all to the New York Armory, or I take them straight to a shelter. We do this during the Christmas holiday.

What is the most rewarding aspect of your career?

Being in a position to give to the homeless and children in need is the most rewarding aspect of my career.

What is your greatest professional accomplishment to date?

My greatest accomplishment is being in a position to give because not too many people can give. I feel honored in what I do. I know what it's like to be homeless, from my personal experiences. That's why I chose instead of giving it to another company, to do it and take it to them myself.

What are your short-term and long-term career goals?

My long-term goal is continuing to be a strong role model for my children. My short-term goal is professional growth and business expansion. I would love to get another 18-wheeler.

And what specific steps have you taken toward achieving these goals?

I've been trying to increase my salary so I can afford another truck. I have a list of people who want to join my team and help out. My workers are willing to divide themselves, enlist other workers and teach each other how to grow.

What is the most difficult obstacle or challenge you have faced in pursuit of your goals?

I would say the cash flow; also, having to sit down with other companies and being the only female. I'm the only president representing myself.

On what topic(s) do you consider yourself to be an expert?

Business operations.

How do you remain current in your profession?
Taking classes, doing research and networking. The research has never stopped. I took some classes with Donald Trump and, at one point, I took classes once a week with Tim Robbins. I'm still doing the research on how to get funding that I know I am entitled to if I apply.

What makes you a valuable resource in your industry?
I get the job done in a timely fashion with honesty and integrity.

What is the most significant issue facing your profession today?
Competition is a significant issue.

What advice can you offer fellow members who work in your industry?
I would tell them to never give up.

What are you passionate about?
Giving to the less fortunate and helping my community.

Who have been your mentors or people who have greatly influenced you?
My dad, Americo Colón and my grandmother, Juanita Castro, because my father taught me how to be a hard worker and my grandmother was a strong female — she always kept our family together. She was the tree and I feel as if I'm the tree now.

Do you have a motto?
"Be a leader, go for what you want."

Disclaimer

The information submitted to Cambridge Who's Who® Publishing, Inc. ("the Company") is obtained primarily from those profiled themselves. Although every effort has been made to verify the information submitted, the Company makes no warranty or representation as to the accuracy, reliability, or currency of the data provided, and accepts no responsibility for errors, factual or otherwise. Furthermore, the Company will not be held responsible for any damage or loss suffered by any person or entity arising from the use of this information, including identity theft or any other misuse of your identity or information, to the fullest extent permitted by law.

By using the information we provide in our publications, you agree to indemnify and hold harmless, and at the Company's request defend, the Company, its parents, subsidiaries, and affiliates, as well as the directors, officers, shareholders, employees, agents and owners from and against any and all claims, proceedings, damages, injuries, liabilities, losses, costs and expenses (including reasonable attorneys' fees) arising out of your acts or omissions.